KNOW YOUR MONTHLY PAYMENTS BEFORE YOU BUY, BORROW OR LEND

ELDON RITTER

Pussywillow Publishing House
P.O.Box 1806
Gilbert, Arizona 85234
or call: 602-892-1316
Fax: 602-497-5689

Cover designed by Terry Latterman

ISBN: 0-934739-06-4

Library of Congress Catalog Card No: 92-61465

Printed in the United States of America

CONTENTS

FOREWORD

As the title indicates, this book will give the reader a fast and accurate monthly payment for any amount of money borrowed or lent. The constants found within are based on yearly interest rates. They range from 1 percent through 20 percent in increments of 1 quarter of 1 percent. The terms (Length of the loan) range from 1 month through 30 years.

Only one calculation is required to obtain the monthly payment amount to amortize your loan. Dividing your loan amount by the correct constant will give you this magical amount.

The listed constants have the greatest possible accuracy within a limit of 8 significant digits. The decision to use a limit of 8 digits was made with the reader of this book in mind. Since most people using this book will do so in conjunction with a handheld calculator, it was determined that most handheld calculators have a capacity for 8 digits. Using your calculator will make short work of all formulas contained within.

The author has taken great care to make the contents within this book correct, though makes no warranty, either expressed or implied for consequental damages in connection with or arising out of the use of materials contained herein.

The information contained between the covers of this book will prove to be a valuable tool for those individuals who borrow or lend money.

It would be of great satisfaction to the author if the contents herein contribute to the well being of those who use it. You can use it for a lifetime.

Eldon Ritter

$$\text{MONTHLY PAYMENT} = \frac{\text{AMOUNT OF LOAN}}{\text{CONSTANT}}$$

LOCATING THE DESIRED CONSTANT TO REVEAL YOUR MONTHLY PAYMENT

There are 27,720 constants listed in this book. The formulas used within will require you to use either 1 or 2 constants. All formulas are easy to solve. Finding the correct constant to use is equally as easy. Simply refer to the index pages in the back of the book. The index will direct you to the page that corresponds with your interest rate and loan term. The loan terms (length of the loan) are given in months. The correct constant is adjacent the specific term you wish to calculate.

EXAMPLE: You wish to know what the monthly payment would be on a $63,000 dollar loan. The term is 20 years (240 months). The yearly interest rate is 9 percent. The index directs you to page 131. On page 131, adjacent 240, is the correct constant of 111.14495. The formula to reveal your monthly payment is:

$$\text{MONTHLY PAYMENT} = \frac{\text{AMOUNT OF LOAN}}{\text{CONSTANT}}$$

$$\text{MONTHLY PAYMENT} = \frac{63{,}000.00}{111.14495}$$

MONTHLY PAYMENT = 566.83 dollars

PRESTO!! YOUR MONTHLY PAYMENT REVEALED!!

Using your calculator makes this, otherwise difficult, division very easy to solve. Don't be surprised when your friends start calling you to make calculations for them.

NOTE: The monthly payment amount shown above has been rounded off 2 places to the right of the decimal point. Using a rounded off monthly payment amount will cause a very slight difference in the calculation results of other formulas listed in this book. All pertinent formula examples listed within have the monthly payment rounded off.

A FAST CALCULATION TO DETERMINE YOUR PRESENT BALANCE

Suppose you wish to determine what your loan balance is after you have made 49 monthly payments. Your original loan was for $63,000 dollars at a 9 percent yearly interest rate. The term was 240 months. The formula to reveal the present balance is:

PRESENT BALANCE = REMAINING CONSTANT X PAYMENT

The "Remaining Constant" in the above formula is the constant that is adjacent the number of months remaining to be paid on the loan. By subtracting 49 months from the original 240 months leaves 191 months remaining to be paid. The index informs you that the constant for 9 percent, with a term of 191 months, is found on page 131. Adjacent 191 is the correct constant of 101.33456. Since the monthly payment has already been determined (as explained on page vi), your present balance can now be revealed.

PRESENT BALANCE = 101.33456 X 566.83

PRESENT BALANCE = 57, 439.47 dollars.

NOTE; Remember not to include your taxes and insurance amounts when making your calculations. Include only the principal and interest of the loan.

CALCULATING THE CURRENT AMOUNT OF MONEY APPLIED TOWARD THE PRINCIPAL

Calculating the current amount of money that has been applied toward the principal is, also, quick and easy. Again 49 payments have been applied toward a loan. The original loan amount was for $63,000 dollars, with a 240 month term. The interest rate is 9 percent. After payment number 49 you want to know the amount applied toward the principal. The formula to reveal the current amount paid to the principal is:

$$\text{CURRENT PRINCIPAL PAID} = \text{ORIGINAL CONSTANT} - \text{REMAINING CONSTANT} \times \text{MONTHLY PAYMENT}$$

The "ORIGINAL CONSTANT" is the constant used to determine the monthly payment. In this case the "ORIGINAL CONSTANT" is 111.14495. The "REMAINING CONSTANT' is the constant that is adjacent the number of months remaining to be paid on the loan. In this case the "REMAINING CONSTANT" is 101.33456, found on page 131. The current amount of money applied toward the principal can now be revealed.

CURRENT PRINCIPAL PAID = 111.14495 - 101.33456 X $566.83

CURRENT PRINCIPAL PAID = $5,560.82

REVEALING THE AMOUNT OF MONEY CURRENTLY PAID IN INTEREST

Again, use the number 49 for the number of payments applied toward a 240 month loan of $63,000 dollars. The yearly interest rate is 9 percent. After making the 49th payment you wish to know the amount of money that has been applied in interest. First, determine the amount of money applied toward the principal. As explained on page viii, the formula to determine the current principal amount is:

CURRENT PRINCIPAL PAID = ORIGINAL CONSTANT − REMAINING CONSTANT X MONTHLY PAYMENT

In this case we have the following: The "ORIGINAL CONSTANT" is 111.14495. The "REMAINING CONSTANT" is 101.33456. We know the "PAYMENT' is $566.83.

CURRENT PRINCIPAL PAID = 111.14495 − 101.33456 x $566.83

CURRENT PRINCIPAL PAID = $5,560.82

The formula to reveal the current amount of interest paid is:

CURRENT INTEREST AMOUNT PAID = TOTAL PAID ON LOAN − CURRENT PRINCIPAL PAID

To determine the total amount paid on the loan, simply multiply the total number of payments made times the amount of the payment. In this case, 49 x 566.83 = 27,774.67 dollars.

CURRENT INTEREST AMOUNT PAID = 27,774.67 − 5,560.82

CURRENT INTEREST AMOUNT PAID = $22,213.85

HOW TO OBTAIN A NEEDED CONSTANT NOT LISTED IN THIS BOOK

As stated previously, there are 27,720 constants listed in this book. Even though they cover a wide range of terms and interest rates, the possibility of you needing to calculate a loan with parameters other than what is listed can always occur. For this reason it is important for you to know how constants are derived. The formula to obtain a needed constant is:

$$\text{CONSTANT} = \frac{1 - (1 + \text{MONTHLY INTEREST RATE})^{-n}}{\text{MONTHLY INTEREST RATE}}$$

Note: n = the number of monthly payments to amortize a loan. The monthly interest rate = the annual interest rate divided by 12. A yearly interest rate of 9.18 percent is expressed as .0918. Thus, .0918 divided by 12 = the monthly interest rate of .00765.

The above formula is not as difficult as it may appear. Suppose you wish to determine the monthly payment on a loan of $95,000. The term is 40 years (480 months.) The interest rate if 9.18 percent per annum. Since the constant is not listed in this book, it will have to be determined by using the formula above. Let's do it!

$$\text{CONSTANT} = \frac{1 - (1 + .00765)^{-480}}{.00765}$$

$$\text{CONSTANT} = \frac{1-(1.00765)^{-480}}{.00765} \qquad \text{CONSTANT} = \frac{1-(.0257834)}{.00765} = 127.34858$$

$$\text{CONSTANT} = 127.34858 \qquad \text{MONTHLY PAYMENT} = \frac{95,000.00}{127.34858} = 745.98$$

Practicing with the negative power key on your calculator will make finding desired constants a simple task.

FORMULAS YOU CAN USE

****

$$\text{MONTHLY PAYMENT} = \frac{\text{AMOUNT OF LOAN}}{\text{CONSTANT}}$$

****

PRESENT BALANCE =
REMAINING CONSTANT X PAYMENT

****

$$\text{CURRENT PRINCIPAL PAID} = \text{ORIGINAL CONSTANT} - \text{REMAINING CONSTANT} \times \text{MONTHLY PAYMENT}$$

****

$$\text{CURRENT INTEREST PAID} = \text{TOTAL PAID ON LOAN} - \text{CURRENT PRINCIPAL PAID}$$

****

$$\text{CONSTANT} = \frac{1 - (1 + \text{MONTHLY INTEREST RATE})^{-n}}{\text{MONTHLY INTEREST RATE}}$$

NOTE: n = the number of monthly payments to amortize a loan. The monthly interest rate = the yearly interest rate divided by 12.

****

$$\text{ORIGINAL LOAN AMOUNT} = \text{ORIGINAL CONSTANT} \times \text{PAYMENT}$$

****

$$\text{EARLY PAYOFF AMOUNT} = \text{PRESENT BALANCE} \div \text{CONSTANT ADJACENT DESIRED TERM}$$

****

REVEALING YOUR PAYMENT FOR AN EARLY PAYOFF

You have been paying on a 30 year, 11 percent, $73,000. dollar loan for 36 months. You decide that an early retirement could be enjoyed if you paid off the loan 10 years early. How much extra money would have to be paid each month to achieve this wonderful goal? Let's make it happen!

Your present principal and interest payment is 695.20 per month. This amount was determined by dividing $73,000. dollars by the constant 105.00635 found on page 164.

First let's reveal your present balance. The formula is:

PRESENT BALANCE = REMAINING CONSTANT X PAYMENT

Since you have already paid 36 payments on a 360 month loan you have 324 payments remaining. The constant for 324 (at 11 percent) is found on page 164, which is 103.41795. By multiplying 103.41795 by 695.20 tells you that the remaining balance is $71,896.16.

Now let's pretend that the existing balance is a new loan you wish to amortize over a 204 month (10 years early) period. Since the yearly interest rate of 11 percent has not changed, the correct constant will be found within its parameter on page 163, adjacent the 204 term. The correct constant is 92.133576. Now let's reveal your new monthly payment.

$$\frac{71{,}896.16}{92.133576} = 780.35 \text{ per month}$$

As you can readily see, for 85.15 dollars more per month your goal will come true. Have a happy retirement!

Just for the fun of it, calculate the amount of money you would save in interest. Nice feeling!

yearly interest rate = 1.00%

term (months)	constant	term (months)	constant
1	0.9991673	46	45.111055
2	1.9975027	47	46.072661
3	2.9950068	48	47.033466
4	3.9916804	49	47.993472
5	4.9875241	50	48.952678
6	5.9825387	51	49.911085
7	6.9767246	52	50.868695
8	7.9700830	53	51.825507
9	8.9626141	54	52.781522
10	9.9543188	55	53.736741
11	10.945198	56	54.691166
12	11.935252	57	55.644795
13	12.924481	58	56.597630
14	13.912887	59	57.549672
15	14.900470	60	58.500921
16	15.887231	61	59.451378
17	16.873170	62	60.401044
18	17.858288	63	61.349919
19	18.842586	64	62.298004
20	19.826064	65	63.245300
21	20.808723	66	64.191807
22	21.790564	67	65.137525
23	22.771588	68	66.082457
24	23.751795	69	67.026601
25	24.731185	70	67.969959
26	25.709761	71	68.912532
27	26.687521	72	69.854320
28	27.664467	73	70.795324
29	28.640600	74	71.735544
30	29.615920	75	72.674982
31	30.590428	76	73.613637
32	31.564125	77	74.551511
33	32.537010	78	75.488604
34	33.509086	79	76.424916
35	34.480352	80	77.360449
36	35.450810	81	78.295203
37	36.420460	82	79.229179
38	37.389302	83	80.162377
39	38.357337	84	81.094798
40	39.324567	85	82.026443
41	40.290991	86	82.957311
42	41.256611	87	83.887405
43	42.221426	88	84.816725
44	43.185438	89	85.745270
45	44.148648	90	86.673043

yearly interest rate = 1.00%

term (months)	constant	term (months)	constant
91	87.600042	136	128.52584
92	88.526271	137	129.41799
93	89.451727	138	130.30940
94	90.376414	139	131.20006
95	91.300330	140	132.08999
96	92.223477	141	132.97917
97	93.145856	142	133.86762
98	94.067466	143	134.75532
99	94.988309	144	135.64229
100	95.908385	145	136.52851
101	96.827696	146	137.41400
102	97.746240	147	138.29875
103	98.664020	148	139.18277
104	99.581033	149	140.06604
105	100.49729	150	140.94859
106	101.41278	151	141.83039
107	102.32750	152	142.71147
108	103.24147	153	143.59181
109	104.15467	154	144.47142
110	105.06712	155	145.35029
111	105.97880	156	146.22843
112	106.88973	157	147.10585
113	107.79989	158	147.98253
114	108.70930	159	148.85848
115	109.61796	160	149.73370
116	110.52585	161	150.60819
117	111.43299	162	151.48196
118	112.33937	163	152.35499
119	113.24500	164	153.22731
120	114.14988	165	154.09889
121	115.05400	166	154.96975
122	115.95737	167	155.83988
123	116.85998	168	156.70929
124	117.76185	169	157.57798
125	118.66296	170	158.44594
126	119.56333	171	159.31318
127	120.46294	172	160.17969
128	121.36181	173	161.04549
129	122.25992	174	161.91056
130	123.15729	175	162.77492
131	124.05391	176	163.63855
132	124.94979	177	164.50147
133	125.84492	178	165.36366
134	126.73930	179	166.22514
135	127.63294	180	167.08590

yearly interest rate = 1.00%

term (months)	constant	term (months)	constant
181	167.94595	226	205.91578
182	168.80528	227	206.74349
183	169.66389	228	207.57051
184	170.52179	229	208.39685
185	171.37897	230	209.22250
186	172.23545	231	210.04746
187	173.09120	232	210.87173
188	173.94625	233	211.69532
189	174.80058	234	212.51822
190	175.65420	235	213.34044
191	176.50711	236	214.16197
192	177.35931	237	214.98282
193	178.21080	238	215.80298
194	179.06159	239	216.62246
195	179.91166	240	217.44126
196	180.76103	241	218.25938
197	181.60968	242	219.07681
198	182.45764	243	219.89357
199	183.30488	244	220.70964
200	184.15142	245	221.52504
201	184.99726	246	222.33976
202	185.84239	247	223.15379
203	186.68682	248	223.96716
204	187.53054	249	224.77984
205	188.37356	250	225.59185
206	189.21588	251	226.40318
207	190.05750	252	227.21383
208	190.89842	253	228.02381
209	191.73864	254	228.83312
210	192.57816	255	229.64175
211	193.41698	256	230.44971
212	194.25510	257	231.25699
213	195.09252	258	232.06361
214	195.92924	259	232.86955
215	196.76527	260	233.67482
216	197.60061	261	234.47942
217	198.43524	262	235.28335
218	199.26919	263	236.08661
219	200.10243	264	236.88920
220	200.93499	265	237.69113
221	201.76685	266	238.49239
222	202.59802	267	239.29297
223	203.42849	268	240.09290
224	204.25828	269	240.89215
225	205.08737	270	241.69074

yearly interest rate = 1.00%

term (months)	constant	term (months)	constant
271	242.48867	316	277.71603
272	243.28593	317	278.48396
273	244.08253	318	279.25125
274	244.87846	319	280.01790
275	245.67374	320	280.78391
276	246.46835	321	281.54929
277	247.26229	322	282.31403
278	248.05558	323	283.07813
279	248.84821	324	283.84160
280	249.64017	325	284.60443
281	250.43148	326	285.36662
282	251.22213	327	286.12818
283	252.01212	328	286.88911
284	252.80145	329	287.64940
285	253.59013	330	288.40906
286	254.37814	331	289.16808
287	255.16551	332	289.92648
288	255.95221	333	290.68424
289	256.73826	334	291.44137
290	257.52366	335	292.19787
291	258.30840	336	292.95375
292	259.09249	337	293.70899
293	259.87593	338	294.46360
294	260.65872	339	295.21759
295	261.44085	340	295.97095
296	262.22233	341	296.72368
297	263.00316	342	297.47578
298	263.78334	343	298.22726
299	264.56287	344	298.97811
300	265.34175	345	299.72833
301	266.11999	346	300.47794
302	266.89757	347	301.22691
303	267.67451	348	301.97527
304	268.45080	349	302.72300
305	269.22645	350	303.47011
306	270.00144	351	304.21659
307	270.77580	352	304.96246
308	271.54951	353	305.70770
309	272.32257	354	306.45232
310	273.09499	355	307.19633
311	273.86677	356	307.93971
312	274.63790	357	308.68248
313	275.40840	358	309.42462
314	276.17825	359	310.16615
315	276.94746	360	310.90706

yearly interest rate = 1.25%

term (months)	constant	term (months)	constant
1	0.9989594	46	44.892491
2	1.9968794	47	45.844736
3	2.9937610	48	46.795990
4	3.9896052	49	47.746254
5	4.9844131	50	48.695530
6	5.9781859	51	49.643818
7	6.9709246	52	50.591119
8	7.9626301	53	51.537434
9	8.9533039	54	52.482764
10	9.9429468	55	53.427111
11	10.931560	56	54.370475
12	11.919144	57	55.312858
13	12.905701	58	56.254260
14	13.891231	59	57.194682
15	14.875735	60	58.134126
16	15.859215	61	59.072592
17	16.841672	62	60.010081
18	17.823106	63	60.946595
19	18.803519	64	61.882135
20	19.782912	65	62.816701
21	20.761286	66	63.750294
22	21.738641	67	64.682916
23	22.714980	68	65.614568
24	23.690303	69	66.545250
25	24.664610	70	67.474963
26	25.637904	71	68.403710
27	26.610185	72	69.331489
28	27.581455	73	70.258304
29	28.551713	74	71.184154
30	29.520962	75	72.109040
31	30.489203	76	73.032964
32	31.456436	77	73.955927
33	32.422662	78	74.877929
34	33.387883	79	75.798972
35	34.352100	80	76.719056
36	35.315313	81	77.638183
37	36.277524	82	78.556353
38	37.238734	83	79.473568
39	38.198943	84	80.389829
40	39.158153	85	81.305136
41	40.116366	86	82.219491
42	41.073581	87	83.132894
43	42.029800	88	84.045347
44	42.985024	89	84.956850
45	43.939254	90	85.867405

yearly interest rate = 1.25%

term (months)	constant	term (months)	constant
91	86.777013	136	126.74448
92	87.685673	137	127.61155
93	88.593389	138	128.47772
94	89.500159	139	129.34299
95	90.405986	140	130.20735
96	91.310871	141	131.07082
97	92.214814	142	131.93339
98	93.117816	143	132.79506
99	94.019879	144	133.65584
100	94.921003	145	134.51572
101	95.821189	146	135.37470
102	96.720439	147	136.23279
103	97.618758	148	137.08999
104	98.516132	149	137.94630
105	99.412577	150	138.80171
106	100.30809	151	139.65624
107	101.20267	152	140.50987
108	102.09632	153	141.36262
109	102.98904	154	142.21448
110	103.88083	155	143.06545
111	104.77169	156	143.91554
112	105.66163	157	144.76474
113	106.55064	158	145.61306
114	107.43872	159	146.46050
115	108.32588	160	147.30706
116	109.21212	161	148.15273
117	110.09744	162	148.99752
118	110.98183	163	149.84144
119	111.86530	164	150.68448
120	112.74786	165	151.52664
121	113.62949	166	152.36792
122	114.51021	167	153.20833
123	115.39002	168	154.04786
124	116.26890	169	154.88652
125	117.14687	170	155.72431
126	118.02393	171	156.56122
127	118.90008	172	157.39727
128	119.77531	173	158.23244
129	120.64964	174	159.06675
130	121.52305	175	159.90019
131	122.39555	176	160.73276
132	123.26715	177	161.56446
133	124.13784	178	162.39530
134	125.00762	179	163.22527
135	125.87650	180	164.05438

yearly interest rate = 1.25%

term (months)	constant	term (months)	constant
181	164.88263	226	201.27520
182	165.71001	227	202.06471
183	166.53654	228	202.85341
184	167.36220	229	203.64128
185	168.18701	230	204.42833
186	169.01096	231	205.21457
187	169.83405	232	205.99999
188	170.65628	233	206.78458
189	171.47766	234	207.56837
190	172.29818	235	208.35134
191	173.11785	236	209.13349
192	173.93666	237	209.91483
193	174.75463	238	210.69535
194	175.57174	239	211.47507
195	176.38800	240	212.25397
196	177.20342	241	213.03206
197	178.01798	242	213.80934
198	178.83170	243	214.58581
199	179.64457	244	215.36148
200	180.45659	245	216.13634
201	181.26777	246	216.91039
202	182.07811	247	217.68364
203	182.88760	248	218.45608
204	183.69625	249	219.22772
205	184.50406	250	219.99855
206	185.31103	251	220.76858
207	186.11715	252	221.53781
208	186.92244	253	222.30625
209	187.72689	254	223.07388
210	188.53051	255	223.84071
211	189.33329	256	224.60674
212	190.13523	257	225.37198
213	190.93634	258	226.13642
214	191.73661	259	226.90007
215	192.53605	260	227.66292
216	193.33466	261	228.42498
217	194.13244	262	229.18624
218	194.92939	263	229.94671
219	195.72551	264	230.70639
220	196.52080	265	231.46529
221	197.31526	266	232.22339
222	198.10890	267	232.98070
223	198.90171	268	233.73722
224	199.69370	269	234.49296
225	200.48486	270	235.24791

yearly interest rate = 1.25%

term (months)	constant	term (months)	constant
271	236.00207	316	269.13950
272	236.75545	317	269.85840
273	237.50805	318	270.57655
274	238.25986	319	271.29395
275	239.01089	320	272.01060
276	239.76114	321	272.72651
277	240.51061	322	273.44168
278	241.25930	323	274.15610
279	242.00721	324	274.86978
280	242.75434	325	275.58271
281	243.50069	326	276.29490
282	244.24627	327	277.00636
283	244.99107	328	277.71707
284	245.73509	329	278.42704
285	246.47835	330	279.13627
286	247.22082	331	279.84477
287	247.96253	332	280.55252
288	248.70346	333	281.25955
289	249.44363	334	281.96583
290	250.18302	335	282.67138
291	250.92164	336	283.37620
292	251.65950	337	284.08028
293	252.39658	338	284.78363
294	253.13290	339	285.48625
295	253.86846	340	286.18814
296	254.60325	341	286.88930
297	255.33727	342	287.58972
298	256.07053	343	288.28942
299	256.80303	344	288.98839
300	257.53476	345	289.68663
301	258.26573	346	290.38415
302	258.99595	347	291.08094
303	259.72540	348	291.77701
304	260.45409	349	292.47235
305	261.18203	350	293.16697
306	261.90921	351	293.86086
307	262.63563	352	294.55403
308	263.36129	353	295.24649
309	264.08620	354	295.93822
310	264.81036	355	296.62923
311	265.53376	356	297.31952
312	266.25641	357	298.00909
313	266.97831	358	298.69795
314	267.69946	359	299.38609
315	268.41985	360	300.07351

yearly interest rate = 1.50%

term (months)	constant	term (months)	constant
1	0.9987515	46	44.675367
2	1.9962562	47	45.618344
3	2.9925156	48	46.560144
4	3.9875312	49	47.500768
5	4.9813046	50	48.440218
6	5.9738373	51	49.378494
7	6.9651310	52	50.315600
8	7.9551870	53	51.251536
9	8.9440070	54	52.186303
10	9.9315925	55	53.119903
11	10.917945	56	54.052337
12	11.903066	57	54.983608
13	12.886958	58	55.913716
14	13.869621	59	56.842662
15	14.851057	60	57.770449
16	15.831268	61	58.697078
17	16.810255	62	59.622550
18	17.788020	63	60.546866
19	18.764564	64	61.470029
20	19.739889	65	62.392039
21	20.713997	66	63.312898
22	21.686888	67	64.232607
23	22.658565	68	65.151168
24	23.629029	69	66.068582
25	24.598281	70	66.984851
26	25.566323	71	67.899976
27	26.533157	72	68.813959
28	27.498783	73	69.726800
29	28.463204	74	70.638502
30	29.426421	75	71.549066
31	30.388436	76	72.458493
32	31.349249	77	73.366784
33	32.308863	78	74.273942
34	33.267279	79	75.179967
35	34.224498	80	76.084861
36	35.180523	81	76.988625
37	36.135353	82	77.891261
38	37.088992	83	78.792770
39	38.041440	84	79.693154
40	38.992700	85	80.592413
41	39.942771	86	81.490550
42	40.891657	87	82.387566
43	41.839357	88	83.283461
44	42.785875	89	84.178238
45	43.731211	90	85.071899

yearly interest rate = 1.50%

term (months)	constant	term (months)	constant
91	85.964443	136	124.99649
92	86.855873	137	125.83919
93	87.746191	138	126.68084
94	88.635396	139	127.52144
95	89.523492	140	128.36099
96	90.410479	141	129.19949
97	91.296358	142	130.03694
98	92.181132	143	130.87335
99	93.064801	144	131.70872
100	93.947367	145	132.54304
101	94.828831	146	133.37632
102	95.709194	147	134.20856
103	96.588459	148	135.03976
104	97.466625	149	135.86992
105	98.343696	150	136.69905
106	99.219671	151	137.52714
107	100.09455	152	138.35419
108	100.96834	153	139.18022
109	101.84104	154	140.00521
110	102.71265	155	140.82918
111	103.58317	156	141.65211
112	104.45261	157	142.47402
113	105.32095	158	143.29490
114	106.18822	159	144.11476
115	107.05440	160	144.93359
116	107.91950	161	145.75140
117	108.78352	162	146.56819
118	109.64646	163	147.38396
119	110.50833	164	148.19871
120	111.36912	165	149.01245
121	112.22883	166	149.82516
122	113.08747	167	150.63687
123	113.94504	168	151.44756
124	114.80154	169	152.25724
125	115.65697	170	153.06591
126	116.51133	171	153.87356
127	117.36462	172	154.68021
128	118.21685	173	155.48586
129	119.06802	174	156.29049
130	119.91812	175	157.09412
131	120.76716	176	157.89675
132	121.61514	177	158.69838
133	122.46206	178	159.49901
134	123.30793	179	160.29863
135	124.15274	180	161.09726

yearly interest rate = 1.50%

term (months)	constant	term (months)	constant
181	161.89489	226	196.77628
182	162.69153	227	197.52937
183	163.48717	228	198.28152
184	164.28182	229	199.03273
185	165.07547	230	199.78300
186	165.86814	231	200.53233
187	166.65981	232	201.28073
188	167.45050	233	202.02820
189	168.24020	234	202.77473
190	169.02891	235	203.52033
191	169.81664	236	204.26500
192	170.60339	237	205.00873
193	171.38915	238	205.75154
194	172.17394	239	206.49343
195	172.95774	240	207.23439
196	173.74056	241	207.97442
197	174.52241	242	208.71353
198	175.30328	243	209.45171
199	176.08318	244	210.18897
200	176.86210	245	210.92532
201	177.64005	246	211.66074
202	178.41703	247	212.39525
203	179.19304	248	213.12884
204	179.96808	249	213.86151
205	180.74215	250	214.59327
206	181.51525	251	215.32411
207	182.28740	252	216.05405
208	183.05857	253	216.78307
209	183.82879	254	217.51118
210	184.59804	255	218.23838
211	185.36633	256	218.96467
212	186.13366	257	219.69006
213	186.90004	258	220.41454
214	187.66546	259	221.13812
215	188.42992	260	221.86079
216	189.19343	261	222.58257
217	189.95598	262	223.30344
218	190.71759	263	224.02341
219	191.47824	264	224.74248
220	192.23794	265	225.46065
221	192.99669	266	226.17793
222	193.75450	267	226.89431
223	194.51136	268	227.60980
224	195.26728	269	228.32440
225	196.02225	270	229.03810

yearly interest rate = 1.50%

term (months)	constant	term (months)	constant
271	229.75091	316	260.92301
272	230.46283	317	261.59062
273	231.17386	318	262.26818
274	231.88401	319	262.93951
275	232.59327	320	263.61000
276	233.30164	321	264.27965
277	234.00913	322	264.94846
278	234.71573	323	265.61644
279	235.42146	324	266.28359
280	236.12630	325	266.94990
281	236.83026	326	267.61538
282	237.53335	327	268.28003
283	238.23555	328	268.94385
284	238.93688	329	269.60684
285	239.63733	330	270.26901
286	240.33691	331	270.93034
287	241.03562	332	271.59085
288	241.73345	333	272.25054
289	242.43041	334	272.90940
290	243.12650	335	273.56744
291	243.82173	336	274.22466
292	244.51608	337	274.88106
293	245.20957	338	275.53664
294	245.90219	339	276.19140
295	246.59395	340	276.84535
296	247.28484	341	277.49847
297	247.97488	342	278.15078
298	248.66405	343	278.80228
299	249.35235	344	279.45297
300	250.03981	345	280.10284
301	250.72640	346	280.75190
302	251.41213	347	281.40015
303	252.09701	348	282.04759
304	252.78103	349	282.69422
305	253.46420	350	283.34004
306	254.14652	351	283.98506
307	254.82799	352	284.62928
308	255.50860	353	285.27269
309	256.18836	354	285.91529
310	256.86728	355	286.55710
311	257.54535	356	287.19810
312	258.22257	357	287.83830
313	258.89895	358	288.47770
314	259.57448	359	289.11631
315	260.24917	360	289.75411

yearly interest rate = 1.75%

term (months)	constant	term (months)	constant
1	0.9985437	46	44.459677
2	1.9956335	47	45.393479
3	2.9912711	48	46.325920
4	3.9854591	49	47.257003
5	4.9781992	50	48.186731
6	5.9694936	51	49.115105
7	6.9593446	52	50.042127
8	7.9477541	53	50.967799
9	8.9347243	54	51.892123
10	9.9202572	55	52.815101
11	10.904355	56	53.736735
12	11.887020	57	54.657026
13	12.868254	58	55.575978
14	13.848058	59	56.493592
15	14.826437	60	57.409869
16	15.803390	61	58.324812
17	16.778921	62	59.238422
18	17.753031	63	60.150703
19	18.725722	64	61.061654
20	19.696998	65	61.971280
21	20.666858	66	62.879580
22	21.635307	67	63.786558
23	22.602345	68	64.692215
24	23.567975	69	65.596554
25	24.532199	70	66.499575
26	25.495019	71	67.401282
27	26.456436	72	68.301675
28	27.416454	73	69.200757
29	28.375074	74	70.098530
30	29.332298	75	70.994996
31	30.288127	76	71.890156
32	31.242565	77	72.784013
33	32.195613	78	73.676568
34	33.147274	79	74.567823
35	34.097548	80	75.457780
36	35.046439	81	76.346442
37	35.993947	82	77.233809
38	36.940076	83	78.119884
39	37.884828	84	79.004669
40	38.828203	85	79.888165
41	39.770205	86	80.770375
42	40.710835	87	81.651300
43	41.650095	88	82.530943
44	42.587988	89	83.409304
45	43.524514	90	84.286387

yearly interest rate = 1.75%

term (months)	constant	term (months)	constant
91	85.162192	136	123.28119
92	86.036721	137	124.10021
93	86.909978	138	124.91803
94	87.781962	139	125.73467
95	88.652677	140	126.55012
96	89.522124	141	127.36438
97	90.390305	142	128.17745
98	91.257221	143	128.98934
99	92.122876	144	129.80005
100	92.987269	145	130.60958
101	93.850404	146	131.41793
102	94.712282	147	132.22510
103	95.572905	148	133.03110
104	96.432274	149	133.83592
105	97.290392	150	134.63957
106	98.147261	151	135.44205
107	99.002882	152	136.24336
108	99.857257	153	137.04351
109	100.71039	154	137.84249
110	101.56228	155	138.64030
111	102.41292	156	139.43696
112	103.26233	157	140.23245
113	104.11050	158	141.02679
114	104.95744	159	141.81997
115	105.80315	160	142.61199
116	106.64762	161	143.40286
117	107.49086	162	144.19258
118	108.33287	163	144.98115
119	109.17366	164	145.76857
120	110.01323	165	146.55484
121	110.85157	166	147.33997
122	111.68869	167	148.12396
123	112.52459	168	148.90680
124	113.35928	169	149.68851
125	114.19274	170	150.46907
126	115.02500	171	151.24850
127	115.85604	172	152.02680
128	116.68588	173	152.80396
129	117.51450	174	153.57999
130	118.34192	175	154.35489
131	119.16813	176	155.12866
132	119.99314	177	155.90130
133	120.81695	178	156.67282
134	121.63956	179	157.44322
135	122.46097	180	158.21249

yearly interest rate = 1.75%

term (months)	constant	term (months)	constant
181	158.98064	226	192.41414
182	159.74768	227	193.13249
183	160.51359	228	193.84979
184	161.27840	229	194.56605
185	162.04209	230	195.28126
186	162.80466	231	195.99544
187	163.56613	232	196.70857
188	164.32649	233	197.42066
189	165.08574	234	198.13172
190	165.84388	235	198.84174
191	166.60092	236	199.55073
192	167.35686	237	200.25869
193	168.11169	238	200.96561
194	168.86543	239	201.67151
195	169.61807	240	202.37638
196	170.36962	241	203.08022
197	171.12007	242	203.78303
198	171.86942	243	204.48483
199	172.61769	244	205.18560
200	173.36487	245	205.88535
201	174.11095	246	206.58408
202	174.85596	247	207.28179
203	175.59987	248	207.97849
204	176.34271	249	208.67418
205	177.08446	250	209.36885
206	177.82513	251	210.06251
207	178.56472	252	210.75515
208	179.30324	253	211.44679
209	180.04068	254	212.13743
210	180.77705	255	212.82705
211	181.51234	256	213.51568
212	182.24656	257	214.20330
213	182.97972	258	214.88992
214	183.71181	259	215.57554
215	184.44283	260	216.26016
216	185.17278	261	216.94378
217	185.90168	262	217.62641
218	186.62951	263	218.30804
219	187.35628	264	218.98868
220	188.08199	265	219.66833
221	188.80665	266	220.34699
222	189.53025	267	221.02467
223	190.25280	268	221.70135
224	190.97430	269	222.37705
225	191.69474	270	223.05177

yearly interest rate = 1.75%

term (months)	constant	term (months)	constant
271	223.72550	316	253.04943
272	224.39825	317	253.67948
273	225.07003	318	254.30862
274	225.74082	319	254.93683
275	226.41064	320	255.56414
276	227.07948	321	256.19052
277	227.74735	322	256.81600
278	228.41425	323	257.44057
279	229.08017	324	258.06422
280	229.74513	325	258.68697
281	230.40911	326	259.30881
282	231.07213	327	259.92975
283	231.73419	328	260.54978
284	232.39528	329	261.16891
285	233.05541	330	261.78714
286	233.71457	331	262.40446
287	234.37278	332	263.02089
288	235.03003	333	263.63642
289	235.68632	334	264.25105
290	236.34165	335	264.86479
291	236.99603	336	265.47764
292	237.64946	337	266.08959
293	238.30194	338	266.70065
294	238.95346	339	267.31082
295	239.60404	340	267.92011
296	240.25367	341	268.52850
297	240.90235	342	269.13601
298	241.55009	343	269.74264
299	242.19689	344	270.34838
300	242.84274	345	270.95324
301	243.48766	346	271.55722
302	244.13163	347	272.16032
303	244.77467	348	272.76254
304	245.41677	349	273.36388
305	246.05794	350	273.96435
306	246.69817	351	274.56395
307	247.33747	352	275.16267
308	247.97584	353	275.76052
309	248.61327	354	276.35750
310	249.24979	355	276.95361
311	249.88537	356	277.54885
312	250.52003	357	278.14322
313	251.15376	358	278.73673
314	251.78657	359	279.32938
315	252.41846	360	279.92116

yearly interest rate = 2.00%

term (months)	constant	term (months)	constant
1	0.9983361	46	44.245414
2	1.9950111	47	45.170131
3	2.9900278	48	46.093309
4	3.9833888	49	47.014950
5	4.9750970	50	47.935059
6	5.9651552	51	48.853636
7	6.9535658	52	49.770685
8	7.9403320	53	50.686208
9	8.9254563	54	51.600207
10	9.9089414	55	52.512686
11	10.890790	56	53.423647
12	11.871005	57	54.333092
13	12.849589	58	55.241023
14	13.826545	59	56.147444
15	14.801875	60	57.052357
16	15.775583	61	57.955764
17	16.747670	62	58.857668
18	17.718140	63	59.758071
19	18.686995	64	60.656976
20	19.654238	65	61.554386
21	20.619871	66	62.450302
22	21.583898	67	63.344728
23	22.546321	68	64.237665
24	23.507142	69	65.129116
25	24.466365	70	66.019085
26	25.423992	71	66.907572
27	26.380025	72	67.794581
28	27.334468	73	68.680114
29	28.287322	74	69.564174
30	29.238591	75	70.446763
31	30.188278	76	71.327883
32	31.136384	77	72.207537
33	32.082912	78	73.085727
34	33.027866	79	73.962457
35	33.971247	80	74.837727
36	34.913059	81	75.711541
37	35.853303	82	76.583901
38	36.791983	83	77.454810
39	37.729101	84	78.324270
40	38.664660	85	79.192283
41	39.598662	86	80.058851
42	40.531111	87	80.923978
43	41.462007	88	81.787665
44	42.391355	89	82.649915
45	43.319157	90	83.510731

yearly interest rate = 2.00%

term (months)	constant	term (months)	constant
91	84.370114	136	121.59787
92	85.228067	137	122.39388
93	86.084593	138	123.18856
94	86.939694	139	123.98193
95	87.793371	140	124.77397
96	88.645629	141	125.56470
97	89.496468	142	126.35411
98	90.345891	143	127.14220
99	91.193902	144	127.92899
100	92.040501	145	128.71446
101	92.885691	146	129.49863
102	93.729476	147	130.28150
103	94.571856	148	131.06306
104	95.412834	149	131.84332
105	96.252414	150	132.62228
106	97.090596	151	133.39995
107	97.927384	152	134.17632
108	98.762779	153	134.95140
109	99.596785	154	135.72519
110	100.42940	155	136.49770
111	101.26063	156	137.26892
112	102.09048	157	138.03885
113	102.91895	158	138.80751
114	103.74604	159	139.57488
115	104.57176	160	140.34098
116	105.39610	161	141.10580
117	106.21906	162	141.86935
118	107.04066	163	142.63163
119	107.86089	164	143.39265
120	108.67976	165	144.15239
121	109.49727	166	144.91087
122	110.31341	167	145.66809
123	111.12820	168	146.42405
124	111.94163	169	147.17876
125	112.75371	170	147.93220
126	113.56443	171	148.68440
127	114.37381	172	149.43534
128	115.18184	173	150.18503
129	115.98852	174	150.93347
130	116.79387	175	151.68067
131	117.59787	176	152.42663
132	118.40054	177	153.17134
133	119.20187	178	153.91482
134	120.00186	179	154.65705
135	120.80053	180	155.39806

yearly interest rate = 2.00%

term (months)	constant	term (months)	constant
181	156.13783	226	188.18405
182	156.87637	227	188.86927
183	157.61368	228	189.55335
184	158.34976	229	190.23629
185	159.08462	230	190.91809
186	159.81826	231	191.59876
187	160.55067	232	192.27830
188	161.28187	233	192.95670
189	162.01185	234	193.63398
190	162.74062	235	194.31013
191	163.46817	236	194.98515
192	164.19451	237	195.65906
193	164.91965	238	196.33184
194	165.64357	239	197.00350
195	166.36630	240	197.67404
196	167.08782	241	198.34347
197	167.80814	242	199.01178
198	168.52726	243	199.67898
199	169.24518	244	200.34507
200	169.96191	245	201.01006
201	170.67745	246	201.67393
202	171.39180	247	202.33671
203	172.10495	248	202.99838
204	172.81693	249	203.65894
205	173.52771	250	204.31841
206	174.23732	251	204.97679
207	174.94574	252	205.63406
208	175.65299	253	206.29025
209	176.35906	254	206.94534
210	177.06395	255	207.59934
211	177.76767	256	208.25225
212	178.47022	257	208.90408
213	179.17160	258	209.55482
214	179.87181	259	210.20448
215	180.57086	260	210.85306
216	181.26875	261	211.50056
217	181.96547	262	212.14698
218	182.66104	263	212.79232
219	183.35544	264	213.43660
220	184.04870	265	214.07980
221	184.74080	266	214.72193
222	185.43174	267	215.36299
223	186.12154	268	216.00298
224	186.81019	269	216.64191
225	187.49769	270	217.27978

yearly interest rate = 2.00%

term (months)	constant	term (months)	constant
271	217.91659	316	245.50247
272	218.55233	317	246.09232
273	219.18702	318	246.68118
274	219.82065	319	247.26907
275	220.45323	320	247.85597
276	221.08476	321	248.44190
277	221.71523	322	249.02686
278	222.34466	323	249.61084
279	222.97303	324	250.19385
280	223.60037	325	250.77589
281	224.22666	326	251.35696
282	224.85190	327	251.93707
283	225.47611	328	252.51621
284	226.09928	329	253.09438
285	226.72141	330	253.67160
286	227.34250	331	254.24785
287	227.96257	332	254.82315
288	228.58160	333	255.39748
289	229.19960	334	255.97087
290	229.81657	335	256.54329
291	230.43252	336	257.11477
292	231.04744	337	257.68529
293	231.66133	338	258.25487
294	232.27421	339	258.82350
295	232.88607	340	259.39118
296	233.49691	341	259.95791
297	234.10673	342	260.52371
298	234.71554	343	261.08856
299	235.32333	344	261.65247
300	235.93011	345	262.21545
301	236.53589	346	262.77749
302	237.14065	347	263.33859
303	237.74441	348	263.89876
304	238.34717	349	264.45799
305	238.94892	350	265.01630
306	239.54967	351	265.57368
307	240.14942	352	266.13013
308	240.74817	353	266.68565
309	241.34593	354	267.24025
310	241.94269	355	267.79393
311	242.53846	356	268.34668
312	243.13324	357	268.89852
313	243.72703	358	269.44944
314	244.31983	359	269.99944
315	244.91164	360	270.54852

yearly interest rate = 2.25%

term (months)	constant	term (months)	constant
1	0.9981285	46	44.032561
2	1.9943890	47	44.948283
3	2.9887851	48	45.862291
4	3.9813201	49	46.774588
5	4.9719976	50	47.685179
6	5.9608211	51	48.594065
7	6.9477939	52	49.501250
8	7.9329197	53	50.406737
9	8.9162019	54	51.310530
10	9.8976438	55	52.212632
11	10.877249	56	53.113045
12	11.855021	57	54.011772
13	12.830963	58	54.908818
14	13.805078	59	55.804186
15	14.777371	60	56.697877
16	15.747843	61	57.589896
17	16.716500	62	58.480246
18	17.683344	63	59.368929
19	18.648378	64	60.255949
20	19.611606	65	61.141309
21	20.573032	66	62.025012
22	21.532658	67	62.907061
23	22.490488	68	63.787460
24	23.446526	69	64.666211
25	24.400775	70	65.543317
26	25.353237	71	66.418782
27	26.303918	72	67.292608
28	27.252819	73	68.164799
29	28.199944	74	69.035358
30	29.145296	75	69.904287
31	30.088880	76	70.771591
32	31.030697	77	71.637271
33	31.970752	78	72.501331
34	32.909048	79	73.363774
35	33.845587	80	74.224603
36	34.780374	81	75.083820
37	35.713411	82	75.941430
38	36.644702	83	76.797435
39	37.574251	84	77.651838
40	38.502059	85	78.504642
41	39.428132	86	79.355849
42	40.352471	87	80.205464
43	41.275080	88	81.053489
44	42.195963	89	81.899927
45	43.115122	90	82.744780

yearly interest rate = 2.25%

term (months)	constant	term (months)	constant
91	83.588053	136	119.94584
92	84.429747	137	120.71950
93	85.269866	138	121.49170
94	86.108412	139	122.26246
95	86.945390	140	123.03177
96	87.780801	141	123.79965
97	88.614648	142	124.56609
98	89.446935	143	125.33109
99	90.277665	144	126.09466
100	91.106840	145	126.85681
101	91.934462	146	127.61752
102	92.760536	147	128.37682
103	93.585064	148	129.13469
104	94.408049	149	129.89114
105	95.229494	150	130.64618
106	96.049401	151	131.39981
107	96.867774	152	132.15202
108	97.684616	153	132.90283
109	98.499928	154	133.65223
110	99.313715	155	134.40023
111	100.12598	156	135.14683
112	100.93672	157	135.89203
113	101.74595	158	136.63584
114	102.55366	159	137.37826
115	103.35986	160	138.11928
116	104.16455	161	138.85892
117	104.96774	162	139.59718
118	105.76942	163	140.33405
119	106.56960	164	141.06955
120	107.36829	165	141.80366
121	108.16548	166	142.53641
122	108.96117	167	143.26778
123	109.75538	168	143.99779
124	110.54811	169	144.72642
125	111.33934	170	145.45370
126	112.12910	171	146.17961
127	112.91738	172	146.90417
128	113.70419	173	147.62736
129	114.48952	174	148.34921
130	115.27338	175	149.06970
131	116.05578	176	149.78885
132	116.83671	177	150.50665
133	117.61618	178	151.22311
134	118.39419	179	151.93822
135	119.17074	180	152.65200

yearly interest rate = 2.25%

term (months)	constant	term (months)	constant
181	153.36444	226	184.08145
182	154.07555	227	184.73507
183	154.78533	228	185.38747
184	155.49378	229	186.03865
185	156.20090	230	186.68861
186	156.90670	231	187.33735
187	157.61118	232	187.98488
188	158.31434	233	188.63120
189	159.01618	234	189.27630
190	159.71672	235	189.92020
191	160.41594	236	190.56290
192	161.11385	237	191.20439
193	161.81045	238	191.84468
194	162.50575	239	192.48377
195	163.19976	240	193.12167
196	163.89246	241	193.75837
197	164.58386	242	194.39388
198	165.27397	243	195.02821
199	165.96279	244	195.66134
200	166.65032	245	196.29329
201	167.33657	246	196.92406
202	168.02153	247	197.55365
203	168.70520	248	198.18205
204	169.38760	249	198.80929
205	170.06872	250	199.43535
206	170.74857	251	200.06023
207	171.42714	252	200.68395
208	172.10445	253	201.30650
209	172.78049	254	201.92789
210	173.45526	255	202.54811
211	174.12877	256	203.16717
212	174.80101	257	203.78507
213	175.47200	258	204.40182
214	176.14174	259	205.01741
215	176.81022	260	205.63185
216	177.47745	261	206.24514
217	178.14343	262	206.85728
218	178.80816	263	207.46828
219	179.47166	264	208.07813
220	180.13390	265	208.68685
221	180.79491	266	209.29442
222	181.45469	267	209.90086
223	182.11322	268	210.50616
224	182.77053	269	211.11033
225	183.42660	270	211.71336

yearly interest rate = 2.25%

term (months)	constant	term (months)	constant
271	212.31527	316	238.26665
272	212.91605	317	238.81886
273	213.51571	318	239.37004
274	214.11425	319	239.92019
275	214.71166	320	240.46931
276	215.30796	321	241.01740
277	215.90314	322	241.56447
278	216.49721	323	242.11051
279	217.09017	324	242.65553
280	217.68201	325	243.19953
281	218.27275	326	243.74252
282	218.86238	327	244.28448
283	219.45091	328	244.82544
284	220.03834	329	245.36538
285	220.62467	330	245.90431
286	221.20990	331	246.44223
287	221.79404	332	246.97914
288	222.37708	333	247.51505
289	222.95903	334	248.04996
290	223.53990	335	248.58386
291	224.11967	336	249.11677
292	224.69836	337	249.64868
293	225.27597	338	250.17959
294	225.85250	339	250.70951
295	226.42794	340	251.23844
296	227.00231	341	251.76638
297	227.57561	342	252.29333
298	228.14783	343	252.81929
299	228.71898	344	253.34427
300	229.28907	345	253.86827
301	229.85808	346	254.39128
302	230.42603	347	254.91332
303	230.99292	348	255.43438
304	231.55875	349	255.95447
305	232.12352	350	256.47358
306	232.68723	351	256.99172
307	233.24989	352	257.50889
308	233.81149	353	258.02509
309	234.37204	354	258.54033
310	234.93155	355	259.05460
311	235.49000	356	259.56791
312	236.04741	357	260.08026
313	236.60378	358	260.59165
314	237.15911	359	261.10209
315	237.71340	360	261.61156

yearly interest rate = 2.50%

term (months)	constant	term (months)	constant
1	0.9979210	46	43.821109
2	1.9937673	47	44.727926
3	2.9875432	48	45.632857
4	3.9792531	49	46.535908
5	4.9689012	50	47.437080
6	5.9564919	51	48.336380
7	6.9420293	52	49.233809
8	7.9255178	53	50.129373
9	8.9069616	54	51.023075
10	9.8863650	55	51.914919
11	10.863732	56	52.804909
12	11.839068	57	53.693048
13	12.812375	58	54.579341
14	13.783659	59	55.463791
15	14.752924	60	56.346403
16	15.720173	61	57.227180
17	16.685412	62	58.106125
18	17.648644	63	58.983244
19	18.609874	64	59.858538
20	19.569105	65	60.732013
21	20.526341	66	61.603672
22	21.481588	67	62.473519
23	22.434849	68	63.341558
24	23.386128	69	64.207791
25	24.335429	70	65.072224
26	25.282756	71	65.934860
27	26.228114	72	66.795702
28	27.171507	73	67.654755
29	28.112939	74	68.512021
30	29.052413	75	69.367506
31	29.989934	76	70.221211
32	30.925505	77	71.073142
33	31.859132	78	71.923302
34	32.790818	79	72.771695
35	33.720567	80	73.618323
36	34.648383	81	74.463191
37	35.574270	82	75.306303
38	36.498232	83	76.147662
39	37.420273	84	76.987272
40	38.340397	85	77.825136
41	39.258608	86	78.661259
42	40.174910	87	79.495643
43	41.089308	88	80.328292
44	42.001804	89	81.159210
45	42.912403	90	81.988401

yearly interest rate = 2.50%

term (months)	constant	term (months)	constant
91	82.815868	136	118.32446
92	83.641615	137	119.07639
93	84.465645	138	119.82675
94	85.287961	139	120.57555
95	86.108569	140	121.32279
96	86.927470	141	122.06848
97	87.744668	142	122.81262
98	88.560168	143	123.55522
99	89.373972	144	124.29627
100	90.186085	145	125.03578
101	90.996508	146	125.77375
102	91.805248	147	126.51018
103	92.612305	148	127.24509
104	93.417685	149	127.97847
105	94.221390	150	128.71032
106	95.023425	151	129.44065
107	95.823792	152	130.16947
108	96.622495	153	130.89677
109	97.419538	154	131.62255
110	98.214923	155	132.34683
111	99.008655	156	133.06960
112	99.800737	157	133.79087
113	100.59117	158	134.51064
114	101.37996	159	135.22891
115	102.16712	160	135.94569
116	102.95263	161	136.66098
117	103.73651	162	137.37479
118	104.51877	163	138.08710
119	105.29939	164	138.79794
120	106.07840	165	139.50730
121	106.85578	166	140.21519
122	107.63155	167	140.92160
123	108.40570	168	141.62654
124	109.17825	169	142.33002
125	109.94919	170	143.03204
126	110.71852	171	143.73260
127	111.48626	172	144.43170
128	112.25240	173	145.12934
129	113.01695	174	145.82554
130	113.77991	175	146.52029
131	114.54128	176	147.21360
132	115.30107	177	147.90546
133	116.05928	178	148.59588
134	116.81591	179	149.28487
135	117.57097	180	149.97243

yearly interest rate = 2.50%

term (months)	constant	term (months)	constant
181	150.65856	226	180.10196
182	151.34326	227	180.72545
183	152.02654	228	181.34764
184	152.70840	229	181.96854
185	153.38884	230	182.58815
186	154.06786	231	183.20647
187	154.74548	232	183.82350
188	155.42168	233	184.43925
189	156.09648	234	185.05373
190	156.76988	235	185.66692
191	157.44187	236	186.27884
192	158.11247	237	186.88949
193	158.78168	238	187.49886
194	159.44949	239	188.10697
195	160.11591	240	188.71382
196	160.78095	241	189.31940
197	161.44461	242	189.92373
198	162.10689	243	190.52680
199	162.76779	244	191.12861
200	163.42732	245	191.72918
201	164.08547	246	192.32849
202	164.74226	247	192.92656
203	165.39768	248	193.52339
204	166.05174	249	194.11898
205	166.70444	250	194.71332
206	167.35578	251	195.30643
207	168.00577	252	195.89831
208	168.65440	253	196.48896
209	169.30169	254	197.07838
210	169.94763	255	197.66658
211	170.59223	256	198.25355
212	171.23549	257	198.83930
213	171.87742	258	199.42383
214	172.51800	259	200.00715
215	173.15726	260	200.58926
216	173.79519	261	201.17015
217	174.43179	262	201.74984
218	175.06706	263	202.32832
219	175.70102	264	202.90560
220	176.33366	265	203.48168
221	176.96498	266	204.05657
222	177.59499	267	204.63025
223	178.22369	268	205.20275
224	178.85108	269	205.77405
225	179.47717	270	206.34417

yearly interest rate = 2.50%

term (months)	constant	term (months)	constant
271	206.91310	316	231.32730
272	207.40805	317	231.84429
273	208.04741	318	232.36020
274	208.61280	319	232.87505
275	209.17702	320	233.38882
276	209.74006	321	233.90153
277	210.30193	322	234.41316
278	210.86263	323	234.92374
279	211.42217	324	235.43325
280	211.98054	325	235.94171
281	212.53776	326	236.44911
282	213.09381	327	236.95545
283	213.64871	328	237.46074
284	214.20246	329	237.96498
285	214.75505	330	238.46817
286	215.30649	331	238.97032
287	215.85679	332	239.47142
288	216.40595	333	239.97148
289	216.95396	334	240.47050
290	217.50083	335	240.96848
291	218.04657	336	241.46543
292	218.59117	337	241.96134
293	219.13464	338	242.45622
294	219.67698	339	242.95008
295	220.21819	340	243.44290
296	220.75828	341	243.93471
297	221.29724	342	244.42549
298	221.83509	343	244.91525
299	222.37181	344	245.40399
300	222.90742	345	245.89171
301	223.44192	346	246.37843
302	223.97530	347	246.86413
303	224.50758	348	247.34882
304	225.03875	349	247.83250
305	225.56881	350	248.31517
306	226.09778	351	248.79685
307	226.62564	352	249.27752
308	227.15240	353	249.75719
309	227.67807	354	250.23587
310	228.20265	355	250.71355
311	228.72614	356	251.19023
312	229.24854	357	251.66593
313	229.76985	358	252.14064
314	230.29008	359	252.61436
315	230.80923	360	253.08709

yearly interest rate = 2.75%

term (months)	constant	term (months)	constant
1	0.9977136	46	43.611051
2	1.9931460	47	44.509051
3	2.9863024	48	45.404998
4	3.9771881	49	46.298896
5	4.9658081	50	47.190751
6	5.9521677	51	48.080566
7	6.9362721	52	48.968347
8	7.9181264	53	49.854098
9	8.8977358	54	50.737824
10	9.8751054	55	51.619529
11	10.850240	56	52.499218
12	11.823146	57	53.376896
13	12.793826	58	54.252567
14	13.762288	59	55.126237
15	14.728535	60	55.997908
16	15.692573	61	56.867587
17	16.654407	62	57.735277
18	17.614041	63	58.600983
19	18.571481	64	59.464709
20	19.526733	65	60.326461
21	20.479800	66	61.186243
22	21.430688	67	62.044058
23	22.379402	68	62.899913
24	23.325946	69	63.753810
25	24.270327	70	64.605756
26	25.212548	71	65.455753
27	26.152615	72	66.303807
28	27.090533	73	67.149921
29	28.026306	74	67.994102
30	28.959939	75	68.836352
31	29.891438	76	69.676676
32	30.820807	77	70.515079
33	31.748051	78	71.351565
34	32.673175	79	72.186138
35	33.596184	80	73.018804
36	34.517082	81	73.849565
37	35.435875	82	74.678427
38	36.352567	83	75.505394
39	37.267163	84	76.330470
40	38.179668	85	77.153659
41	39.090087	86	77.974967
42	39.998424	87	78.794396
43	40.904684	88	79.611952
44	41.808872	89	80.427639
45	42.710993	90	81.241461

yearly interest rate = 2.75%

term (months)	constant	term (months)	constant
91	82.053422	136	116.73308
92	82.863526	137	117.46389
93	83.671778	138	118.19303
94	84.478182	139	118.92050
95	85.282743	140	119.64632
96	86.085464	141	120.37047
97	86.886349	142	121.09296
98	87.685403	143	121.81381
99	88.482631	144	122.53300
100	89.278035	145	123.25055
101	90.071621	146	123.96646
102	90.863393	147	124.68073
103	91.653354	148	125.39337
104	92.441509	149	126.10439
105	93.227861	150	126.81377
106	94.012416	151	127.52153
107	94.795177	152	128.22768
108	95.576149	153	128.93221
109	96.355334	154	129.63513
110	97.132739	155	130.33644
111	97.908365	156	131.03615
112	98.682218	157	131.73426
113	99.454302	158	132.43077
114	100.22462	159	133.12569
115	100.99318	160	133.81902
116	101.75998	161	134.51077
117	102.52503	162	135.20093
118	103.28832	163	135.88952
119	104.04988	164	136.57653
120	104.80969	165	137.26197
121	105.56776	166	137.94585
122	106.32410	167	138.62816
123	107.07871	168	139.30891
124	107.83160	169	139.98810
125	108.58276	170	140.66574
126	109.33221	171	141.34184
127	110.07994	172	142.01638
128	110.82597	173	142.68939
129	111.57029	174	143.36085
130	112.31290	175	144.03078
131	113.05382	176	144.69918
132	113.79304	177	145.36605
133	114.53058	178	146.03139
134	115.26643	179	146.69521
135	116.00059	180	147.35752

yearly interest rate = 2.75%

term (months)	constant	term (months)	constant
181	148.01831	226	176.24137
182	148.67759	227	176.83612
183	149.33537	228	177.42951
184	149.99163	229	178.02154
185	150.64640	230	178.61222
186	151.29967	231	179.20155
187	151.95145	232	179.78953
188	152.60174	233	180.37617
189	153.25054	234	180.96147
190	153.89786	235	181.54543
191	154.54370	236	182.12805
192	155.18806	237	182.70934
193	155.83094	238	183.28930
194	156.47236	239	183.86794
195	157.11231	240	184.44525
196	157.75080	241	185.02125
197	158.38783	242	185.59592
198	159.02340	243	186.16928
199	159.65752	244	186.74134
200	160.29019	245	187.31208
201	160.92141	246	187.88152
202	161.55119	247	188.44965
203	162.17953	248	189.01649
204	162.80643	249	189.58203
205	163.43190	250	190.14628
206	164.05593	251	190.70924
207	164.67855	252	191.27091
208	165.29973	253	191.83129
209	165.91950	254	192.39040
210	166.53785	255	192.94823
211	167.15479	256	193.50478
212	167.77032	257	194.06006
213	168.38444	258	194.61407
214	168.99715	259	195.16681
215	169.60846	260	195.71829
216	170.21838	261	196.26851
217	170.82690	262	196.81747
218	171.43403	263	197.36517
219	172.03977	264	197.91162
220	172.64413	265	198.45683
221	173.24711	266	199.00078
222	173.84870	267	199.54350
223	174.44893	268	200.08497
224	175.04777	269	200.62520
225	175.64525	270	201.16420

yearly interest rate = 2.75%

term (months)	constant	term (months)	constant
271	201.70197	316	224.67050
272	202.23850	317	225.15452
273	202.77381	318	225.63744
274	203.30790	319	226.11925
275	203.84077	320	226.59995
276	204.37241	321	227.07956
277	204.90284	322	227.55808
278	205.43206	323	228.03550
279	205.96007	324	228.51182
280	206.48687	325	228.98706
281	207.01247	326	229.46121
282	207.53686	327	229.93428
283	208.06006	328	230.40627
284	208.58206	329	230.87717
285	209.10286	330	231.34700
286	209.62248	331	231.81576
287	210.14091	332	232.28344
288	210.65815	333	232.75006
289	211.17421	334	233.21560
290	211.68909	335	233.68009
291	212.20279	336	234.14351
292	212.71531	337	234.60587
293	213.22667	338	235.06717
294	213.73686	339	235.52742
295	214.24588	340	235.98662
296	214.75373	341	236.44477
297	215.26043	342	236.90187
298	215.76596	343	237.35792
299	216.27034	344	237.81293
300	216.77357	345	238.26691
301	217.27565	346	238.71984
302	217.77658	347	239.17174
303	218.27636	348	239.62260
304	218.77500	349	240.07244
305	219.27250	350	240.52124
306	219.76886	351	240.96902
307	220.26409	352	241.41578
308	220.75819	353	241.86151
309	221.25115	354	242.30623
310	221.74299	355	242.74992
311	222.23371	356	243.19261
312	222.72330	357	243.63428
313	223.21177	358	244.07494
314	223.69913	359	244.51459
315	224.18537	360	244.95324

yearly interest rate = 3.00%

term (months)	constant	term (months)	constant
1	0.9975062	46	43.402371
2	1.9925249	47	44.291642
3	2.9850623	48	45.178695
4	3.9751245	49	46.063536
5	4.9627177	50	46.946171
6	5.9478481	51	47.826604
7	6.9305218	52	48.704842
8	7.9107449	53	49.580890
9	8.8885236	54	50.454753
10	9.8638640	55	51.326437
11	10.836772	56	52.195947
12	11.807254	57	53.063289
13	12.775316	58	53.928468
14	13.740963	59	54.791489
15	14.704203	60	55.652358
16	15.665040	61	56.511080
17	16.623481	62	57.367661
18	17.579533	63	58.222106
19	18.533200	64	59.074420
20	19.484488	65	59.924608
21	20.433405	66	60.772677
22	21.379955	67	61.618630
23	22.324145	68	62.462474
24	23.265980	69	63.304213
25	24.205466	70	64.143854
26	25.142610	71	64.981400
27	26.077416	72	65.816858
28	27.009891	73	66.650233
29	27.940041	74	67.481529
30	28.867872	75	68.310752
31	29.793388	76	69.137907
32	30.716597	77	69.963000
33	31.637503	78	70.786035
34	32.556113	79	71.607017
35	33.472431	80	72.425952
36	34.386465	81	73.242845
37	35.298220	82	74.057701
38	36.207700	83	74.870524
39	37.114913	84	75.681321
40	38.019864	85	76.490096
41	38.922557	86	77.296854
42	39.823000	87	78.101600
43	40.721197	88	78.904339
44	41.617154	89	79.705076
45	42.510877	90	80.503817

yearly interest rate = 3.00%

term (months)	constant	term (months)	constant
91	81.300565	136	115.17105
92	82.095327	137	115.88134
93	82.888107	138	116.58987
94	83.678909	139	117.29663
95	84.467740	140	118.00162
96	85.254604	141	118.70486
97	86.039505	142	119.40634
98	86.822449	143	120.10608
99	87.603440	144	120.80407
100	88.382484	145	121.50032
101	89.159585	146	122.19483
102	89.934748	147	122.88761
103	90.707978	148	123.57867
104	91.479280	149	124.26800
105	92.248658	150	124.95561
106	93.016118	151	125.64150
107	93.781664	152	126.32569
108	94.545301	153	127.00817
109	95.307033	154	127.68895
110	96.066866	155	128.36803
111	96.824804	156	129.04541
112	97.580852	157	129.72111
113	98.335014	158	130.39512
114	99.087296	159	131.06745
115	99.837702	160	131.73811
116	100.58624	161	132.40709
117	101.33290	162	133.07440
118	102.07771	163	133.74005
119	102.82066	164	134.40404
120	103.56175	165	135.06638
121	104.30100	166	135.72706
122	105.03841	167	136.38610
123	105.77397	168	137.04349
124	106.50770	169	137.69924
125	107.23960	170	138.35335
126	107.96968	171	139.00584
127	108.69793	172	139.65670
128	109.42437	173	140.30593
129	110.14900	174	140.95355
130	110.87182	175	141.59955
131	111.59284	176	142.24394
132	112.31206	177	142.88672
133	113.02948	178	143.52790
134	113.74512	179	144.16749
135	114.45897	180	144.80547

yearly interest rate = 3.00%

term (months)	constant	term (months)	constant
181	145.44187	226	172.49559
182	146.07668	227	173.06293
183	146.70990	228	173.62886
184	147.34155	229	174.19338
185	147.97162	230	174.75649
186	148.60012	231	175.31819
187	149.22705	232	175.87850
188	149.85242	233	176.43740
189	150.47623	234	176.99491
190	151.09848	235	177.55104
191	151.71918	236	178.10577
192	152.33834	237	178.65912
193	152.95595	238	179.21110
194	153.57202	239	179.76169
195	154.18655	240	180.31092
196	154.79955	241	180.85877
197	155.41103	242	181.40526
198	156.02097	243	181.95038
199	156.62940	244	182.49414
200	157.23631	245	183.03655
201	157.84170	246	183.57761
202	158.44559	247	184.11732
203	159.04797	248	184.65568
204	159.64885	249	185.19269
205	160.24823	250	185.72837
206	160.84611	251	186.26272
207	161.44251	252	186.79573
208	162.03741	253	187.32741
209	162.63084	254	187.85776
210	163.22278	255	188.38680
211	163.81325	256	188.91451
212	164.40224	257	189.44091
213	164.98977	258	189.96599
214	165.57583	259	190.48977
215	166.16043	260	191.01224
216	166.74357	261	191.53341
217	167.32525	262	192.05327
218	167.90549	263	192.57184
219	168.48428	264	193.08912
220	169.06163	265	193.60511
221	169.63753	266	194.11981
222	170.21200	267	194.63322
223	170.78504	268	195.14536
224	171.35665	269	195.65622
225	171.92683	270	196.16581

yearly interest rate = 3.00%

term (months)	constant	term (months)	constant
271	196.67412	316	218.28302
272	197.18117	317	218.73618
273	197.68695	318	219.18821
274	198.19147	319	219.63912
275	198.69473	320	220.08889
276	199.19674	321	220.53755
277	199.69750	322	220.98509
278	200.19701	323	221.43151
279	200.69527	324	221.87682
280	201.19229	325	222.32101
281	201.68807	326	222.76410
282	202.18261	327	223.20609
283	202.67592	328	223.64697
284	203.16800	329	224.08675
285	203.65885	330	224.52544
286	204.14848	331	224.96303
287	204.63689	332	225.39953
288	205.12408	333	225.83495
289	205.61006	334	226.26927
290	206.09482	335	226.70252
291	206.57837	336	227.13468
292	207.06072	337	227.56577
293	207.54187	338	227.99578
294	208.02181	339	228.42471
295	208.50056	340	228.85258
296	208.97811	341	229.27938
297	209.45448	342	229.70512
298	209.92965	343	230.12980
299	210.40365	344	230.55341
300	210.87645	345	230.97597
301	211.34808	346	231.39748
302	211.81854	347	231.81794
303	212.28782	348	232.23734
304	212.75593	349	232.65570
305	213.22287	350	233.07302
306	213.68865	351	233.48930
307	214.15327	352	233.90454
308	214.61672	353	234.31874
309	215.07903	354	234.73191
310	215.54018	355	235.14405
311	216.00018	356	235.55516
312	216.45903	357	235.96525
313	216.91674	358	236.37431
314	217.37330	359	236.78236
315	217.82873	360	237.18938

yearly interest rate = 3.25%

term (months)	constant	term (months)	constant
1	0.9972990	46	43.195061
2	1.9919042	47	44.075689
3	2.9838230	48	44.953939
4	3.9730626	49	45.829817
5	4.9596303	50	46.703329
6	5.9435332	51	47.574481
7	6.9247786	52	48.443280
8	7.9033736	53	49.309733
9	8.8793254	54	50.173846
10	9.8526412	55	51.035624
11	10.823328	56	51.895075
12	11.791393	57	52.752204
13	12.756843	58	53.607019
14	13.719686	59	54.459524
15	14.679928	60	55.309727
16	15.637576	61	56.157633
17	16.592637	62	57.003250
18	17.545119	63	57.846582
19	18.495029	64	58.687636
20	19.442372	65	59.526419
21	20.387157	66	60.362936
22	21.329390	67	61.197193
23	22.269078	68	62.029198
24	23.206228	69	62.858955
25	24.140846	70	63.686470
26	25.072940	71	64.511751
27	26.002517	72	65.334803
28	26.929582	73	66.155631
29	27.854144	74	66.974243
30	28.776209	75	67.790643
31	29.695782	76	68.604838
32	30.612873	77	69.416834
33	31.527486	78	70.226637
34	32.439628	79	71.034253
35	33.349307	80	71.839687
36	34.256529	81	72.642945
37	35.161301	82	73.444035
38	36.063628	83	74.242960
39	36.963519	84	75.039727
40	37.860979	85	75.834343
41	38.756014	86	76.626812
42	39.648633	87	77.417140
43	40.538840	88	78.205334
44	41.426643	89	78.991399
45	42.312048	90	79.775341

yearly interest rate = 3.25%

term (months)	constant	term (months)	constant
91	80.557165	136	113.63775
92	81.336878	137	114.32812
93	82.114484	138	115.01661
94	82.889991	139	115.70325
95	83.663402	140	116.38803
96	84.434725	141	117.07096
97	85.203964	142	117.75205
98	85.971126	143	118.43130
99	86.736215	144	119.10871
100	87.499238	145	119.78430
101	88.260200	146	120.45806
102	89.019106	147	121.13000
103	89.775963	148	121.80012
104	90.530776	149	122.46844
105	91.283549	150	123.13495
106	92.034290	151	123.79966
107	92.783003	152	124.46257
108	93.529693	153	125.12369
109	94.274367	154	125.78303
110	95.017029	155	126.44059
111	95.757685	156	127.09637
112	96.496341	157	127.75038
113	97.233001	158	128.40262
114	97.967672	159	129.05310
115	98.700359	160	129.70183
116	99.431066	161	130.34880
117	100.15980	162	130.99402
118	100.88657	163	131.63750
119	101.61137	164	132.27925
120	102.33421	165	132.91926
121	103.05511	166	133.55754
122	103.77405	167	134.19410
123	104.49105	168	134.82894
124	105.20612	169	135.46206
125	105.91926	170	136.09347
126	106.63047	171	136.72318
127	107.33975	172	137.35119
128	108.04713	173	137.97750
129	108.75259	174	138.60212
130	109.45614	175	139.22505
131	110.15780	176	139.84630
132	110.85756	177	140.46587
133	111.55543	178	141.08377
134	112.25142	179	141.70000
135	112.94552	180	142.31456

yearly interest rate = 3.25%

term (months)	constant	term (months)	constant
181	142.92747	226	168.86072
182	143.53872	227	169.40193
183	144.14832	228	169.94167
184	144.75627	229	170.47995
185	145.36258	230	171.01678
186	145.96725	231	171.55216
187	146.57029	232	172.08610
188	147.17170	233	172.61859
189	147.77148	234	173.14964
190	148.36965	235	173.67926
191	148.96620	236	174.20745
192	149.56114	237	174.73421
193	150.15447	238	175.25955
194	150.74620	239	175.78347
195	151.33633	240	176.30597
196	151.92487	241	176.82706
197	152.51181	242	177.34675
198	153.09718	243	177.86503
199	153.68096	244	178.38191
200	154.26316	245	178.89740
201	154.84379	246	179.41149
202	155.42285	247	179.92420
203	156.00035	248	180.43552
204	156.57629	249	180.94546
205	157.15068	250	181.45402
206	157.72351	251	181.96121
207	158.29479	252	182.46703
208	158.86454	253	182.97148
209	159.43274	254	183.47457
210	159.99941	255	183.97630
211	160.56454	256	184.47668
212	161.12816	257	184.97570
213	161.69024	258	185.47338
214	162.25082	259	185.96971
215	162.80987	260	186.46470
216	163.36742	261	186.95836
217	163.92346	262	187.45068
218	164.47800	263	187.94167
219	165.03104	264	188.43133
220	165.58259	265	188.91968
221	166.13264	266	189.40670
222	166.68121	267	189.89241
223	167.22830	268	190.37680
224	167.77392	269	190.85989
225	168.31806	270	191.34167

yearly interest rate = 3.25%

term (months)	constant	term (months)	constant
271	191.82216	316	212.15232
272	192.30134	317	212.57659
273	192.77923	318	212.99972
274	193.25583	319	213.42170
275	193.73114	320	213.84254
276	194.20517	321	214.26225
277	194.67791	322	214.68082
278	195.14938	323	215.09826
279	195.61958	324	215.51458
280	196.08851	325	215.92977
281	196.55617	326	216.34384
282	197.02257	327	216.75679
283	197.48770	328	217.16862
284	197.95158	329	217.57935
285	198.41421	330	217.98896
286	198.87559	331	218.39747
287	199.33572	332	218.80487
288	199.79461	333	219.21117
289	200.25226	334	219.61638
290	200.70868	335	220.02049
291	201.16386	336	220.42351
292	201.61781	337	220.82544
293	202.07054	338	221.22628
294	202.52204	339	221.62605
295	202.97232	340	222.02473
296	203.42139	341	222.42234
297	203.86924	342	222.81887
298	204.31589	343	223.21433
299	204.76133	344	223.60872
300	205.20556	345	224.00205
301	205.64860	346	224.39432
302	206.09043	347	224.78552
303	206.53108	348	225.17567
304	206.97053	349	225.56477
305	207.40880	350	225.95281
306	207.84589	351	226.33981
307	208.28179	352	226.72576
308	208.71652	353	227.11067
309	209.15007	354	227.49454
310	209.58245	355	227.87737
311	210.01366	356	228.25917
312	210.44371	357	228.63993
313	210.87260	358	229.01967
314	211.30032	359	229.39838
315	211.72690	360	229.77607

yearly interest rate = 3.50%

term (months)	constant	term (months)	constant
1	0.9970918	46	42.989113
2	1.9912839	47	43.861184
3	2.9825847	48	44.730720
4	3.9710026	49	45.597726
5	4.9565461	50	46.462211
6	5.9392234	51	47.324183
7	6.9190428	52	48.183647
8	7.8960128	53	49.040612
9	8.8701416	54	49.895085
10	9.8414374	55	50.747072
11	10.809909	56	51.596582
12	11.775563	57	52.443622
13	12.738409	58	53.288198
14	13.698456	59	54.130318
15	14.655710	60	54.969989
16	15.610180	61	55.807218
17	16.561875	62	56.642012
18	17.510802	63	57.474378
19	18.456969	64	58.304324
20	19.400384	65	59.131856
21	20.341056	66	59.956981
22	21.278993	67	60.779707
23	22.214201	68	61.600041
24	23.146690	69	62.417988
25	24.076467	70	63.233557
26	25.003540	71	64.046754
27	25.927917	72	64.857586
28	26.849606	73	65.666060
29	27.768614	74	66.472183
30	28.684949	75	67.275961
31	29.598620	76	68.077402
32	30.509634	77	68.876512
33	31.417998	78	69.673299
34	32.323720	79	70.467768
35	33.226809	80	71.259926
36	34.127271	81	72.049781
37	35.025114	82	72.837339
38	35.920347	83	73.622606
39	36.812976	84	74.405590
40	37.703008	85	75.186297
41	38.590453	86	75.964733
42	39.475317	87	76.740905
43	40.357607	88	77.514820
44	41.237331	89	78.286485
45	42.114498	90	79.055905

yearly interest rate = 3.50%

term (months)	constant	term (months)	constant
91	79.823088	136	112.13260
92	80.588039	137	112.80359
93	81.350766	138	113.47263
94	82.111275	139	114.13972
95	82.869572	140	114.80487
96	83.625664	141	115.46809
97	84.379557	142	116.12938
98	85.131257	143	116.78875
99	85.880772	144	117.44619
100	86.628106	145	118.10173
101	87.373268	146	118.75536
102	88.116262	147	119.40709
103	88.857095	148	120.05692
104	89.595774	149	120.70487
105	90.332305	150	121.35093
106	91.066694	151	121.99511
107	91.798947	152	122.63742
108	92.529071	153	123.27786
109	93.257071	154	123.91643
110	93.982954	155	124.55315
111	94.706726	156	125.18802
112	95.428393	157	125.82104
113	96.147962	158	126.45223
114	96.865437	159	127.08157
115	97.580827	160	127.70909
116	98.294136	161	128.33478
117	99.005370	162	128.95865
118	99.714536	163	129.58070
119	100.42164	164	130.20095
120	101.12669	165	130.81939
121	101.82968	166	131.43604
122	102.53064	167	132.05089
123	103.22955	168	132.66395
124	103.92643	169	133.27523
125	104.62129	170	133.88474
126	105.31412	171	134.49247
127	106.00494	172	135.09843
128	106.69375	173	135.70263
129	107.38055	174	136.30507
130	108.06536	175	136.90577
131	108.74818	176	137.50471
132	109.42901	177	138.10191
133	110.10787	178	138.69738
134	110.78474	179	139.29111
135	111.45965	180	139.88312

yearly interest rate = 3.50%

term (months)	constant	term (months)	constant
181	140.47341	226	165.33300
182	141.06198	227	165.84927
183	141.64883	228	166.36405
184	142.23398	229	166.87732
185	142.81743	230	167.38910
186	143.39919	231	167.89940
187	143.97925	232	168.40820
188	144.55762	233	168.91553
189	145.13431	234	169.42139
190	145.70933	235	169.92577
191	146.28267	236	170.42869
192	146.85434	237	170.93014
193	147.42436	238	171.43014
194	147.99271	239	171.92868
195	148.55941	240	172.42577
196	149.12447	241	172.92142
197	149.68788	242	173.41562
198	150.24965	243	173.90839
199	150.80979	244	174.39972
200	151.36830	245	174.88963
201	151.92518	246	175.37811
202	152.48045	247	175.86517
203	153.03410	248	176.35081
204	153.58614	249	176.83504
205	154.13657	250	177.31787
206	154.68541	251	177.79928
207	155.23264	252	178.27930
208	155.77829	253	178.75793
209	156.32235	254	179.23516
210	156.86483	255	179.71100
211	157.40573	256	180.18546
212	157.94506	257	180.65854
213	158.48281	258	181.13024
214	159.01901	259	181.60057
215	159.55364	260	182.06954
216	160.08672	261	182.53714
217	160.61825	262	183.00338
218	161.14824	263	183.46826
219	161.67668	264	183.93179
220	162.20359	265	184.39398
221	162.72896	266	184.85482
222	163.25281	267	185.31432
223	163.77513	268	185.77248
224	164.29593	269	186.22931
225	164.81522	270	186.68481

yearly interest rate = 3.50%

term (months)	constant	term (months)	constant
271	187.13899	316	206.26647
272	187.59185	317	206.66370
273	188.04339	318	207.05977
274	188.49362	319	207.45470
275	188.94253	320	207.84847
276	189.39015	321	208.24110
277	189.83646	322	208.63259
278	190.28147	323	209.02294
279	190.72519	324	209.41216
280	191.16762	325	209.80024
281	191.60876	326	210.18719
282	192.04861	327	210.57302
283	192.48719	328	210.95773
284	192.92450	329	211.34132
285	193.36053	330	211.72379
286	193.79529	331	212.10515
287	194.22879	332	212.48540
288	194.66103	333	212.86454
289	195.09201	334	213.24259
290	195.52174	335	213.61953
291	195.95022	336	213.99538
292	196.37745	337	214.37013
293	196.80344	338	214.74379
294	197.22819	339	215.11637
295	197.65171	340	215.48787
296	198.07399	341	215.85828
297	198.49505	342	216.22762
298	198.91488	343	216.59588
299	199.33349	344	216.96307
300	199.75088	345	217.32919
301	200.16706	346	217.69425
302	200.58203	347	218.05825
303	200.99580	348	218.42119
304	201.40835	349	218.78307
305	201.81971	350	219.14390
306	202.22988	351	219.50368
307	202.63885	352	219.86241
308	203.04663	353	220.22011
309	203.45322	354	220.57676
310	203.85863	355	220.93237
311	204.26287	356	221.28695
312	204.66593	357	221.64050
313	205.06781	358	221.99302
314	205.46853	359	222.34451
315	205.86808	360	222.69499

yearly interest rate = 3.75%

term (months)	constant	term (months)	constant
1	0.9968847	46	42.784512
2	1.9906639	47	43.648112
3	2.9813472	48	44.509021
4	3.9689443	49	45.367249
5	4.9534647	50	46.222802
6	5.9349181	51	47.075691
7	6.9133140	52	47.925922
8	7.8886619	53	48.773505
9	8.8609714	54	49.618447
10	9.8302518	55	50.460758
11	10.796513	56	51.300444
12	11.759763	57	52.137514
13	12.720013	58	52.971977
14	13.677272	59	53.803840
15	14.631548	60	54.633111
16	15.582852	61	55.459799
17	16.531192	62	56.283912
18	17.476578	63	57.105457
19	18.419018	64	57.924444
20	19.358523	65	58.740878
21	20.295101	66	59.554770
22	21.228761	67	60.366126
23	22.159512	68	61.174954
24	23.087364	69	61.981262
25	24.012326	70	62.785059
26	24.934406	71	63.586352
27	25.853613	72	64.385148
28	26.769957	73	65.181456
29	27.683446	74	65.975283
30	28.594090	75	66.766638
31	29.501896	76	67.555527
32	30.406875	77	68.341958
33	31.309034	78	69.125939
34	32.208383	79	69.907479
35	33.104930	80	70.686583
36	33.998684	81	71.463260
37	34.889654	82	72.237518
38	35.777848	83	73.009364
39	36.663276	84	73.778805
40	37.545945	85	74.545849
41	38.425864	86	75.310504
42	39.303042	87	76.072777
43	40.177487	88	76.832674
44	41.049208	89	77.590205
45	41.918214	90	78.345376

yearly interest rate = 3.75%

term (months)	constant	term (months)	constant
91	79.098194	136	110.65499
92	79.848667	137	111.30715
93	80.596802	138	111.95728
94	81.342606	139	112.60539
95	82.086087	140	113.25148
96	82.827252	141	113.89556
97	83.566108	142	114.53763
98	84.302662	143	115.17770
99	85.036922	144	115.81577
100	85.768894	145	116.45186
101	86.498586	146	117.08597
102	87.226005	147	117.71810
103	87.951157	148	118.34826
104	88.674051	149	118.97646
105	89.394692	150	119.60270
106	90.113089	151	120.22699
107	90.829248	152	120.84934
108	91.543175	153	121.46974
109	92.254879	154	122.08822
110	92.964365	155	122.70477
111	93.671641	156	123.31939
112	94.376714	157	123.93211
113	95.079590	158	124.54291
114	95.780277	159	125.15181
115	96.478781	160	125.75881
116	97.175109	161	126.36393
117	97.869267	162	126.96715
118	98.561263	163	127.56850
119	99.251103	164	128.16798
120	99.938795	165	128.76558
121	100.62434	166	129.36133
122	101.30776	167	129.95522
123	101.98904	168	130.54726
124	102.66820	169	131.13746
125	103.34525	170	131.72581
126	104.02019	171	132.31234
127	104.69302	172	132.89703
128	105.36376	173	133.47991
129	106.03241	174	134.06097
130	106.69897	175	134.64022
131	107.36346	176	135.21766
132	108.02588	177	135.79331
133	108.68624	178	136.36716
134	109.34454	179	136.93923
135	110.00078	180	137.50951

yearly interest rate = 3.75%

term (months)	constant	term (months)	constant
181	138.07801	226	161.90878
182	138.64475	227	162.40128
183	139.20972	228	162.89224
184	139.77293	229	163.38167
185	140.33438	230	163.86958
186	140.89409	231	164.35596
187	141.45205	232	164.84084
188	142.00828	233	165.32420
189	142.56277	234	165.80605
190	143.11553	235	166.28641
191	143.66657	236	166.76527
192	144.21590	237	167.24263
193	144.76351	238	167.71851
194	145.30942	239	168.19291
195	145.85363	240	168.66583
196	146.39614	241	169.13728
197	146.93696	242	169.60725
198	147.47610	243	170.07577
199	148.01356	244	170.54282
200	148.54934	245	171.00842
201	149.08345	246	171.47257
202	149.61590	247	171.93527
203	150.14670	248	172.39653
204	150.67583	249	172.85636
205	151.20332	250	173.31475
206	151.72917	251	173.77171
207	152.25338	252	174.22725
208	152.77595	253	174.68137
209	153.29690	254	175.13408
210	153.81623	255	175.58537
211	154.33393	256	176.03526
212	154.85003	257	176.48375
213	155.36451	258	176.93084
214	155.87739	259	177.37654
215	156.38868	260	177.82085
216	156.89837	261	178.26378
217	157.40648	262	178.70532
218	157.91300	263	179.14549
219	158.41794	264	179.58429
220	158.92131	265	180.02172
221	159.42312	266	180.45779
222	159.92336	267	180.89250
223	160.42204	268	181.32586
224	160.91917	269	181.75787
225	161.41474	270	182.18853

yearly interest rate = 3.75%

term (months)	constant	term (months)	constant
271	182.61785	316	200.61414
272	183.04583	317	200.98606
273	183.47248	318	201.35682
274	183.89780	319	201.72643
275	184.32179	320	202.09488
276	184.74446	321	202.46218
277	185.16582	322	202.82835
278	185.58587	323	203.19337
279	186.00460	324	203.55725
280	186.42203	325	203.92000
281	186.83816	326	204.28162
282	187.25300	327	204.64211
283	187.66654	328	205.00148
284	188.07879	329	205.35973
285	188.48976	330	205.71687
286	188.89945	331	206.07289
287	189.30786	332	206.42780
288	189.71501	333	206.78161
289	190.12088	334	207.13432
290	190.52549	335	207.48592
291	190.92883	336	207.83644
292	191.33092	337	208.18585
293	191.73176	338	208.53419
294	192.13135	339	208.88143
295	192.52970	340	209.22759
296	192.92680	341	209.57268
297	193.32267	342	209.91669
298	193.71730	343	210.25963
299	194.11070	344	210.60150
300	194.50288	345	210.94230
301	194.89384	346	211.28205
302	195.28358	347	211.62073
303	195.67210	348	211.95836
304	196.05942	349	212.29494
305	196.44552	350	212.63047
306	196.83043	351	212.96496
307	197.21414	352	213.29840
308	197.59665	353	213.63080
309	197.97796	354	213.96217
310	198.35810	355	214.29251
311	198.73704	356	214.62181
312	199.11481	357	214.95009
313	199.49140	358	215.27735
314	199.86681	359	215.60359
315	200.24106	360	215.92881

yearly interest rate = 4.00%

term (months)	constant	term (months)	constant
1	0.9966777	46	42.581251
2	1.9900442	47	43.436463
3	2.9801105	48	44.288834
4	3.9668876	49	45.138372
5	4.9503863	50	45.985089
6	5.9306175	51	46.828992
7	6.9075923	52	47.670092
8	7.8813212	53	48.508397
9	8.8518151	54	49.343917
10	9.8190848	55	50.176662
11	10.783141	56	51.006640
12	11.743994	57	51.833860
13	12.701655	58	52.658332
14	13.656135	59	53.480066
15	14.607444	60	54.299069
16	15.555592	61	55.115351
17	16.500590	62	55.928921
18	17.442448	63	56.739788
19	18.381178	64	57.547962
20	19.316788	65	58.353450
21	20.249291	66	59.156263
22	21.178695	67	59.956408
23	22.105012	68	60.753895
24	23.028251	69	61.548733
25	23.948423	70	62.340930
26	24.865537	71	63.130495
27	25.779605	72	63.917436
28	26.690637	73	64.701764
29	27.598641	74	65.483486
30	28.503629	75	66.262610
31	29.405610	76	67.039146
32	30.304595	77	67.813103
33	31.200593	78	68.584488
34	32.093614	79	69.353310
35	32.983669	80	70.119578
36	33.870766	81	70.883300
37	34.754917	82	71.644486
38	35.636129	83	72.403142
39	36.514415	84	73.159277
40	37.389782	85	73.912901
41	38.262241	86	74.664021
42	39.131802	87	75.412646
43	39.998474	88	76.158783
44	40.862266	89	76.902441
45	41.723189	90	77.643629

yearly interest rate = 4.00%

term (months)	constant	term (months)	constant
91	78.382355	136	109.20434
92	79.118626	137	109.83821
93	79.852451	138	110.46998
94	80.583838	139	111.09964
95	81.312796	140	111.72722
96	82.039331	141	112.35271
97	82.763453	142	112.97612
98	83.485169	143	113.59747
99	84.204488	144	114.21674
100	84.921416	145	114.83396
101	85.635963	146	115.44913
102	86.348136	147	116.06226
103	87.057943	148	116.67335
104	87.765391	149	117.28241
105	88.470490	150	117.88944
106	89.173246	151	118.49446
107	89.873667	152	119.09747
108	90.571761	153	119.69847
109	91.267536	154	120.29748
110	91.960999	155	120.89450
111	92.652159	156	121.48954
112	93.341022	157	122.08259
113	94.027596	158	122.67368
114	94.711890	159	123.26281
115	95.393910	160	123.84997
116	96.073665	161	124.43519
117	96.751161	162	125.01846
118	97.426406	163	125.59979
119	98.099408	164	126.17920
120	98.770174	165	126.75667
121	99.438712	166	127.33223
122	100.10503	167	127.90588
123	100.76913	168	128.47762
124	101.43103	169	129.04746
125	102.09073	170	129.61541
126	102.74823	171	130.18147
127	103.40355	172	130.74566
128	104.05670	173	131.30796
129	104.70767	174	131.86840
130	105.35648	175	132.42698
131	106.00314	176	132.98370
132	106.64765	177	133.53857
133	107.29001	178	134.09160
134	107.93025	179	134.64279
135	108.56835	180	135.19215

yearly interest rate = 4.00%

term (months)	constant	term (months)	constant
181	135.73968	226	158.58456
182	136.28540	227	159.05438
183	136.82930	228	159.52264
184	137.37140	229	159.98934
185	137.91169	230	160.45449
186	138.45019	231	160.91810
187	138.98690	232	161.38017
188	139.52183	233	161.84070
189	140.05498	234	162.29970
190	140.58636	235	162.75717
191	141.11597	236	163.21313
192	141.64382	237	163.66757
193	142.16992	238	164.12050
194	142.69428	239	164.57193
195	143.21689	240	165.02186
196	143.73776	241	165.47029
197	144.25690	242	165.91723
198	144.77432	243	166.36269
199	145.29002	244	166.80667
200	145.80401	245	167.24917
201	146.31629	246	167.69020
202	146.82687	247	168.12977
203	147.33575	248	168.56788
204	147.84294	249	169.00453
205	148.34844	250	169.43973
206	148.85227	251	169.87349
207	149.35442	252	170.30580
208	149.85490	253	170.73668
209	150.35372	254	171.16612
210	150.85089	255	171.59414
211	151.34640	256	172.02074
212	151.84027	257	172.44592
213	152.33249	258	172.86969
214	152.82308	259	173.29205
215	153.31204	260	173.71300
216	153.79938	261	174.13256
217	154.28509	262	174.55073
218	154.76919	263	174.96750
219	155.25169	264	175.38289
220	155.73258	265	175.79690
221	156.21187	266	176.20954
222	156.68958	267	176.62080
223	157.16569	268	177.03070
224	157.64022	269	177.43924
225	158.11318	270	177.84641

yearly interest rate = 4.00%

term (months)	constant	term (months)	constant
271	178.25224	316	195.18459
272	178.65672	317	195.53281
273	179.05985	318	195.87988
274	179.46165	319	196.22579
275	179.86211	320	196.57056
276	180.26123	321	196.91418
277	180.65904	322	197.25666
278	181.05552	323	197.59800
279	181.45068	324	197.93820
280	181.84454	325	198.27728
281	182.23708	326	198.61523
282	182.62832	327	198.95205
283	183.01826	328	199.28776
284	183.40690	329	199.62235
285	183.79425	330	199.95583
286	184.18032	331	200.28821
287	184.56510	332	200.61947
288	184.94861	333	200.94964
289	185.33084	334	201.27871
290	185.71180	335	201.60669
291	186.09149	336	201.93358
292	186.46993	337	202.25938
293	186.84710	338	202.58410
294	187.22303	339	202.90774
295	187.59770	340	203.23031
296	187.97113	341	203.55180
297	188.34332	342	203.87223
298	188.71427	343	204.19159
299	189.08399	344	204.50989
300	189.45248	345	204.82713
301	189.81975	346	205.14332
302	190.18580	347	205.45846
303	190.55063	348	205.77255
304	190.91425	349	206.08560
305	191.27666	350	206.39761
306	191.63787	351	206.70858
307	191.99787	352	207.01852
308	192.35668	353	207.32743
309	192.71430	354	207.63531
310	193.07073	355	207.94217
311	193.42598	356	208.24801
312	193.78005	357	208.55283
313	194.13294	358	208.85664
314	194.48466	359	209.15944
315	194.83520	360	209.46124

yearly interest rate = 4.25%

term (months)	constant	term (months)	constant
1	0.9964708	46	42.379321
2	1.9894250	47	43.226228
3	2.9788748	48	44.070146
4	3.9648327	49	44.911086
5	4.9473110	50	45.749058
6	5.9263219	51	46.584073
7	6.9018778	52	47.416141
8	7.8739908	53	48.245272
9	8.8426730	54	49.071477
10	9.8079365	55	49.894767
11	10.769794	56	50.715150
12	11.728256	57	51.532639
13	12.683336	58	52.347242
14	13.635045	59	53.158971
15	14.583396	60	53.967835
16	15.528399	61	54.773844
17	16.470068	62	55.577009
18	17.408413	63	56.377339
19	18.343447	64	57.174845
20	19.275180	65	57.969536
21	20.203626	66	58.761423
22	21.128795	67	59.550515
23	22.050698	68	60.336822
24	22.969349	69	61.120354
25	23.884757	70	61.901121
26	24.796934	71	62.679132
27	25.705893	72	63.454398
28	26.611643	73	64.226928
29	27.514197	74	64.996731
30	28.413566	75	65.763818
31	29.309760	76	66.528197
32	30.202792	77	67.289879
33	31.092672	78	68.048872
34	31.979412	79	68.805187
35	32.863022	80	69.558833
36	33.743514	81	70.309819
37	34.620898	82	71.058155
38	35.495186	83	71.803849
39	36.366388	84	72.546912
40	37.234516	85	73.287353
41	38.099580	86	74.025181
42	38.961591	87	74.760404
43	39.820560	88	75.493033
44	40.676497	89	76.223076
45	41.529414	90	76.950543

yearly interest rate = 4.25%

term (months)	constant	term (months)	constant
91	77.675443	136	107.78009
92	78.397784	137	108.39619
93	79.117576	138	109.01011
94	79.834827	139	109.62187
95	80.549548	140	110.23147
96	81.261746	141	110.83891
97	81.971430	142	111.44421
98	82.678610	143	112.04738
99	83.383294	144	112.64841
100	84.085492	145	113.24733
101	84.785211	146	113.84413
102	85.482460	147	114.43883
103	86.177249	148	115.03143
104	86.869586	149	115.62193
105	87.559480	150	116.21035
106	88.246938	151	116.79670
107	88.931971	152	117.38097
108	89.614586	153	117.96319
109	90.294792	154	118.54335
110	90.972597	155	119.12146
111	91.648011	156	119.69753
112	92.321040	157	120.27157
113	92.991695	158	120.84358
114	93.659982	159	121.41357
115	94.325911	160	121.98156
116	94.989490	161	122.54753
117	95.650727	162	123.11151
118	96.309631	163	123.67350
119	96.966209	164	124.23351
120	97.620470	165	124.79154
121	98.272421	166	125.34760
122	98.922072	167	125.90170
123	99.569431	168	126.45384
124	100.21450	169	127.00403
125	100.85730	170	127.55229
126	101.49783	171	128.09860
127	102.13610	172	128.64299
128	102.77211	173	129.18546
129	103.40588	174	129.72602
130	104.03742	175	130.26466
131	104.66672	176	130.80141
132	105.29381	177	131.33626
133	105.91868	178	131.86922
134	106.54135	179	132.40030
135	107.16181	180	132.92951

yearly interest rate = 4.25%

term (months)	constant	term (months)	constant
181	133.45685	226	155.35699
182	133.98233	227	155.80518
183	134.50595	228	156.25178
184	135.02773	229	156.69682
185	135.54767	230	157.14028
186	136.06577	231	157.58217
187	136.58204	232	158.02251
188	137.09649	233	158.46129
189	137.60912	234	158.89853
190	138.11995	235	159.33422
191	138.62897	236	159.76837
192	139.13620	237	160.20099
193	139.64163	238	160.63209
194	140.14529	239	161.06166
195	140.64716	240	161.48972
196	141.14726	241	161.91627
197	141.64560	242	162.34131
198	142.14218	243	162.76485
199	142.63701	244	163.18690
200	143.13009	245	163.60745
201	143.62143	246	164.02652
202	144.11104	247	164.44412
203	144.59892	248	164.86024
204	145.08507	249	165.27489
205	145.56951	250	165.68808
206	146.05225	251	166.09981
207	146.53327	252	166.51008
208	147.01260	253	166.91891
209	147.49024	254	167.32630
210	147.96620	255	167.73225
211	148.44047	256	168.13676
212	148.91307	257	168.53985
213	149.38400	258	168.94152
214	149.85327	259	169.34176
215	150.32088	260	169.74060
216	150.78685	261	170.13803
217	151.25117	262	170.53405
218	151.71385	263	170.92868
219	152.17489	264	171.32192
220	152.63431	265	171.71376
221	153.09211	266	172.10423
222	153.54830	267	172.49311
223	154.00287	268	172.88103
224	154.45584	269	173.26737
225	154.90721	270	173.65235

yearly interest rate = 4.25%

term (months)	constant	term (months)	constant
271	174.03597	316	189.96760
272	174.41824	317	190.29364
273	174.79916	318	190.61853
274	175.17874	319	190.94228
275	175.55697	320	191.26488
276	175.93388	321	191.58635
277	176.30945	322	191.90668
278	176.68369	323	192.22588
279	177.05662	324	192.54395
280	177.42822	325	192.86090
281	177.79852	326	193.17673
282	178.16751	327	193.49145
283	178.53520	328	193.80506
284	178.90159	329	194.11756
285	179.26669	330	194.42896
286	179.63049	331	194.73926
287	179.99302	332	195.04846
288	180.35426	333	195.35657
289	180.71424	334	195.66360
290	181.07294	335	195.96954
291	181.43037	336	196.27440
292	181.78654	337	196.57818
293	182.14146	338	196.88090
294	182.49512	339	197.18254
295	182.84754	340	197.48312
296	183.19871	341	197.78264
297	183.54864	342	198.08111
298	183.89734	343	198.37852
299	184.24480	344	198.67488
300	184.59104	345	198.97019
301	184.93606	346	199.26446
302	185.27986	347	199.55769
303	185.62245	348	199.84989
304	185.96383	349	200.14106
305	186.30400	350	200.43120
306	186.64297	351	200.72031
307	186.98075	352	201.00841
308	187.31733	353	201.29549
309	187.65273	354	201.58155
310	187.98694	355	201.86661
311	188.31998	356	202.15066
312	188.65183	357	202.43371
313	188.98252	358	202.71575
314	189.31204	359	202.99681
315	189.64040	360	203.27687

yearly interest rate = 4.50%

term (months)	constant	term (months)	constant
1	0.9962640	46	42.178708
2	1.9888060	47	43.017393
3	2.9776398	48	43.852944
4	3.9627794	49	44.685374
5	4.9442385	50	45.514694
6	5.9220309	51	46.340916
7	6.8961703	52	47.164050
8	7.8666703	53	47.984110
9	8.8335445	54	48.801106
10	9.7968065	55	49.615049
11	10.756470	56	50.425952
12	11.712548	57	51.233825
13	12.665054	58	52.038680
14	13.614001	59	52.840528
15	14.559403	60	53.639381
16	15.501274	61	54.435248
17	16.439625	62	55.228143
18	17.374471	63	56.018075
19	18.305824	64	56.805056
20	19.233698	65	57.589097
21	20.158105	66	58.370209
22	21.079058	67	59.148402
23	21.996571	68	59.923688
24	22.910656	69	60.696078
25	23.821326	70	61.465582
26	24.728594	71	62.232211
27	25.632472	72	62.995976
28	26.532974	73	63.756888
29	27.430111	74	64.514957
30	28.323896	75	65.270194
31	29.214342	76	66.022609
32	30.101462	77	66.772213
33	30.985267	78	67.519017
34	31.865770	79	68.263031
35	32.742984	80	69.004265
36	33.616921	81	69.742729
37	34.487592	82	70.478435
38	35.355011	83	71.211392
39	36.219189	84	71.941611
40	37.080139	85	72.669102
41	37.937871	86	73.393875
42	38.792400	87	74.115940
43	39.643736	88	74.835308
44	40.491891	89	75.551988
45	41.336878	90	76.265991

yearly interest rate = 4.50%

term (months)	constant	term (months)	constant
91	76.977326	136	106.38170
92	77.686003	137	106.98052
93	78.392033	138	107.57710
94	79.095425	139	108.17146
95	79.796190	140	108.76360
96	80.494336	141	109.35352
97	81.189874	142	109.94124
98	81.882813	143	110.52677
99	82.573164	144	111.11010
100	83.260935	145	111.69126
101	83.946137	146	112.27025
102	84.628779	147	112.84707
103	85.308871	148	113.42174
104	85.986422	149	113.99426
105	86.661442	150	114.56464
106	87.333939	151	115.13290
107	88.003925	152	115.69902
108	88.671407	153	116.26304
109	89.336395	154	116.82494
110	89.998900	155	117.38475
111	90.658929	156	117.94247
112	91.316492	157	118.49810
113	91.971598	158	119.05166
114	92.624257	159	119.60314
115	93.274478	160	120.15257
116	93.922269	161	120.69995
117	94.567641	162	121.24528
118	95.210601	163	121.78857
119	95.851159	164	122.32983
120	96.489324	165	122.86907
121	97.125105	166	123.40630
122	97.758511	167	123.94152
123	98.389550	168	124.47474
124	99.018231	169	125.00597
125	99.644564	170	125.53521
126	100.26856	171	126.06248
127	100.89022	172	126.58777
128	101.50956	173	127.11111
129	102.12658	174	127.63248
130	102.74130	175	128.15191
131	103.35373	176	128.66940
132	103.96386	177	129.18496
133	104.57172	178	129.69859
134	105.17730	179	130.21030
135	105.78063	180	130.72010

yearly interest rate = 4.50%

term (months)	constant	term (months)	constant
181	131.22800	226	152.22279
182	131.73399	227	152.65035
183	132.23810	228	153.07632
184	132.74032	229	153.50069
185	133.24067	230	153.92348
186	133.73915	231	154.34468
187	134.23577	232	154.76432
188	134.73053	233	155.18238
189	135.22344	234	155.59889
190	135.71451	235	156.01383
191	136.20375	236	156.42723
192	136.69115	237	156.83909
193	137.17674	238	157.24940
194	137.66051	239	157.65818
195	138.14248	240	158.06544
196	138.62264	241	158.47117
197	139.10102	242	158.87539
198	139.57760	243	159.27809
199	140.05240	244	159.67930
200	140.52543	245	160.07900
201	140.99670	246	160.47721
202	141.46620	247	160.87393
203	141.93394	248	161.26917
204	142.39995	249	161.66294
205	142.86420	250	162.05523
206	143.32673	251	162.44606
207	143.78753	252	162.83543
208	144.24660	253	163.22334
209	144.70396	254	163.60980
210	145.15961	255	163.99482
211	145.61356	256	164.37840
212	146.06582	257	164.76055
213	146.51638	258	165.14127
214	146.96526	259	165.52057
215	147.41246	260	165.89845
216	147.85799	261	166.27492
217	148.30186	262	166.64998
218	148.74407	263	167.02364
219	149.18463	264	167.39591
220	149.62354	265	167.76678
221	150.06081	266	168.13627
222	150.49645	267	168.50438
223	150.93046	268	168.87111
224	151.36285	269	169.23648
225	151.79363	270	169.60047

yearly interest rate = 4.50%

term (months)	constant	term (months)	constant
271	169.96311	316	184.95345
272	170.32440	317	185.25873
273	170.68433	318	185.56287
274	171.04292	319	185.86587
275	171.40017	320	186.16774
276	171.75608	321	186.46849
277	172.11067	322	186.76810
278	172.46393	323	187.06661
279	172.81587	324	187.36399
280	173.16649	325	187.66026
281	173.51581	326	187.95543
282	173.86382	327	188.24950
283	174.21053	328	188.54246
284	174.55595	329	188.83433
285	174.90007	330	189.12511
286	175.24291	331	189.41481
287	175.58447	332	189.70342
288	175.92475	333	189.99095
289	176.26376	334	190.27741
290	176.60151	335	190.56280
291	176.93799	336	190.84713
292	177.27321	337	191.13039
293	177.60719	338	191.41259
294	177.93991	339	191.69374
295	178.27139	340	191.97384
296	178.60164	341	192.25289
297	178.93065	342	192.53090
298	179.25843	343	192.80787
299	179.58499	344	193.08380
300	179.91032	345	193.35871
301	180.23444	346	193.63259
302	180.55735	347	193.90544
303	180.87906	348	194.17728
304	181.19956	349	194.44810
305	181.51886	350	194.71790
306	181.83697	351	194.98670
307	182.15390	352	195.25450
308	182.46964	353	195.52129
309	182.78419	354	195.78709
310	183.09758	355	196.05190
311	183.40979	356	196.31571
312	183.72084	357	196.57854
313	184.03072	358	196.84039
314	184.33945	359	197.10126
315	184.64702	360	197.36116

yearly interest rate = 4.75%

term (months)	constant	term (months)	constant
1	0.9960573	46	41.979405
2	1.9881873	47	42.809949
3	2.9764058	48	43.637218
4	3.9607279	49	44.461226
5	4.9411690	50	45.281984
6	5.9177446	51	46.099507
7	6.8904699	52	46.913807
8	7.8593599	53	47.724896
9	8.8244298	54	48.532787
10	9.7856948	55	49.337492
11	10.743170	56	50.139025
12	11.696870	57	50.937398
13	12.646809	58	51.732623
14	13.593004	59	52.524713
15	14.535467	60	53.313680
16	15.474215	61	54.099536
17	16.409262	62	54.882293
18	17.340622	63	55.661965
19	18.268310	64	56.438562
20	19.192340	65	57.212097
21	20.112727	66	57.982583
22	21.029486	67	58.750031
23	21.942629	68	59.514453
24	22.852173	69	60.275861
25	23.758130	70	61.034267
26	24.660516	71	61.789683
27	25.559343	72	62.542120
28	26.454627	73	63.291591
29	27.346381	74	64.038107
30	28.234619	75	64.781679
31	29.119355	76	65.522320
32	30.000603	77	66.260041
33	30.878376	78	66.994853
34	31.752688	79	67.726768
35	32.623553	80	68.455797
36	33.490984	81	69.181952
37	34.354996	82	69.905243
38	35.215601	83	70.625683
39	36.072813	84	71.343283
40	36.926645	85	72.058053
41	37.777110	86	72.770005
42	38.624223	87	73.479150
43	39.467995	88	74.185499
44	40.308441	89	74.889063
45	41.145573	90	75.589853

yearly interest rate = 4.75%

term (months)	constant	term (months)	constant
91	76.287881	136	105.00861
92	76.983156	137	105.59064
93	77.675689	138	106.17039
94	78.365493	139	106.74784
95	79.052576	140	107.32302
96	79.736951	141	107.89593
97	80.418627	142	108.46659
98	81.097615	143	109.03499
99	81.773927	144	109.60115
100	82.447572	145	110.16508
101	83.118561	146	110.72679
102	83.786905	147	111.28628
103	84.452613	148	111.84357
104	85.115697	149	112.39866
105	85.776166	150	112.95156
106	86.434031	151	113.50228
107	87.089303	152	114.05082
108	87.741991	153	114.59721
109	88.392105	154	115.14144
110	89.039657	155	115.68353
111	89.684655	156	116.22348
112	90.327110	157	116.76130
113	90.967032	158	117.29700
114	91.604431	159	117.83058
115	92.239317	160	118.36207
116	92.871700	161	118.89146
117	93.501590	162	119.41876
118	94.128996	163	119.94398
119	94.753928	164	120.46713
120	95.376397	165	120.98822
121	95.996411	166	121.50725
122	96.613981	167	122.02424
123	97.229115	168	122.53919
124	97.841825	169	123.05211
125	98.452118	170	123.56300
126	99.060006	171	124.07188
127	99.665497	172	124.57876
128	100.26860	173	125.08364
129	100.86933	174	125.58652
130	101.46768	175	126.08743
131	102.06368	176	126.58636
132	102.65733	177	127.08332
133	103.24864	178	127.57832
134	103.83761	179	128.07137
135	104.42427	180	128.56248

yearly interest rate = 4.75%

term (months)	constant	term (months)	constant
181	129.05165	226	149.17885
182	129.53889	227	149.58674
183	130.02421	228	149.99302
184	130.50762	229	150.39769
185	130.98912	230	150.80077
186	131.46872	231	151.20226
187	131.94644	232	151.60217
188	132.42226	233	152.00050
189	132.89622	234	152.39726
190	133.36830	235	152.79246
191	133.83852	236	153.18610
192	134.30689	237	153.57818
193	134.77341	238	153.96872
194	135.23810	239	154.35773
195	135.70095	240	154.74519
196	136.16197	241	155.13113
197	136.62118	242	155.51555
198	137.07858	243	155.89845
199	137.53417	244	156.27984
200	137.98797	245	156.65973
201	138.43998	246	157.03812
202	138.89020	247	157.41502
203	139.33865	248	157.79043
204	139.78534	249	158.16437
205	140.23026	250	158.53683
206	140.67343	251	158.90782
207	141.11485	252	159.27734
208	141.55453	253	159.64541
209	141.99247	254	160.01203
210	142.42869	255	160.37721
211	142.86319	256	160.74094
212	143.29598	257	161.10324
213	143.72706	258	161.46411
214	144.15644	259	161.82356
215	144.58413	260	162.18159
216	145.01013	261	162.53821
217	145.43445	262	162.89342
218	145.85710	263	163.24724
219	146.27808	264	163.59965
220	146.69741	265	163.95068
221	147.11508	266	164.30033
222	147.53110	267	164.64859
223	147.94548	268	164.99549
224	148.35823	269	165.34101
225	148.76935	270	165.68517

yearly interest rate = 4.75%

term (months)	constant	term (months)	constant
271	166.02798	316	180.13293
272	166.36943	317	180.41877
273	166.70954	318	180.70348
274	167.04831	319	180.98708
275	167.38574	320	181.26955
276	167.72184	321	181.55091
277	168.05662	322	181.83116
278	168.39007	323	182.11031
279	168.72222	324	182.38836
280	169.05305	325	182.66531
281	169.38257	326	182.94116
282	169.71080	327	183.21593
283	170.03774	328	183.48962
284	170.36338	329	183.76223
285	170.68774	330	184.03376
286	171.01082	331	184.30422
287	171.33263	332	184.57362
288	171.65317	333	184.84195
289	171.97245	334	185.10923
290	172.29046	335	185.37545
291	172.60723	336	185.64063
292	172.92274	337	185.90475
293	173.23701	338	186.16784
294	173.55004	339	186.42989
295	173.86184	340	186.69090
296	174.17241	341	186.95089
297	174.48175	342	187.20985
298	174.78987	343	187.46779
299	175.09678	344	187.72471
300	175.40248	345	187.98062
301	175.70697	346	188.23552
302	176.01027	347	188.48942
303	176.31236	348	188.74231
304	176.61327	349	188.99421
305	176.91299	350	189.24512
306	177.21153	351	189.49503
307	177.50889	352	189.74396
308	177.80508	353	189.99191
309	178.10010	354	190.23888
310	178.39395	355	190.48488
311	178.68665	356	190.72991
312	178.97820	357	190.97397
313	179.26859	358	191.21707
314	179.55784	359	191.45921
315	179.84595	360	191.70039

yearly interest rate = 5.00%

term (months)	constant	term (months)	constant
1	0.9958506	46	41.781402
2	1.9875691	47	42.603885
3	2.9751726	48	43.422956
4	3.9586781	49	44.238629
5	4.9381027	50	45.050917
6	5.9134632	51	45.859834
7	6.8847767	52	46.665395
8	7.8520598	53	47.467613
9	8.8153293	54	48.266503
10	9.7746018	55	49.062077
11	10.729894	56	49.854351
12	11.681222	57	50.643337
13	12.628603	58	51.429049
14	13.572053	59	52.211501
15	14.511588	60	52.990707
16	15.447224	61	53.766679
17	16.378979	62	54.539431
18	17.306867	63	55.308977
19	18.230905	64	56.075330
20	19.151108	65	56.838503
21	20.067494	66	57.598509
22	20.980077	67	58.355362
23	21.888873	68	59.109074
24	22.793899	69	59.859659
25	23.695169	70	60.607129
26	24.592699	71	61.351498
27	25.486505	72	62.092778
28	26.376603	73	62.830982
29	27.263007	74	63.566123
30	28.145733	75	64.298214
31	29.024797	76	65.027267
32	29.900212	77	65.753295
33	30.771996	78	66.476311
34	31.640162	79	67.196326
35	32.504725	80	67.913354
36	33.365702	81	68.627406
37	34.223105	82	69.338496
38	35.076951	83	70.046635
39	35.927255	84	70.751836
40	36.774029	85	71.454110
41	37.617291	86	72.153471
42	38.457053	87	72.849929
43	39.293331	88	73.543498
44	40.126139	89	74.234189
45	40.955491	90	74.922014

yearly interest rate = 5.00%

term (months)	constant	term (months)	constant
91	75.606985	136	103.66030
92	76.289113	137	104.22603
93	76.968412	138	104.78941
94	77.644891	139	105.35045
95	78.318564	140	105.90916
96	78.989441	141	106.46555
97	79.657535	142	107.01964
98	80.322856	143	107.57142
99	80.985417	144	108.12092
100	81.645229	145	108.66813
101	82.302302	146	109.21308
102	82.956650	147	109.75576
103	83.608282	148	110.29620
104	84.257210	149	110.83439
105	84.903446	150	111.37034
106	85.547000	151	111.90408
107	86.187884	152	112.43560
108	86.826108	153	112.96491
109	87.461685	154	113.49202
110	88.094624	155	114.01695
111	88.724937	156	114.53971
112	89.352634	157	115.06029
113	89.977727	158	115.57871
114	90.600226	159	116.09498
115	91.220142	160	116.60911
116	91.837486	161	117.12110
117	92.452268	162	117.63098
118	93.064499	163	118.13873
119	93.674190	164	118.64438
120	94.281351	165	119.14793
121	94.885993	166	119.64939
122	95.488126	167	120.14877
123	96.087760	168	120.64608
124	96.684906	169	121.14132
125	97.279575	170	121.63451
126	97.871776	171	122.12566
127	98.461519	172	122.61476
128	99.048816	173	123.10184
129	99.633676	174	123.58689
130	100.21611	175	124.06993
131	100.79612	176	124.55097
132	101.37373	177	125.03001
133	101.94895	178	125.50707
134	102.52177	179	125.98214
135	103.09222	180	126.45524

yearly interest rate = 5.00%

term (months)	constant	term (months)	constant
181	126.92638	226	146.22216
182	127.39557	227	146.61128
183	127.86281	228	146.99878
184	128.32811	229	147.38468
185	128.79148	230	147.76897
186	129.25292	231	148.15168
187	129.71245	232	148.53279
188	130.17008	233	148.91232
189	130.62580	234	149.29028
190	131.07964	235	149.66667
191	131.53159	236	150.04149
192	131.98167	237	150.41477
193	132.42988	238	150.78649
194	132.87622	239	151.15667
195	133.32072	240	151.52531
196	133.76337	241	151.89243
197	134.20419	242	152.25802
198	134.64318	243	152.62210
199	135.08034	244	152.98466
200	135.51569	245	153.34572
201	135.94924	246	153.70528
202	136.38098	247	154.06335
203	136.81094	248	154.41993
204	137.23911	249	154.77504
205	137.66550	250	155.12867
206	138.09013	251	155.48083
207	138.51299	252	155.83153
208	138.93410	253	156.18078
209	139.35346	254	156.52858
210	139.77108	255	156.87493
211	140.18697	256	157.21985
212	140.60113	257	157.56333
213	141.01357	258	157.90540
214	141.42430	259	158.24604
215	141.83333	260	158.58527
216	142.24066	261	158.92308
217	142.64630	262	159.25950
218	143.05026	263	159.59453
219	143.45254	264	159.92816
220	143.85315	265	160.26041
221	144.25210	266	160.59128
222	144.64940	267	160.92077
223	145.04504	268	161.24890
224	145.43905	269	161.57567
225	145.83142	270	161.90108

yearly interest rate = 5.00%

term (months)	constant	term (months)	constant
271	162.22515	316	175.49726
272	162.54786	317	175.76491
273	162.86924	318	176.03144
274	163.18929	319	176.29687
275	163.50800	320	176.56120
276	163.82540	321	176.82443
277	164.14147	322	177.08657
278	164.45624	323	177.34762
279	164.76970	324	177.60759
280	165.08186	325	177.86648
281	165.39272	326	178.12430
282	165.70230	327	178.38104
283	166.01059	328	178.63672
284	166.31760	329	178.89134
285	166.62333	330	179.14490
286	166.92780	331	179.39742
287	167.23100	332	179.64888
288	167.53295	333	179.89930
289	167.83364	334	180.14868
290	168.13309	335	180.39702
291	168.43129	336	180.64434
292	168.72826	337	180.89063
293	169.02399	338	181.13590
294	169.31850	339	181.38014
295	169.61178	340	181.62338
296	169.90385	341	181.86561
297	170.19470	342	182.10683
298	170.48435	343	182.34705
299	170.77280	344	182.58627
300	171.06005	345	182.82450
301	171.34611	346	183.06175
302	171.63098	347	183.29801
303	171.91467	348	183.53328
304	172.19718	349	183.76759
305	172.47852	350	184.00091
306	172.75869	351	184.23328
307	173.03770	352	184.46467
308	173.31555	353	184.69511
309	173.59225	354	184.92459
310	173.86780	355	185.15312
311	174.14221	356	185.38070
312	174.41548	357	185.60734
313	174.68761	358	185.83303
314	174.95862	359	186.05779
315	175.22850	360	186.28162

yearly interest rate = 5.25%

term (months)	constant	term (months)	constant
1	0.9956440	46	41.584687
2	1.9869512	47	42.399191
3	2.9739402	48	43.210146
4	3.9566299	49	44.017569
5	4.9350391	50	44.821475
6	5.9091864	51	45.621880
7	6.8790904	52	46.418797
8	7.8447696	53	47.212244
9	8.8062422	54	48.002234
10	9.7635268	55	48.788783
11	10.716642	56	49.571906
12	11.665604	57	50.351618
13	12.610434	58	51.127933
14	13.551148	59	51.900867
15	14.487764	60	52.670434
16	15.420300	61	53.436648
17	16.348774	62	54.199525
18	17.273204	63	54.959079
19	18.193607	64	55.715325
20	19.110000	65	56.468276
21	20.022402	66	57.217948
22	20.930830	67	57.964354
23	21.835301	68	58.707508
24	22.735831	69	59.447426
25	23.632439	70	60.184120
26	24.525142	71	60.917606
27	25.413956	72	61.647896
28	26.298898	73	62.375006
29	27.179986	74	63.098948
30	28.057235	75	63.819736
31	28.930664	76	64.537385
32	29.800287	77	65.251908
33	30.666123	78	65.963319
34	31.528187	79	66.671630
35	32.386496	80	67.376857
36	33.241067	81	68.079011
37	34.091915	82	68.778107
38	34.939056	83	69.474157
39	35.782508	84	70.167176
40	36.622285	85	70.857176
41	37.458405	86	71.544170
42	38.290882	87	72.228172
43	39.119733	88	72.909194
44	39.944974	89	73.587250
45	40.766620	90	74.262352

yearly interest rate = 5.25%

term (months)	constant	term (months)	constant
91	74.934513	136	102.33627
92	75.603747	137	102.88614
93	76.270066	138	103.43362
94	76.933482	139	103.97871
95	77.594008	140	104.52143
96	78.251657	141	105.06178
97	78.906441	142	105.59978
98	79.558373	143	106.13544
99	80.207466	144	106.66877
100	80.853731	145	107.19977
101	81.497180	146	107.72846
102	82.137827	147	108.25484
103	82.775684	148	108.77893
104	83.410762	149	109.30074
105	84.043073	150	109.82028
106	84.672630	151	110.33755
107	85.299445	152	110.85257
108	85.923530	153	111.36535
109	86.544896	154	111.87589
110	87.163555	155	112.38421
111	87.779520	156	112.89031
112	88.392802	157	113.39422
113	89.003412	158	113.89592
114	89.611362	159	114.39544
115	90.216664	160	114.89278
116	90.819329	161	115.38796
117	91.419370	162	115.88098
118	92.016796	163	116.37186
119	92.611620	164	116.86059
120	93.203854	165	117.34720
121	93.793507	166	117.83168
122	94.380592	167	118.31406
123	94.965119	168	118.79433
124	95.547101	169	119.27252
125	96.126547	170	119.74862
126	96.703470	171	120.22264
127	97.277879	172	120.69460
128	97.849786	173	121.16451
129	98.419202	174	121.63237
130	98.986138	175	122.09819
131	99.550604	176	122.56198
132	100.11261	177	123.02375
133	100.67217	178	123.48351
134	101.22929	179	123.94127
135	101.78399	180	124.39703

yearly interest rate = 5.25%

term (months)	constant	term (months)	constant
181	124.85081	226	143.34979
182	125.30261	227	143.72101
183	125.75244	228	144.09062
184	126.20032	229	144.45861
185	126.64624	230	144.82500
186	127.09022	231	145.18979
187	127.53226	232	145.55300
188	127.97239	233	145.91462
189	128.41059	234	146.27467
190	128.84688	235	146.63315
191	129.28128	236	146.99007
192	129.71378	237	147.34543
193	130.14440	238	147.69925
194	130.57314	239	148.05152
195	131.00002	240	148.40226
196	131.42503	241	148.75148
197	131.84820	242	149.09917
198	132.26952	243	149.44534
199	132.68900	244	149.79001
200	133.10666	245	150.13318
201	133.52250	246	150.47485
202	133.93653	247	150.81504
203	134.34875	248	151.15374
204	134.75918	249	151.49097
205	135.16782	250	151.82672
206	135.57468	251	152.16102
207	135.97977	252	152.49386
208	136.38309	253	152.82525
209	136.78466	254	153.15520
210	137.18448	255	153.48370
211	137.58256	256	153.81078
212	137.97890	257	154.13643
213	138.37351	258	154.46067
214	138.76641	259	154.78349
215	139.15760	260	155.10491
216	139.54708	261	155.42492
217	139.93486	262	155.74355
218	140.32096	263	156.06078
219	140.70537	264	156.37663
220	141.08811	265	156.69111
221	141.46918	266	157.00422
222	141.84860	267	157.31596
223	142.22636	268	157.62634
224	142.60247	269	157.93538
225	142.97695	270	158.24306

yearly interest rate = 5.25%

term (months)	constant	term (months)	constant
271	158.54941	316	171.03811
272	158.85442	317	171.28872
273	159.15810	318	171.53824
274	159.46046	319	171.78668
275	159.76151	320	172.03403
276	160.06124	321	172.28030
277	160.35967	322	172.52550
278	160.65679	323	172.76964
279	160.95262	324	173.01271
280	161.24717	325	173.25472
281	161.54043	326	173.49567
282	161.83241	327	173.73558
283	162.12312	328	173.97444
284	162.41257	329	174.21226
285	162.70075	330	174.44905
286	162.98768	331	174.68480
287	163.27336	332	174.91953
288	163.55780	333	175.15323
289	163.84099	334	175.38592
290	164.12295	335	175.61759
291	164.40369	336	175.84826
292	164.68320	337	176.07792
293	164.96149	338	176.30658
294	165.23857	339	176.53424
295	165.51445	340	176.76091
296	165.78912	341	176.98659
297	166.06260	342	177.21129
298	166.33488	343	177.43502
299	166.60598	344	177.65776
300	166.87590	345	177.87954
301	167.14464	346	178.10035
302	167.41221	347	178.32020
303	167.67862	348	178.53909
304	167.94386	349	178.75703
305	168.20795	350	178.97402
306	168.47089	351	179.19006
307	168.73269	352	179.40516
308	168.99334	353	179.61933
309	169.25286	354	179.83256
310	169.51125	355	180.04487
311	169.76851	356	180.25624
312	170.02465	357	180.46670
313	170.27968	358	180.67624
314	170.53360	359	180.88487
315	170.78640	360	181.09259

yearly interest rate = 5.50%

term (months)	constant	term (months)	constant
1	0.9954376	46	41.389253
2	1.9863335	47	42.195855
3	2.9727086	48	42.998777
4	3.9545834	49	43.798036
5	4.9319785	50	44.593649
6	5.9049143	51	45.385631
7	6.8734112	52	46.174000
8	7.8374894	53	46.958773
9	8.7971690	54	47.739964
10	9.7524702	55	48.517592
11	10.703413	56	49.291672
12	11.650017	57	50.062220
13	12.592302	58	50.829253
14	13.530288	59	51.592786
15	14.463995	60	52.352835
16	15.393442	61	53.109417
17	16.318648	62	53.862547
18	17.239633	63	54.612241
19	18.156416	64	55.358514
20	19.069016	65	56.101383
21	19.977453	66	56.840862
22	20.881745	67	57.576968
23	21.781911	68	58.309715
24	22.677971	69	59.039119
25	23.569942	70	59.765195
26	24.457843	71	60.487959
27	25.341694	72	61.207425
28	26.221512	73	61.923608
29	27.097316	74	62.636524
30	27.969124	75	63.346188
31	28.836955	76	64.052613
32	29.700826	77	64.755816
33	30.560756	78	65.455810
34	31.416762	79	66.152610
35	32.268863	80	66.846232
36	33.117077	81	67.536689
37	33.961420	82	68.223995
38	34.801911	83	68.908166
39	35.638568	84	69.589216
40	36.471407	85	70.267158
41	37.300447	86	70.942007
42	38.125704	87	71.613777
43	38.947196	88	72.282482
44	39.764940	89	72.948137
45	40.578953	90	73.610754

yearly interest rate = 5.50%

term (months)	constant	term (months)	constant
91	74.270348	136	101.03599
92	74.926933	137	101.57046
93	75.580523	138	102.10249
94	76.231130	139	102.63209
95	76.878769	140	103.15928
96	77.523453	141	103.68406
97	78.165196	142	104.20645
98	78.804011	143	104.72645
99	79.439911	144	105.24408
100	80.072910	145	105.75935
101	80.703022	146	106.27227
102	81.330258	147	106.78285
103	81.954632	148	107.29110
104	82.576158	149	107.79703
105	83.194849	150	108.30065
106	83.810716	151	108.80198
107	84.423774	152	109.30101
108	85.034035	153	109.79777
109	85.641511	154	110.29227
110	86.246216	155	110.78451
111	86.848162	156	111.27450
112	87.447361	157	111.76225
113	88.043827	158	112.24778
114	88.637572	159	112.73110
115	89.228607	160	113.21221
116	89.816946	161	113.69113
117	90.402601	162	114.16786
118	90.985584	163	114.64241
119	91.565907	164	115.11480
120	92.143582	165	115.58504
121	92.718621	166	116.05313
122	93.291037	167	116.51908
123	93.860842	168	116.98291
124	94.428047	169	117.44462
125	94.992664	170	117.90423
126	95.554705	171	118.36174
127	96.114181	172	118.81716
128	96.671105	173	119.27050
129	97.225489	174	119.72178
130	97.777342	175	120.17099
131	98.326678	176	120.61816
132	98.873508	177	121.06329
133	99.417843	178	121.50638
134	99.959695	179	121.94746
135	100.49907	180	122.38652

yearly interest rate = 5.50%

term (months)	constant	term (months)	constant
181	122.82358	226	140.55896
182	123.25864	227	140.91311
183	123.69172	228	141.26564
184	124.12283	229	141.61656
185	124.55196	230	141.96589
186	124.97914	231	142.31362
187	125.40437	232	142.65976
188	125.82766	233	143.00432
189	126.24902	234	143.34731
190	126.66846	235	143.68874
191	127.08598	236	144.02861
192	127.50160	237	144.36693
193	127.91532	238	144.70370
194	128.32715	239	145.03894
195	128.73711	240	145.37265
196	129.14519	241	145.70483
197	129.55141	242	146.03551
198	129.95578	243	146.36467
199	130.35831	244	146.69233
200	130.75900	245	147.01849
201	131.15786	246	147.34317
202	131.55490	247	147.66637
203	131.95012	248	147.98809
204	132.34355	249	148.30834
205	132.73518	250	148.62713
206	133.12502	251	148.94447
207	133.51309	252	149.26036
208	133.89938	253	149.57481
209	134.28391	254	149.88782
210	134.66669	255	150.19941
211	135.04772	256	150.50957
212	135.42702	257	150.81832
213	135.80458	258	151.12566
214	136.18042	259	151.43160
215	136.55454	260	151.73615
216	136.92696	261	152.03930
217	137.29768	262	152.34107
218	137.66671	263	152.64146
219	138.03405	264	152.94048
220	138.39972	265	153.23814
221	138.76372	266	153.53444
222	139.12606	267	153.82939
223	139.48674	268	154.12299
224	139.84578	269	154.41526
225	140.20319	270	154.70619

yearly interest rate = 5.50%

term (months)	constant	term (months)	constant
271	154.99579	316	166.74756
272	155.28407	317	166.98223
273	155.57104	318	167.21582
274	155.85670	319	167.44835
275	156.14105	320	167.67982
276	156.42410	321	167.91023
277	156.70587	322	168.13959
278	156.98635	323	168.36790
279	157.26555	324	168.59517
280	157.54347	325	168.82141
281	157.82013	326	169.04661
282	158.09553	327	169.27079
283	158.36967	328	169.49394
284	158.64255	329	169.71608
285	158.91420	330	169.93720
286	159.18460	331	170.15731
287	159.45377	332	170.37642
288	159.72171	333	170.59453
289	159.98843	334	170.81164
290	160.25394	335	171.02776
291	160.51823	336	171.24290
292	160.78131	337	171.45705
293	161.04320	338	171.67023
294	161.30389	339	171.88244
295	161.56339	340	172.09367
296	161.82171	341	172.30395
297	162.07885	342	172.51326
298	162.33481	343	172.72162
299	162.58961	344	172.92903
300	162.84324	345	173.13549
301	163.09572	346	173.34101
302	163.34705	347	173.54560
303	163.59723	348	173.74925
304	163.84627	349	173.95197
305	164.09417	350	174.15376
306	164.34094	351	174.35464
307	164.58658	352	174.55459
308	164.83111	353	174.75364
309	165.07452	354	174.95178
310	165.31681	355	175.14901
311	165.55801	356	175.34534
312	165.79810	357	175.54078
313	166.03709	358	175.73533
314	166.27500	359	175.92899
315	166.51182	360	176.12176

yearly interest rate = 5.75%

term (months)	constant	term (months)	constant
1	0.9952312	46	41.195089
2	1.9857163	47	41.993869
3	2.9714780	48	42.788839
4	3.9525388	49	43.580018
5	4.9289210	50	44.367424
6	5.9006471	51	45.151075
7	6.8677392	52	45.930989
8	7.8302194	53	46.707184
9	8.7881097	54	47.479677
10	9.7414320	55	48.248486
11	10.690208	56	49.013629
12	11.634460	57	49.775124
13	12.574208	58	50.532986
14	13.509475	59	51.287235
15	14.440282	60	52.037887
16	15.366651	61	52.784959
17	16.288601	62	53.528468
18	17.206155	63	54.268432
19	18.119333	64	55.004867
20	19.028156	65	55.737790
21	19.932646	66	56.467218
22	20.832822	67	57.193168
23	21.728705	68	57.915655
24	22.620316	69	58.634697
25	23.507675	70	59.350310
26	24.390803	71	60.062511
27	25.269719	72	60.771315
28	26.144443	73	61.476739
29	27.014996	74	62.178799
30	27.881398	75	62.877511
31	28.743668	76	63.572891
32	29.601826	77	64.264954
33	30.455891	78	64.953718
34	31.305884	79	65.639197
35	32.151823	80	66.321407
36	32.993728	81	67.000363
37	33.831618	82	67.676082
38	34.665513	83	68.348578
39	35.495431	84	69.017868
40	36.321391	85	69.683965
41	37.143412	86	70.346887
42	37.961513	87	71.006646
43	38.775713	88	71.663260
44	39.586030	89	72.316742
45	40.392482	90	72.967108

yearly interest rate = 5.75%

term (months)	constant	term (months)	constant
91	73.614373	136	99.758991
92	74.258550	137	100.27849
93	74.899656	138	100.79551
94	75.537705	139	101.31007
95	76.172711	140	101.82217
96	76.804688	141	102.33183
97	77.433652	142	102.83906
98	78.059616	143	103.34387
99	78.682595	144	103.84627
100	79.302604	145	104.34628
101	79.919655	146	104.84390
102	80.533765	147	105.33915
103	81.144945	148	105.83204
104	81.753211	149	106.32258
105	82.358576	150	106.81078
106	82.961054	151	107.29665
107	83.560659	152	107.78020
108	84.157405	153	108.26145
109	84.751305	154	108.74040
110	85.342373	155	109.21707
111	85.930622	156	109.69146
112	86.516066	157	110.16360
113	87.098718	158	110.63348
114	87.678591	159	111.10112
115	88.255700	160	111.56653
116	88.830056	161	112.02972
117	89.401673	162	112.49070
118	89.970564	163	112.94949
119	90.536742	164	113.40608
120	91.100220	165	113.86050
121	91.661011	166	114.31275
122	92.219128	167	114.76285
123	92.774583	168	115.21079
124	93.327389	169	115.65661
125	93.877559	170	116.10029
126	94.425105	171	116.54186
127	94.970041	172	116.98133
128	95.512377	173	117.41870
129	96.052127	174	117.85398
130	96.589304	175	118.28719
131	97.123918	176	118.71833
132	97.655983	177	119.14741
133	98.185511	178	119.57445
134	98.712514	179	119.99945
135	99.237003	180	120.42243

yearly interest rate = 5.75%

term (months)	constant	term (months)	constant
181	120.84339	226	137.84696
182	121.26234	227	138.18482
183	121.67929	228	138.52108
184	122.09426	229	138.85573
185	122.50724	230	139.18878
186	122.91826	231	139.52024
187	123.32732	232	139.85013
188	123.73442	233	140.17844
189	124.13959	234	140.50519
190	124.54282	235	140.83037
191	124.94413	236	141.15401
192	125.34353	237	141.47611
193	125.74102	238	141.79666
194	126.13661	239	142.11569
195	126.53032	240	142.43320
196	126.92215	241	142.74919
197	127.31212	242	143.06368
198	127.70022	243	143.37667
199	128.08647	244	143.68816
200	128.47088	245	143.99817
201	128.85346	246	144.30670
202	129.23420	247	144.61376
203	129.61315	248	144.91935
204	129.99028	249	145.22349
205	130.36561	250	145.52618
206	130.73915	251	145.82742
207	131.11091	252	146.12723
208	131.48090	253	146.42561
209	131.84912	254	146.72256
210	132.21559	255	147.01810
211	132.58031	256	147.31223
212	132.94329	257	147.60495
213	133.30454	258	147.89628
214	133.66406	259	148.18623
215	134.02188	260	148.47478
216	134.37798	261	148.76197
217	134.73239	262	149.04778
218	135.08511	263	149.33223
219	135.43614	264	149.61532
220	135.78550	265	149.89707
221	136.13320	266	150.17746
222	136.47923	267	150.45653
223	136.82362	268	150.73426
224	137.16636	269	151.01067
225	137.50747	270	151.28576

yearly interest rate = 5.75%

term (months)	constant	term (months)	constant
271	151.55953	316	162.61807
272	151.83200	317	162.83781
273	152.10318	318	163.05650
274	152.37306	319	163.27414
275	152.64165	320	163.49075
276	152.90896	321	163.70632
277	153.17500	322	163.92087
278	153.43976	323	164.13439
279	153.70327	324	164.34690
280	153.96552	325	164.55839
281	154.22651	326	164.76887
282	154.48627	327	164.97835
283	154.74478	328	165.18683
284	155.00206	329	165.39431
285	155.25812	330	165.60081
286	155.51295	331	165.80632
287	155.76657	332	166.01085
288	156.01898	333	166.21441
289	156.27019	334	166.41699
290	156.52019	335	166.61861
291	156.76901	336	166.81927
292	157.01664	337	167.01897
293	157.26308	338	167.21772
294	157.50836	339	167.41552
295	157.75246	340	167.61238
296	157.99540	341	167.80830
297	158.23718	342	168.00328
298	158.47781	343	168.19734
299	158.71729	344	168.39046
300	158.95562	345	168.58267
301	159.19282	346	168.77396
302	159.42889	347	168.96434
303	159.66384	348	169.15381
304	159.89766	349	169.34238
305	160.13037	350	169.53005
306	160.36197	351	169.71682
307	160.59246	352	169.90271
308	160.82186	353	170.08770
309	161.05016	354	170.27182
310	161.27737	355	170.45505
311	161.50350	356	170.63742
312	161.72855	357	170.81891
313	161.95253	358	170.99954
314	162.17544	359	171.17930
315	162.39729	360	171.35821

yearly interest rate = 6.00%

term (months)	constant	term (months)	constant
1	0.9950249	46	41.002186
2	1.9850994	47	41.793219
3	2.9702481	48	42.580318
4	3.9504957	49	43.363500
5	4.9258663	50	44.142786
6	5.8963844	51	44.918195
7	6.8620740	52	45.689747
8	7.8229592	53	46.457459
9	8.7790639	54	47.221353
10	9.7304119	55	47.981445
11	10.677027	56	48.737757
12	11.618932	57	49.490305
13	12.556151	58	50.239110
14	13.488708	59	50.984189
15	14.416625	60	51.725561
16	15.339925	61	52.463245
17	16.258632	62	53.197258
18	17.172768	63	53.927620
19	18.082356	64	54.654349
20	18.987419	65	55.377461
21	19.887979	66	56.096976
22	20.784059	67	56.812912
23	21.675681	68	57.525285
24	22.562866	69	58.234115
25	23.445638	70	58.939418
26	24.324018	71	59.641212
27	25.198028	72	60.339514
28	26.067689	73	61.034342
29	26.933024	74	61.725714
30	27.794054	75	62.413646
31	28.650800	76	63.098155
32	29.503284	77	63.779259
33	30.351526	78	64.456974
34	31.195548	79	65.131317
35	32.035371	80	65.802306
36	32.871016	81	66.469956
37	33.702504	82	67.134284
38	34.529855	83	67.795308
39	35.353089	84	68.453043
40	36.172228	85	69.107505
41	36.987292	86	69.758712
42	37.798300	87	70.406678
43	38.605274	88	71.051421
44	39.408232	89	71.692956
45	40.207197	90	72.331300

yearly interest rate = 6.00%

term (months)	constant	term (months)	constant
91	72.966467	136	98.504778
92	73.598475	137	99.009730
93	74.227338	138	99.512169
94	74.853073	139	100.01211
95	75.475695	140	100.50956
96	76.095218	141	101.00454
97	76.711660	142	101.49705
98	77.325035	143	101.98712
99	77.935358	144	102.47474
100	78.542645	145	102.95994
101	79.146910	146	103.44273
102	79.748170	147	103.92311
103	80.346437	148	104.40111
104	80.941729	149	104.87673
105	81.534058	150	105.34998
106	82.123441	151	105.82087
107	82.709892	152	106.28942
108	83.293425	153	106.75565
109	83.874054	154	107.21955
110	84.451795	155	107.68114
111	85.026662	156	108.14044
112	85.598669	157	108.59745
113	86.167830	158	109.05219
114	86.734159	159	109.50467
115	87.297670	160	109.95489
116	87.858379	161	110.40288
117	88.416297	162	110.84864
118	88.971440	163	111.29218
119	89.523821	164	111.73351
120	90.073454	165	112.17264
121	90.620352	166	112.60960
122	91.164529	167	113.04437
123	91.705999	168	113.47699
124	92.244775	169	113.90745
125	92.780871	170	114.33577
126	93.314299	171	114.76196
127	93.845074	172	115.18603
128	94.373208	173	115.60799
129	94.898714	174	116.02785
130	95.421606	175	116.44563
131	95.941897	176	116.86132
132	96.459599	177	117.27495
133	96.974725	178	117.68651
134	97.487289	179	118.09603
135	97.997302	180	118.50351

yearly interest rate = 6.00%

term (months)	constant	term (months)	constant
181	118.90897	226	135.21118
182	119.31241	227	135.53352
183	119.71384	228	135.85425
184	120.11327	229	136.17338
185	120.51072	230	136.49092
186	120.90619	231	136.80689
187	121.29969	232	137.12128
188	121.69123	233	137.43411
189	122.08083	234	137.74539
190	122.46849	235	138.05511
191	122.85422	236	138.36329
192	123.23803	237	138.66994
193	123.61993	238	138.97507
194	123.99993	239	139.27868
195	124.37804	240	139.58077
196	124.75426	241	139.88137
197	125.12862	242	140.18046
198	125.50112	243	140.47807
199	125.87176	244	140.77420
200	126.24055	245	141.06886
201	126.60752	246	141.36205
202	126.97265	247	141.65378
203	127.33597	248	141.94406
204	127.69749	249	142.23289
205	128.05720	250	142.52029
206	128.41512	251	142.80626
207	128.77127	252	143.09081
208	129.12564	253	143.37394
209	129.47825	254	143.65566
210	129.82910	255	143.93598
211	130.17821	256	144.21490
212	130.52558	257	144.49244
213	130.87123	258	144.76860
214	131.21515	259	145.04338
215	131.55737	260	145.31680
216	131.89788	261	145.58885
217	132.23669	262	145.85956
218	132.57382	263	146.12891
219	132.90928	264	146.39693
220	133.24306	265	146.66361
221	133.57519	266	146.92896
222	133.90566	267	147.19300
223	134.23449	268	147.45572
224	134.56168	269	147.71713
225	134.88724	270	147.97725

yearly interest rate = 6.00%

term (months)	constant	term (months)	constant
271	148.23607	316	158.64248
272	148.49360	317	158.84824
273	148.74985	318	159.05297
274	149.00483	319	159.25669
275	149.25853	320	159.45939
276	149.51098	321	159.66109
277	149.76217	322	159.86178
278	150.01211	323	160.06147
279	150.26080	324	160.26017
280	150.50826	325	160.45788
281	150.75449	326	160.65461
282	150.99949	327	160.85036
283	151.24328	328	161.04513
284	151.48585	329	161.23894
285	151.72721	330	161.43178
286	151.96737	331	161.62366
287	152.20634	332	161.81459
288	152.44412	333	162.00456
289	152.68072	334	162.19360
290	152.91614	335	162.38169
291	153.15039	336	162.56884
292	153.38347	337	162.75507
293	153.61539	338	162.94037
294	153.84616	339	163.12474
295	154.07578	340	163.30820
296	154.30426	341	163.49075
297	154.53160	342	163.67239
298	154.75781	343	163.85312
299	154.98290	344	164.03296
300	155.20686	345	164.21190
301	155.42972	346	164.38995
302	155.65146	347	164.56711
303	155.87210	348	164.74339
304	156.09164	349	164.91880
305	156.31009	350	165.09333
306	156.52745	351	165.26700
307	156.74373	352	165.43980
308	156.95894	353	165.61174
309	157.17307	354	165.78283
310	157.38614	355	165.95306
311	157.59815	356	166.12245
312	157.80911	357	166.29099
313	158.01901	358	166.45870
314	158.22787	359	166.62557
315	158.43569	360	166.79161

yearly interest rate = 6.25%

term (months)	constant	term (months)	constant
1	0.9948186	46	40.810533
2	1.9844828	47	41.593898
3	2.9690192	48	42.373205
4	3.9484543	49	43.148473
5	4.9228146	50	43.919724
6	5.8921265	51	44.686980
7	6.8564160	52	45.450260
8	7.8157091	53	46.209585
9	8.7700319	54	46.964976
10	9.7194099	55	47.716452
11	10.663869	56	48.464035
12	11.603434	57	49.207745
13	12.538132	58	49.947601
14	13.467986	59	50.683624
15	14.393022	60	51.415833
16	15.313266	61	52.144249
17	16.228741	62	52.868890
18	17.139473	63	53.589776
19	18.045486	64	54.306928
20	18.946805	65	55.020364
21	19.843453	66	55.730103
22	20.735456	67	56.436164
23	21.622837	68	57.138567
24	22.505620	69	57.837331
25	23.383830	70	58.532475
26	24.257489	71	59.224016
27	25.126621	72	59.911975
28	25.991250	73	60.596369
29	26.851399	74	61.277217
30	27.707091	75	61.954537
31	28.558349	76	62.628347
32	29.405197	77	63.298667
33	30.247657	78	63.965513
34	31.085753	79	64.628904
35	31.919505	80	65.288858
36	32.748938	81	65.945392
37	33.574073	82	66.598525
38	34.394932	83	67.248274
39	35.211539	84	67.894656
40	36.023914	85	68.537689
41	36.832081	86	69.177390
42	37.636060	87	69.813776
43	38.435873	88	70.446865
44	39.231542	89	71.076674
45	40.023088	90	71.703220

yearly interest rate = 6.25%

term (months)	constant	term (months)	constant
91	72.326520	136	97.272886
92	72.946589	137	97.763700
93	73.563446	138	98.251971
94	74.177107	139	98.737712
95	74.787589	140	99.220936
96	75.394907	141	99.701656
97	75.999078	142	100.17989
98	76.600119	143	100.65564
99	77.198046	144	101.12892
100	77.792875	145	101.59976
101	78.384622	146	102.06815
102	78.973302	147	102.53412
103	79.558933	148	102.99768
104	80.141529	149	103.45883
105	80.721107	150	103.91759
106	81.297681	151	104.37398
107	81.871269	152	104.82800
108	82.441884	153	105.27967
109	83.009542	154	105.72899
110	83.574260	155	106.17599
111	84.136051	156	106.62068
112	84.694932	157	107.06306
113	85.250917	158	107.50315
114	85.804021	159	107.94095
115	86.354259	160	108.37649
116	86.901646	161	108.80977
117	87.446197	162	109.24081
118	87.987927	163	109.66962
119	88.526849	164	110.09620
120	89.062980	165	110.52057
121	89.596332	166	110.94274
122	90.126921	167	111.36273
123	90.654761	168	111.78054
124	91.179866	169	112.19618
125	91.702250	170	112.60968
126	92.221927	171	113.02102
127	92.738912	172	113.43024
128	93.253218	173	113.83734
129	93.764860	174	114.24233
130	94.273850	175	114.64522
131	94.780203	176	115.04602
132	95.283933	177	115.44474
133	95.785052	178	115.84140
134	96.283575	179	116.23601
135	96.779515	180	116.62857

yearly interest rate = 6.25%

term (months)	constant	term (months)	constant
181	117.01909	226	132.64913
182	117.40759	227	132.95665
183	117.79408	228	133.26257
184	118.17857	229	133.56691
185	118.56106	230	133.86967
186	118.94158	231	134.17087
187	119.32012	232	134.47050
188	119.69670	233	134.76858
189	120.07133	234	135.06512
190	120.44401	235	135.36012
191	120.81477	236	135.65359
192	121.18361	237	135.94554
193	121.55053	238	136.23597
194	121.91555	239	136.52491
195	122.27868	240	136.81234
196	122.63994	241	137.09829
197	122.99931	242	137.38275
198	123.35683	243	137.66575
199	123.71249	244	137.94727
200	124.06632	245	138.22734
201	124.41830	246	138.50595
202	124.76847	247	138.78312
203	125.11682	248	139.05886
204	125.46336	249	139.33316
205	125.80811	250	139.60605
206	126.15108	251	139.87752
207	126.49226	252	140.14758
208	126.83168	253	140.41625
209	127.16934	254	140.68352
210	127.50525	255	140.94941
211	127.83942	256	141.21392
212	128.17186	257	141.47706
213	128.50257	258	141.73884
214	128.83158	259	141.99926
215	129.15887	260	142.25833
216	129.48447	261	142.51606
217	129.80839	262	142.77245
218	130.13063	263	143.02752
219	130.45119	264	143.28126
220	130.77010	265	143.53369
221	131.08735	266	143.78481
222	131.40296	267	144.03463
223	131.71694	268	144.28316
224	132.02928	269	144.53039
225	132.34001	270	144.77635

yearly interest rate = 6.25%

term (months)	constant	term (months)	constant
271	145.02103	316	154.81397
272	145.26445	317	155.00664
273	145.50660	318	155.19832
274	145.74750	319	155.38900
275	145.98715	320	155.57869
276	146.22556	321	155.76740
277	146.46273	322	155.95514
278	146.69867	323	156.14190
279	146.93340	324	156.32769
280	147.16690	325	156.51252
281	147.39920	326	156.69640
282	147.63029	327	156.87932
283	147.86019	328	157.06129
284	148.08889	329	157.24232
285	148.31641	330	157.42241
286	148.54275	331	157.60157
287	148.76791	332	157.77980
288	148.99192	333	157.95710
289	149.21476	334	158.13349
290	149.43644	335	158.30897
291	149.65698	336	158.48353
292	149.87637	337	158.65719
293	150.09463	338	158.82995
294	150.31175	339	159.00182
295	150.52776	340	159.17279
296	150.74264	341	159.34288
297	150.95641	342	159.51209
298	151.16907	343	159.68042
299	151.38063	344	159.84788
300	151.59109	345	160.01447
301	151.80046	346	160.18020
302	152.00875	347	160.34507
303	152.21596	348	160.50908
304	152.42209	349	160.67225
305	152.62716	350	160.83457
306	152.83116	351	160.99605
307	153.03411	352	161.15669
308	153.23601	353	161.31650
309	153.43686	354	161.47548
310	153.63667	355	161.63364
311	153.83544	356	161.79098
312	154.03318	357	161.94750
313	154.22990	358	162.10322
314	154.42560	359	162.25812
315	154.62029	360	162.41222

yearly interest rate = 6.50%

term (months)	constant	term (months)	constant
1	0.9946125	46	40.620124
2	1.9838666	47	41.395896
3	2.9677911	48	42.167489
4	3.9464147	49	42.934924
5	4.9197659	50	43.698226
6	5.8878733	51	44.457415
7	6.8507650	52	45.212514
8	7.8084691	53	45.963544
9	8.7610136	54	46.710529
10	9.7084264	55	47.453489
11	10.650735	56	48.192447
12	11.587967	57	48.927423
13	12.520149	58	49.658440
14	13.447310	59	50.385519
15	14.369475	60	51.108680
16	15.286672	61	51.827945
17	16.198928	62	52.543336
18	17.106269	63	53.254872
19	18.008722	64	53.962574
20	18.906313	65	54.666464
21	19.799068	66	55.366562
22	20.687013	67	56.062888
23	21.570175	68	56.755463
24	22.448578	69	57.444306
25	23.322249	70	58.129438
26	24.191214	71	58.810879
27	25.055496	72	59.488649
28	25.915123	73	60.162768
29	26.770118	74	60.833254
30	27.620507	75	61.500128
31	28.466314	76	62.163410
32	29.307565	77	62.823118
33	30.144284	78	63.479272
34	30.976494	79	64.131891
35	31.804221	80	64.780994
36	32.627489	81	65.426600
37	33.446322	82	66.068728
38	34.260743	83	66.707396
39	35.070776	84	67.342623
40	35.876445	85	67.974429
41	36.677774	86	68.602830
42	37.474785	87	69.227846
43	38.267503	88	69.849494
44	39.055950	89	70.467794
45	39.840149	90	71.082762

yearly interest rate = 6.50%

term (months)	constant	term (months)	constant
91	71.694417	136	96.062853
92	72.302777	137	96.539929
93	72.907860	138	97.014434
94	73.509682	139	97.486383
95	74.108263	140	97.955789
96	74.703618	141	98.422666
97	75.295766	142	98.887028
98	75.884724	143	99.348888
99	76.470508	144	99.808260
100	77.053137	145	100.26516
101	77.632627	146	100.71959
102	78.208995	147	101.17158
103	78.782258	148	101.62113
104	79.352432	149	102.06826
105	79.919535	150	102.51298
106	80.483582	151	102.95531
107	81.044591	152	103.39525
108	81.602577	153	103.83282
109	82.157556	154	104.26804
110	82.709546	155	104.70091
111	83.258563	156	105.13145
112	83.804621	157	105.55967
113	84.347737	158	105.98558
114	84.887928	159	106.40919
115	85.425208	160	106.83053
116	85.959593	161	107.24959
117	86.491100	162	107.66640
118	87.019743	163	108.08096
119	87.545538	164	108.49329
120	88.068500	165	108.90340
121	88.588645	166	109.31129
122	89.105988	167	109.71699
123	89.620543	168	110.12051
124	90.132326	169	110.52185
125	90.641352	170	110.92102
126	91.147636	171	111.31805
127	91.651192	172	111.71294
128	92.152035	173	112.10570
129	92.650180	174	112.49635
130	93.145641	175	112.88489
131	93.638433	176	113.27133
132	94.128570	177	113.65570
133	94.616066	178	114.03799
134	95.100936	179	114.41823
135	95.583194	180	114.79641

yearly interest rate = 6.50%

term (months)	constant	term (months)	constant
181	115.17256	226	130.15838
182	115.54668	227	130.45176
183	115.91879	228	130.74357
184	116.28889	229	131.03380
185	116.65700	230	131.32247
186	117.02312	231	131.60959
187	117.38728	232	131.89516
188	117.74947	233	132.17919
189	118.10971	234	132.46169
190	118.46800	235	132.74266
191	118.82437	236	133.02213
192	119.17882	237	133.30008
193	119.53136	238	133.57654
194	119.88200	239	133.85152
195	120.23075	240	134.12500
196	120.57762	241	134.39702
197	120.92262	242	134.66757
198	121.26577	243	134.93666
199	121.60706	244	135.20431
200	121.94652	245	135.47051
201	122.28414	246	135.73528
202	122.61995	247	135.99862
203	122.95395	248	136.26054
204	123.28615	249	136.52105
205	123.61656	250	136.78016
206	123.94519	251	137.03787
207	124.27205	252	137.29419
208	124.59715	253	137.54913
209	124.92050	254	137.80270
210	125.24210	255	138.05491
211	125.56198	256	138.30575
212	125.88013	257	138.55524
213	126.19656	258	138.80339
214	126.51129	259	139.05020
215	126.82433	260	139.29568
216	127.13568	261	139.53984
217	127.44535	262	139.78269
218	127.75335	263	140.02422
219	128.05969	264	140.26446
220	128.36439	265	140.50340
221	128.66744	266	140.74105
222	128.96886	267	140.97742
223	129.26865	268	141.21252
224	129.56683	269	141.44635
225	129.86340	270	141.67893

yearly interest rate = 6.50%

term (months)	constant	term (months)	constant
271	141.91024	316	151.12605
272	142.14032	317	151.30647
273	142.36915	318	151.48592
274	142.59675	319	151.66441
275	142.82313	320	151.84193
276	143.04828	321	152.01850
277	143.27222	322	152.19411
278	143.49496	323	152.36878
279	143.71650	324	152.54251
280	143.93684	325	152.71530
281	144.15599	326	152.88716
282	144.37397	327	153.05810
283	144.59077	328	153.22811
284	144.80640	329	153.39721
285	145.02087	330	153.56540
286	145.23418	331	153.73268
287	145.44635	332	153.89906
288	145.65737	333	154.06454
289	145.86726	334	154.22914
290	146.07601	335	154.39284
291	146.28364	336	154.55566
292	146.49016	337	154.71761
293	146.69555	338	154.87868
294	146.89985	339	155.03889
295	147.10304	340	155.19823
296	147.30514	341	155.35672
297	147.50614	342	155.51435
298	147.70607	343	155.67113
299	147.90492	344	155.82707
300	148.10270	345	155.98216
301	148.29941	346	156.13642
302	148.49506	347	156.28985
303	148.68966	348	156.44246
304	148.88321	349	156.59424
305	149.07571	350	156.74520
306	149.26718	351	156.89535
307	149.45762	352	157.04469
308	149.64703	353	157.19323
309	149.83542	354	157.34097
310	150.02280	355	157.48791
311	150.20917	356	157.63406
312	150.39453	357	157.77942
313	150.57889	358	157.92400
314	150.76226	359	158.06780
315	150.94465	360	158.21082

yearly interest rate = 6.75%

term (months)	constant	term (months)	constant
1	0.9944065	46	40.430946
2	1.9832507	47	41.199200
3	2.9665638	48	41.963158
4	3.9443766	49	42.722842
5	4.9167201	50	43.478276
6	5.8836247	51	44.229485
7	6.8451209	52	44.976493
8	7.8012389	53	45.719321
9	8.7520089	54	46.457995
10	9.6974607	55	47.192537
11	10.637624	56	47.922970
12	11.572529	57	48.649318
13	12.502204	58	49.371603
14	13.426679	59	50.089847
15	14.345982	60	50.804075
16	15.260144	61	51.514307
17	16.169192	62	52.220566
18	17.073156	63	52.922875
19	17.972063	64	53.621255
20	18.865942	65	54.315729
21	19.754821	66	55.006319
22	20.638728	67	55.693045
23	21.517691	68	56.375931
24	22.391738	69	57.054996
25	23.260895	70	57.730264
26	24.125191	71	58.401754
27	24.984653	72	59.069488
28	25.839306	73	59.733487
29	26.689180	74	60.393772
30	27.534299	75	61.050364
31	28.374692	76	61.703283
32	29.210383	77	62.352550
33	30.041400	78	62.998185
34	30.867769	79	63.640209
35	31.689516	80	64.278641
36	32.506666	81	64.913503
37	33.319245	82	65.544813
38	34.127279	83	66.172592
39	34.930793	84	66.796860
40	35.729813	85	67.417636
41	36.524364	86	68.034939
42	37.314470	87	68.648790
43	38.100156	88	69.259207
44	38.881448	89	69.866209
45	39.658370	90	70.469817

yearly interest rate = 6.75%

term (months)	constant	term (months)	constant
91	71.070048	136	94.874230
92	71.666921	137	95.337954
93	72.260456	138	95.799084
94	72.850671	139	96.257635
95	73.437585	140	96.713621
96	74.021215	141	97.167056
97	74.601582	142	97.617955
98	75.178701	143	98.066332
99	75.752593	144	98.512201
100	76.323275	145	98.955576
101	76.890764	146	99.396471
102	77.455079	147	99.834899
103	78.016238	148	100.27088
104	78.574258	149	100.70441
105	79.129156	150	101.13553
106	79.680951	151	101.56423
107	80.229659	152	101.99053
108	80.775298	153	102.41445
109	81.317885	154	102.83600
110	81.857437	155	103.25519
111	82.393971	156	103.67203
112	82.927504	157	104:08654
113	83.458052	158	104.49874
114	83.985633	159	104.90863
115	84.510263	160	105.31622
116	85.031958	161	105.72154
117	85.550735	162	106.12459
118	86.066610	163	106.52538
119	86.579600	164	106.92394
120	87.089720	165	107.32026
121	87.596987	166	107.71437
122	88.101417	167	108.10627
123	88.603025	168	108.49598
124	89.101827	169	108.88351
125	89.597839	170	109.26887
126	90.091077	171	109.65208
127	90.581556	172	110.03314
128	91.069291	173	110.41208
129	91.554298	174	110.78889
130	92.036592	175	111.16359
131	92.516189	176	111.53620
132	92.993102	177	111.90673
133	93.467349	178	112.27518
134	93.938942	179	112.64157
135	94.407898	180	113.00591

yearly interest rate = 6.75%

term (months)	constant	term (months)	constant
181	113.36822	226	127.73659
182	113.72849	227	128.01650
183	114.08675	228	128.29484
184	114.44301	229	128.57163
185	114.79728	230	128.84686
186	115.14956	231	129.12056
187	115.49987	232	129.39273
188	115.84823	233	129.66337
189	116.19463	234	129.93250
190	116.53910	235	130.20012
191	116.88164	236	130.46625
192	117.22227	237	130.73089
193	117.56099	238	130.99405
194	117.89781	239	131.25573
195	118.23275	240	131.51596
196	118.56582	241	131.77472
197	118.89702	242	132.03204
198	119.22637	243	132.28792
199	119.55388	244	132.54237
200	119.87956	245	132.79540
201	120.20342	246	133.04701
202	120.52546	247	133.29721
203	120.84570	248	133.54602
204	121.16416	249	133.79343
205	121.48083	250	134.03946
206	121.79573	251	134.28411
207	122.10886	252	134.52739
208	122.42025	253	134.76931
209	122.72989	254	135.00988
210	123.03781	255	135.24911
211	123.34400	256	135.48699
212	123.64847	257	135.72355
213	123.95125	258	135.95878
214	124.25233	259	136.19270
215	124.55172	260	136.42530
216	124.84945	261	136.65661
217	125.14550	262	136.88662
218	125.43990	263	137.11535
219	125.73266	264	137.34280
220	126.02377	265	137.56897
221	126.31326	266	137.79388
222	126.60113	267	138.01753
223	126.88739	268	138.23993
224	127.17205	269	138.46109
225	127.45511	270	138.68101

yearly interest rate = 6.75%

term (months)	constant	term (months)	constant
271	138.89970	316	147.57255
272	139.11716	317	147.74151
273	139.33341	318	147.90952
274	139.54845	319	148.07659
275	139.76229	320	148.24272
276	139.97493	321	148.40793
277	140.18638	322	148.57221
278	140.39665	323	148.73557
279	140.60574	324	148.89802
280	140.81367	325	149.05956
281	141.02043	326	149.22020
282	141.22603	327	149.37993
283	141.43048	328	149.53878
284	141.63379	329	149.69673
285	141.83597	330	149.85381
286	142.03701	331	150.01000
287	142.23693	332	150.16532
288	142.43572	333	150.31977
289	142.63341	334	150.47336
290	142.82999	335	150.62609
291	143.02547	336	150.77796
292	143.21986	337	150.92898
293	143.41316	338	151.07916
294	143.60538	339	151.22850
295	143.79653	340	151.37701
296	143.98660	341	151.52468
297	144.17562	342	151.67153
298	144.36357	343	151.81756
299	144.55047	344	151.96277
300	144.73633	345	152.10716
301	144.92115	346	152.25075
302	145.10494	347	152.39354
303	145.28769	348	152.53553
304	145.46943	349	152.67672
305	145.65014	350	152.81712
306	145.82985	351	152.95674
307	146.00855	352	153.09558
308	146.18626	353	153.23364
309	146.36296	354	153.37093
310	146.53868	355	153.50745
311	146.71342	356	153.64321
312	146.88718	357	153.77820
313	147.05997	358	153.91245
314	147.23179	359	154.04594
315	147.40265	360	154.17868

yearly interest rate = 7.00%

term (months)	constant	term (months)	constant
1	0.9942005	46	40.242991
2	1.9826351	47	41.003802
3	2.9653373	48	41.760201
4	3.9423403	49	42.512213
5	4.9136772	50	43.259864
6	5.8793808	51	44.003179
7	6.8394838	52	44.742183
8	7.7940187	53	45.476901
9	8.7430178	54	46.207358
10	9.6865131	55	46.933579
11	10.624537	56	47.655588
12	11.557120	57	48.373410
13	12.484295	58	49.087068
14	13.406093	59	49.796588
15	14.322545	60	50.501993
16	15.233682	61	51.203307
17	16.139534	62	51.900554
18	17.040133	63	52.593757
19	17.935510	64	53.282940
20	18.825693	65	53.968126
21	19.710714	66	54.649338
22	20.590602	67	55.326600
23	21.465387	68	55.999933
24	22.335099	69	56.669362
25	23.199767	70	57.334908
26	24.059421	71	57.996595
27	24.914088	72	58.654444
28	25.763800	73	59.308478
29	26.608583	74	59.958719
30	27.448467	75	60.605189
31	28.283480	76	61.247909
32	29.113650	77	61.886902
33	29.939006	78	62.522189
34	30.759575	79	63.153792
35	31.575385	80	63.781732
36	32.386464	81	64.406030
37	33.192839	82	65.026708
38	33.994538	83	65.643786
39	34.791587	84	66.257285
40	35.584014	85	66.867226
41	36.371845	86	67.473630
42	37.155106	87	68.076517
43	37.933826	88	68.675907
44	38.708029	89	69.271822
45	39.477742	90	69.864280

yearly interest rate = 7.00%

term (months)	constant	term (months)	constant
91	70.453303	136	93.706577
92	71.038909	137	94.157326
93	71.621119	138	94.605461
94	72.199953	139	95.050997
95	72.775429	140	95.493949
96	73.347568	141	95.934332
97	73.916390	142	96.372161
98	74.481912	143	96.807451
99	75.044154	144	97.240216
100	75.603136	145	97.670472
101	76.158876	146	98.098232
102	76.711393	147	98.523511
103	77.260705	148	98.946324
104	77.806832	149	99.366685
105	78.349792	150	99.784609
106	78.889602	151	100.20011
107	79.426282	152	100.61320
108	79.959850	153	101.02389
109	80.490323	154	101.43220
110	81.017719	155	101.83815
111	81.542057	156	102.24174
112	82.063355	157	102.64299
113	82.581628	158	103.04191
114	83.096897	159	103.43852
115	83.609176	160	103.83283
116	84.118485	161	104.22485
117	84.624840	162	104.61460
118	85.128259	163	105.00208
119	85.628758	164	105.38732
120	86.126354	165	105.77033
121	86.621064	166	106.15112
122	87.112906	167	106.52969
123	87.601895	168	106.90607
124	88.088048	169	107.28027
125	88.571381	170	107.65230
126	89.051912	171	108.02217
127	89.529656	172	108.38990
128	90.004629	173	108.75549
129	90.476847	174	109.11896
130	90.946327	175	109.48033
131	91.413084	176	109.83960
132	91.877134	177	110.19678
133	92.338493	178	110.55190
134	92.797176	179	110.90495
135	93.253199	180	111.25596

yearly interest rate = 7.00%

term (months)	constant	term (months)	constant
181	111.60493	226	125.38153
182	111.95188	227	125.64858
183	112.29681	228	125.91408
184	112.63975	229	126.17804
185	112.98069	230	126.44047
186	113.31966	231	126.70138
187	113.65666	232	126.96077
188	113.99171	233	127.21866
189	114.32482	234	127.47506
190	114.65599	235	127.72997
191	114.98524	236	127.98340
192	115.31259	237	128.23536
193	115.63803	238	128.48586
194	115.96159	239	128.73490
195	116.28327	240	128.98251
196	116.60308	241	129.22867
197	116.92105	242	129.47341
198	117.23716	243	129.71673
199	117.55145	244	129.95864
200	117.86391	245	130.19914
201	118.17455	246	130.43825
202	118.48340	247	130.67598
203	118.79046	248	130.91232
204	119.09573	249	131.14730
205	119.39924	250	131.38091
206	119.70098	251	131.61316
207	120.00097	252	131.84407
208	120.29923	253	132.07364
209	120.59575	254	132.30188
210	120.89056	255	132.52880
211	121.18365	256	132.75440
212	121.47505	257	132.97869
213	121.76476	258	133.20168
214	122.05278	259	133.42338
215	122.33914	260	133.64379
216	122.62383	261	133.86292
217	122.90687	262	134.08078
218	123.18828	263	134.29738
219	123.46805	264	134.51272
220	123.74619	265	134.72682
221	124.02273	266	134.93967
222	124.29766	267	135.15129
223	124.57099	268	135.36168
224	124.84274	269	135.57085
225	125.11292	270	135.77880

yearly interest rate = 7.00%

term (months)	constant	term (months)	constant
271	135.98555	316	144.14761
272	136.19111	317	144.30583
273	136.39547	318	144.46313
274	136.59864	319	144.61951
275	136.80064	320	144.77499
276	137.00146	321	144.92957
277	137.20112	322	145.08325
278	137.39962	323	145.23604
279	137.59697	324	145.38795
280	137.79318	325	145.53897
281	137.98825	326	145.68912
282	138.18219	327	145.83839
283	138.37500	328	145.98680
284	138.56669	329	146.13435
285	138.75728	330	146.28105
286	138.94675	331	146.42689
287	139.13513	332	146.57189
288	139.32242	333	146.71604
289	139.50862	334	146.85936
290	139.69374	335	147.00185
291	139.87778	336	147.14351
292	140.06076	337	147.28436
293	140.24268	338	147.42438
294	140.42354	339	147.56359
295	140.60336	340	147.70200
296	140.78213	341	147.83960
297	140.95986	342	147.97640
298	141.13656	343	148.11242
299	141.31224	344	148.24764
300	141.48690	345	148.38208
301	141.66055	346	148.51573
302	141.83319	347	148.64862
303	142.00483	348	148.78073
304	142.17547	349	148.91207
305	142.34512	350	149.04266
306	142.51379	351	149.17249
307	142.68149	352	149.30156
308	142.84820	353	149.42989
309	143.01396	354	149.55747
310	143.17875	355	149.68431
311	143.34258	356	149.81042
312	143.50547	357	149.93579
313	143.66741	358	150.06044
314	143.82841	359	150.18436
315	143.98848	360	150.30757

yearly interest rate = 7.25%

term (months)	constant	term (months)	constant
1	0.9939946	46	40.056252
2	1.9820199	47	40.809693
3	2.9641118	48	41.558610
4	3.9403057	49	42.303029
5	4.9106373	50	43.042978
6	5.8751417	51	43.778483
7	6.8338538	52	44.509571
8	7.7868085	53	45.236268
9	8.7340404	54	45.958602
10	9.6755837	55	46.676597
11	10.611473	56	47.390281
12	11.541741	57	48.099679
13	12.466423	58	48.804816
14	13.385552	59	49.505719
15	14.299162	60	50.202413
16	15.207284	61	50.894923
17	16.109953	62	51.583274
18	17.007202	63	52.267491
19	17.899061	64	52.947599
20	18.785565	65	53.623623
21	19.666745	66	54.295588
22	20.542634	67	54.963516
23	21.413262	68	55.627434
24	22.278662	69	56.287364
25	23.138864	70	56.943332
26	23.993901	71	57.595360
27	24.843803	72	58.243472
28	25.688601	73	58.887692
29	26.528326	74	59.528044
30	27.363008	75	60.164550
31	28.192677	76	60.797233
32	29.017364	77	61.426117
33	29.837098	78	62.051224
34	30.651909	79	62.672577
35	31.461827	80	63.290199
36	32.266882	81	63.904112
37	33.067101	82	64.514338
38	33.862515	83	65.120899
39	34.653153	84	65.723817
40	35.439042	85	66.323115
41	36.220211	86	66.918814
42	36.996690	87	67.510936
43	37.768505	88	68.099501
44	38.535685	89	68.684532
45	39.298258	90	69.266050

yearly interest rate = 7.25%

term (months)	constant	term (months)	constant
91	69.844075	136	92.559466
92	70.418629	137	92.997605
93	70.989733	138	93.433113
94	71.557407	139	93.866006
95	72.121672	140	94.296299
96	72.682548	141	94.724009
97	73.240056	142	95.149149
98	73.794216	143	95.571737
99	74.345048	144	95.991786
100	74.892572	145	96.409313
101	75.436808	146	96.824333
102	75.977776	147	97.236860
103	76.515495	148	97.646910
104	77.049984	149	98.054498
105	77.581264	150	98.459637
106	78.109353	151	98.862344
107	78.634271	152	99.262632
108	79.156037	153	99.660517
109	79.674669	154	100.05601
110	80.190187	155	100.44913
111	80.702609	156	100.83989
112	81.211953	157	101.22830
113	81.718239	158	101.61438
114	82.221484	159	101.99814
115	82.721707	160	102.37960
116	83.218926	161	102.75877
117	83.713159	162	103.13565
118	84.204424	163	103.51028
119	84.692739	164	103.88266
120	85.178121	165	104.25280
121	85.660588	166	104.62071
122	86.140158	167	104.98642
123	86.616848	168	105.34993
124	87.090675	169	105.71126
125	87.561657	170	106.07042
126	88.029810	171	106.42742
127	88.495152	172	106.78227
128	88.957699	173	107.13500
129	89.417468	174	107.48561
130	89.874477	175	107.83411
131	90.328741	176	108.18052
132	90.780276	177	108.52485
133	91.229101	178	108.86711
134	91.675229	179	109.20732
135	92.118679	180	109.54548

yearly interest rate = 7.25%

term (months)	constant	term (months)	constant
181	109.88161	226	123.09101
182	110.21572	227	123.34580
183	110.54783	228	123.59905
184	110.87794	229	123.85079
185	111.20607	230	124.10101
186	111.53223	231	124.34973
187	111.85643	232	124.59696
188	112.17869	233	124.82470
189	112.49900	234	125.08696
190	112.81740	235	125.32976
191	113.13388	236	125.57110
192	113.44846	237	125.81100
193	113.76116	238	126.04945
194	114.07197	239	126.28647
195	114.38092	240	126.52206
196	114.68801	241	126.75624
197	114.99326	242	126.98902
198	115.29668	243	127.22040
199	115.59827	244	127.45038
200	115.89806	245	127.67899
201	116.19604	246	127.90622
202	116.49223	247	128.13209
203	116.78665	248	128.35660
204	117.07929	249	128.57977
205	117.37018	250	128.80159
206	117.65932	251	129.02208
207	117.94673	252	129.24125
208	118.23241	253	129.45910
209	118.51637	254	129.67564
210	118.79863	255	129.89089
211	119.07919	256	130.10484
212	119.35807	257	130.31750
213	119.63527	258	130.52889
214	119.91081	259	130.73901
215	120.18470	260	130.94786
216	120.45693	261	131.15547
217	120.72754	262	131.36182
218	120.99652	263	131.56694
219	121.26388	264	131.77082
220	121.52964	265	131.97348
221	121.79380	266	132.17493
222	122.05638	267	132.37516
223	122.31738	268	132.57419
224	122.57681	269	132.77203
225	122.83468	270	132.96867

yearly interest rate = 7.25%

term (months)	constant	term (months)	constant
271	133.16414	316	140.84564
272	133.35843	317	140.99380
273	133.55156	318	141.14108
274	133.74353	319	141.28746
275	133.93434	320	141.43297
276	134.12401	321	141.57761
277	134.31254	322	141.72137
278	134.49993	323	141.86428
279	134.68620	324	142.00632
280	134.87136	325	142.14752
281	135.05540	326	142.28786
282	135.23833	327	142.42736
283	135.42017	328	142.56602
284	135.60091	329	142.70386
285	135.78057	330	142.84086
286	135.95915	331	142.97704
287	136.13666	332	143.11240
288	136.31310	333	143.24695
289	136.48848	334	143.38069
290	136.66281	335	143.51363
291	136.83609	336	143.64577
292	137.00833	337	143.77712
293	137.17954	338	143.90768
294	137.34972	339	144.03745
295	137.51888	340	144.16644
296	137.68702	341	144.29466
297	137.85415	342	144.42211
298	138.02028	343	144.54880
299	138.18541	344	144.67472
300	138.34954	345	144.79989
301	138.51270	346	144.92430
302	138.67487	347	145.04797
303	138.83607	348	145.17090
304	138.99630	349	145.29309
305	139.15557	350	145.41454
306	139.31388	351	145.53526
307	139.47124	352	145.65526
308	139.62766	353	145.77454
309	139.78313	354	145.89311
310	139.93768	355	146.01096
311	140.09129	356	146.12810
312	140.24398	357	146.24454
313	140.39576	358	146.36028
314	140.54662	359	146.47532
315	140.69658	360	146.58968

yearly interest rate = 7.50%

term (months)	constant	term (months)	constant
1	0.9937888	46	39.870716
2	1.9814050	47	40.616861
3	2.9628870	48	41.358371
4	3.9382728	49	42.095276
5	4.9076003	50	42.827603
6	5.8709071	51	43.555382
7	6.8282307	52	44.278641
8	7.7796081	53	44.997407
9	8.7250764	54	45.711709
10	9.6646722	55	46.421574
11	10.598432	56	47.127030
12	11.526392	57	47.828104
13	12.448588	58	48.524824
14	13.365057	59	49.217216
15	14.275833	60	49.905308
16	15.180952	61	50.589126
17	16.080449	62	51.268697
18	16.974359	63	51.944047
19	17.862717	64	52.615202
20	18.745558	65	53.282188
21	19.622914	66	53.945031
22	20.494822	67	54.603758
23	21.361314	68	55.258393
24	22.222423	69	55.908962
25	23.078185	70	56.555490
26	23.928631	71	57.198003
27	24.773795	72	57.836524
28	25.613709	73	58.471080
29	26.448406	74	59.101695
30	27.277919	75	59.728392
31	28.102280	76	60.351197
32	28.921521	77	60.970134
33	29.735673	78	61.585226
34	30.544768	79	62.196498
35	31.348838	80	62.803973
36	32.147913	81	63.407675
37	32.942026	82	64.007628
38	33.731206	83	64.603853
39	34.515484	84	65.196376
40	35.294891	85	65.785219
41	36.069457	86	66.370404
42	36.839212	87	66.951954
43	37.604185	88	67.529892
44	38.364408	89	68.104240
45	39.119908	90	68.675022

yearly interest rate = 7.50%

term (months)	constant	term (months)	constant
91	69.242257	136	91.432474
92	69.805970	137	91.858359
93	70.366182	138	92.281599
94	70.922913	139	92.702210
95	71.476187	140	93.120209
96	72.026025	141	93.535611
97	72.572447	142	93.948433
98	73.115475	143	94.358692
99	73.655130	144	94.766402
100	74.191434	145	95.171579
101	74.724406	146	95.574240
102	75.254069	147	95.974400
103	75.780441	148	96.372075
104	76.303544	149	96.767279
105	76.823397	150	97.160029
106	77.340022	151	97.550339
107	77.853438	152	97.938226
108	78.363665	153	98.323702
109	78.870723	154	98.706785
110	79.374632	155	99.087488
111	79.875411	156	99.465827
112	80.373079	157	99.841815
113	80.867656	158	100.21547
114	81.359161	159	100.58680
115	81.847614	160	100.95583
116	82.333032	161	101.32256
117	82.815436	162	101.68702
118	83.294843	163	102.04921
119	83.771272	164	102.40915
120	84.244743	165	102.76686
121	84.715272	166	103.12235
122	85.182879	167	103.47562
123	85.647582	168	103.82671
124	86.109398	169	104.17561
125	86.568346	170	104.52234
126	87.024443	171	104.86693
127	87.477708	172	105.20937
128	87.928157	173	105.54968
129	88.375808	174	105.88788
130	88.820679	175	106.22398
131	89.262786	176	106.55799
132	89.702148	177	106.88993
133	90.138780	178	107.21981
134	90.572701	179	107.54764
135	91.003927	180	107.87343

yearly interest rate = 7.50%

term (months)	constant	term (months)	constant
181	108.19719	226	120.86295
182	108.51895	227	121.10604
183	108.83871	228	121.34762
184	109.15648	229	121.58769
185	109.47228	230	121.82628
186	109.78612	231	122.06338
187	110.09800	232	122.29901
188	110.40795	233	122.53318
189	110.71598	234	122.76589
190	111.02209	235	122.99716
191	111.32630	236	123.22699
192	111.62862	237	123.45540
193	111.92907	238	123.68238
194	112.22764	239	123.90796
195	112.52437	240	124.13213
196	112.81925	241	124.35491
197	113.11229	242	124.57631
198	113.40352	243	124.79633
199	113.69294	244	125.01499
200	113.98056	245	125.23229
201	114.26640	246	125.44824
202	114.55046	247	125.66284
203	114.83275	248	125.87612
204	115.11329	249	126.08807
205	115.39209	250	126.29870
206	115.66916	251	126.50803
207	115.94451	252	126.71605
208	116.21814	253	126.92278
209	116.49008	254	127.12823
210	116.76033	255	127.33240
211	117.02890	256	127.53531
212	117.29580	257	127.73695
213	117.56104	258	127.93734
214	117.82464	259	128.13649
215	118.08660	260	128.33440
216	118.34693	261	128.53108
217	118.60565	262	128.72654
218	118.86275	263	128.92079
219	119.11826	264	129.11382
220	119.37219	265	129.30566
221	119.62453	266	129.49631
222	119.87531	267	129.68578
223	120.12454	268	129.87406
224	120.37221	269	130.06118
225	120.61834	270	130.24714

yearly interest rate = 7.50%

term (months)	constant	term (months)	constant
271	130.43194	316	137.66131
272	130.61559	317	137.80006
273	130.79810	318	137.93795
274	130.97948	319	138.07498
275	131.15973	320	138.21116
276	131.33886	321	138.34649
277	131.51688	322	138.48099
278	131.69380	323	138.61465
279	131.86961	324	138.74748
280	132.04433	325	138.87948
281	132.21797	326	139.01066
282	132.39053	327	139.14103
283	132.56202	328	139.27059
284	132.73244	329	139.39934
285	132.90180	330	139.52730
286	133.07012	331	139.65446
287	133.23738	332	139.78083
288	133.40361	333	139.90641
289	133.56881	334	140.03122
290	133.73297	335	140.15525
291	133.89612	336	140.27851
292	134.05826	337	140.40100
293	134.21939	338	140.52273
294	134.37952	339	140.64371
295	134.53865	340	140.76394
296	134.69679	341	140.88341
297	134.85396	342	141.00215
298	135.01014	343	141.12015
299	135.16536	344	141.23742
300	135.31961	345	141.35395
301	135.47291	346	141.46977
302	135.62525	347	141.58486
303	135.77665	348	141.69924
304	135.92710	349	141.81291
305	136.07662	350	141.92587
306	136.22521	351	142.03814
307	136.37288	352	142.14970
308	136.51964	353	142.26057
309	136.66548	354	142.37075
310	136.81041	355	142.48025
311	136.95445	356	142.58907
312	137.09759	357	142.69721
313	137.23984	358	142.80468
314	137.38121	359	142.91149
315	137.52169	360	143.01763

yearly interest rate = 7.75%

term (months)	constant	term (months)	constant
1	0.9935831	46	39.686377
2	1.9807905	47	40.425297
3	2.9616631	48	41.159476
4	3.9362415	49	41.888943
5	4.9045662	50	42.613729
6	5.8666772	51	43.333865
7	6.8226145	52	44.049379
8	7.7724177	53	44.760302
9	8.7161260	54	45.466663
10	9.6537787	55	46.168492
11	10.585415	56	46.865817
12	11.511072	57	47.558667
13	12.430790	58	48.247071
14	13.344606	59	48.931058
15	14.252558	60	49.610656
16	15.154684	61	50.285893
17	16.051021	62	50.956797
18	16.941607	63	51.623396
19	17.826478	64	52.285717
20	18.705670	65	52.943789
21	19.579221	66	53.597637
22	20.447166	67	54.247290
23	21.309542	68	54.892774
24	22.166384	69	55.534117
25	23.017728	70	56.171343
26	23.863609	71	56.804481
27	24.704062	72	57.433556
28	25.539122	73	58.058594
29	26.368823	74	58.679622
30	27.193200	75	59.296664
31	28.012288	76	59.909747
32	28.826119	77	60.518896
33	29.634728	78	61.124136
34	30.438148	79	61.725492
35	31.236413	80	62.322989
36	32.029556	81	62.916652
37	32.817609	82	63.506506
38	33.600605	83	64.092575
39	34.378576	84	64.674883
40	35.151556	85	65.253455
41	35.919575	86	65.828313
42	36.682666	87	66.399483
43	37.440861	88	66.966988
44	38.194190	89	67.530851
45	38.942685	90	68.091096

yearly interest rate = 7.75%

term (months)	constant	term (months)	constant
91	68.647746	136	90.325191
92	69.200824	137	90.739167
93	69.750353	138	91.150487
94	70.296356	139	91.559167
95	70.838855	140	91.965225
96	71.377873	141	92.368678
97	71.913432	142	92.769541
98	72.445555	143	93.167832
99	72.974263	144	93.563567
100	73.499578	145	93.956763
101	74.021522	146	94.347436
102	74.540117	147	94.735602
103	75.055384	148	95.121277
104	75.567345	149	95.504477
105	76.076021	150	95.885219
106	76.581433	151	96.263517
107	77.083601	152	96.639387
108	77.582547	153	97.012846
109	78.078291	154	97.383908
110	78.570855	155	97.752589
111	79.060257	156	98.118905
112	79.546519	157	98.482870
113	80.029661	158	98.844499
114	80.509703	159	99.203808
115	80.986664	160	99.560811
116	81.460564	161	99.915523
117	81.931424	162	100.26796
118	82.399262	163	100.61813
119	82.864098	164	100.96606
120	83.325951	165	101.31176
121	83.784841	166	101.65523
122	84.240786	167	101.99651
123	84.693805	168	102.33559
124	85.143917	169	102.67249
125	85.591141	170	103.00724
126	86.035495	171	103.33984
127	86.476998	172	103.67030
128	86.915667	173	103.99864
129	87.351522	174	104.32488
130	87.784580	175	104.64902
131	88.214859	176	104.97108
132	88.642377	177	105.29108
133	89.067152	178	105.60902
134	89.489201	179	105.92492
135	89.908541	180	106.23879

yearly interest rate = 7.75%

term (months)	constant	term (months)	constant
181	106.55065	226	118.69533
182	106.86051	227	118.92726
183	107.16838	228	119.15770
184	107.47428	229	119.38666
185	107.77821	230	119.61415
186	108.08019	231	119.84019
187	108.38024	232	120.06477
188	108.67836	233	120.28791
189	108.97456	234	120.50962
190	109.26887	235	120.72990
191	109.56128	236	120.94878
192	109.85182	237	121.16624
193	110.14050	238	121.38232
194	110.42732	239	121.59700
195	110.71231	240	121.81031
196	110.99546	241	122.02225
197	111.27680	242	122.23283
198	111.55633	243	122.44206
199	111.83407	244	122.64994
200	112.11003	245	122.85650
201	112.38421	246	123.06172
202	112.65664	247	123.26563
203	112.92731	248	123.46823
204	113.19625	249	123.66953
205	113.46347	250	123.86954
206	113.72897	251	124.06827
207	113.99277	252	124.26572
208	114.25487	253	124.46190
209	114.51529	254	124.65683
210	114.77404	255	124.85050
211	115.03113	256	125.04293
212	115.28658	257	125.23413
213	115.54038	258	125.42410
214	115.79255	259	125.61285
215	116.04311	260	125.80039
216	116.29205	261	125.98672
217	116.53940	262	126.17186
218	116.78516	263	126.35582
219	117.02935	264	126.53859
220	117.27197	265	126.72019
221	117.51303	266	126.90062
222	117.75255	267	127.07990
223	117.99052	268	127.25802
224	118.22697	269	127.43500
225	118.46191	270	127.61085

yearly interest rate = 7.75%

term (months)	constant	term (months)	constant
271	127.78557	316	134.58956
272	127.95916	317	134.71950
273	128.13165	318	134.84860
274	128.30302	319	134.97688
275	128.47330	320	135.10433
276	128.64248	321	135.23096
277	128.81058	322	135.35678
278	128.97760	323	135.48180
279	129.14355	324	135.60601
280	129.30843	325	135.72942
281	129.47226	326	135.85204
282	129.63503	327	135.97388
283	129.79676	328	136.09493
284	129.95745	329	136.21521
285	130.11711	330	136.33471
286	130.27575	331	136.45345
287	130.43337	332	136.57143
288	130.58997	333	136.68865
289	130.74557	334	136.80511
290	130.90018	335	136.92083
291	131.05379	336	137.03581
292	131.20641	337	137.15005
293	131.35806	338	137.26356
294	131.50873	339	137.37633
295	131.65844	340	137.48839
296	131.80718	341	137.59972
297	131.95497	342	137.71034
298	132.10182	343	137.82026
299	132.24772	344	137.92946
300	132.39268	345	138.03797
301	132.53671	346	138.14577
302	132.67982	347	138.25289
303	132.82202	348	138.35932
304	132.96329	349	138.46507
305	133.10367	350	138.57013
306	133.24314	351	138.67453
307	133.38171	352	138.77825
308	133.51940	353	138.88131
309	133.65620	354	138.98371
310	133.79213	355	139.08545
311	133.92718	356	139.18653
312	134.06137	357	139.28697
313	134.19470	358	139.38677
314	134.32717	359	139.48592
315	134.45879	360	139.58444

yearly interest rate = 8.00%

term (months)	constant	term (months)	constant
1	0.9933775	46	39.503226
2	1.9801763	47	40.234993
3	2.9604401	48	40.961913
4	3.934212	49	41.684020
5	4.9015351	50	42.401344
6	5.8624521	51	43.113918
7	6.8170054	52	43.821773
8	7.7652372	53	44.524940
9	8.7071892	54	45.223450
10	9.6429032	55	45.917335
11	10.572420	56	46.606624
12	11.495782	57	47.291348
13	12.413028	58	47.971538
14	13.324200	59	48.647223
15	14.229338	60	49.318434
16	15.128482	61	49.985199
17	16.021670	62	50.647549
18	16.908944	63	51.305512
19	17.790342	64	51.959118
20	18.665903	65	52.608395
21	19.535665	66	53.253373
22	20.399667	67	53.894079
23	21.257947	68	54.530542
24	22.110544	69	55.162790
25	22.957494	70	55.790851
26	23.798835	71	56.414753
27	24.634604	72	57.034522
28	25.464839	73	57.650188
29	26.289575	74	58.261776
30	27.108849	75	58.869314
31	27.922698	76	59.472828
32	28.731157	77	60.072346
33	29.534262	78	60.667894
34	30.332048	79	61.259497
35	31.124551	80	61.847182
36	31.911806	81	62.430976
37	32.693847	82	63.010903
38	33.470709	83	63.586990
39	34.242426	84	64.159262
40	35.009032	85	64.727743
41	35.770562	86	65.292460
42	36.527048	87	65.853437
43	37.278525	88	66.410699
44	38.025025	89	66.964271
45	38.766581	90	67.514176

yearly interest rate = 8.00%

term (months)	constant	term (months)	constant
91	68.060440	136	89.237217
92	68.603086	137	89.639620
93	69.142139	138	90.039357
94	69.677621	139	90.436448
95	70.209557	140	90.830908
96	70.737971	141	91.222757
97	71.262885	142	91.612010
98	71.784323	143	91.998685
99	72.302307	144	92.382800
100	72.816862	145	92.764371
101	73.328008	146	93.143415
102	73.835770	147	93.519948
103	74.340169	148	93.893988
104	74.841227	149	94.265551
105	75.338967	150	94.634654
106	75.833411	151	95.001312
107	76.324581	152	95.365541
108	76.812498	153	95.727359
109	77.297183	154	96.086780
110	77.778659	155	96.443822
111	78.256946	156	96.798498
112	78.732065	157	97.150826
113	79.204038	158	97.500821
114	79.672886	159	97.848497
115	80.138628	160	98.193872
116	80.601286	161	98.536959
117	81.060880	162	98.877773
118	81.517431	163	99.216331
119	81.970958	164	99.552647
120	82.421481	165	99.886735
121	82.869021	166	100.21861
122	83.313597	167	100.54829
123	83.755229	168	100.87578
124	84.193936	169	101.20111
125	84.629738	170	101.52428
126	85.062653	171	101.84531
127	85.492702	172	102.16422
128	85.919903	173	102.48101
129	86.344274	174	102.79571
130	86.765835	175	103.10832
131	87.184605	176	103.41886
132	87.600601	177	103.72734
133	88.013842	178	104.03378
134	88.424346	179	104.33820
135	88.832132	180	104.64059

yearly interest rate = 8.00%

term (months)	constant	term (months)	constant
181	104.94099	226	116.58621
182	105.23939	227	116.80750
183	105.53582	228	117.02731
184	105.83028	229	117.24568
185	106.12280	230	117.46259
186	106.41337	231	117.67807
187	106.70203	232	117.89212
188	106.98877	233	118.10476
189	107.27361	234	118.31599
190	107.55657	235	118.52581
191	107.83765	236	118.73425
192	108.11687	237	118.94131
193	108.39424	238	119.14700
194	108.66978	239	119.35132
195	108.94349	240	119.55429
196	109.21539	241	119.75592
197	109.48548	242	119.95621
198	109.75379	243	120.15518
199	110.02032	244	120.35282
200	110.28509	245	120.54916
201	110.54810	246	120.74420
202	110.80937	247	120.93795
203	111.06891	248	121.13041
204	111.32673	249	121.32160
205	111.58285	250	121.51153
206	111.83727	251	121.70019
207	112.09000	252	121.88761
208	112.34106	253	122.07378
209	112.59046	254	122.25872
210	112.83820	255	122.44244
211	113.08431	256	122.62494
212	113.32878	257	122.80623
213	113.57164	258	122.98632
214	113.81288	259	123.16522
215	114.05253	260	123.34294
216	114.29060	261	123.51947
217	114.52708	262	123.69484
218	114.76200	263	123.86905
219	114.99537	264	124.04210
220	115.22719	265	124.21401
221	115.45747	266	124.38477
222	115.68623	267	124.55441
223	115.91347	268	124.72293
224	116.13921	269	124.89032
225	116.36345	270	125.05661

yearly interest rate = 8.00%

term (months)	constant	term (months)	constant
271	125.22180	316	131.62557
272	125.38589	317	131.74726
273	125.54890	318	131.86814
274	125.71083	319	131.98822
275	125.87169	320	132.10750
276	126.03148	321	132.22599
277	126.19021	322	132.34370
278	126.34789	323	132.46063
279	126.50452	324	132.57679
280	126.66012	325	132.69217
281	126.81469	326	132.80679
282	126.96824	327	132.92066
283	127.12077	328	133.03376
284	127.27228	329	133.14612
285	127.42280	330	133.25774
286	127.57232	331	133.36861
287	127.72084	332	133.47876
288	127.86839	333	133.58817
289	128.01496	334	133.69686
290	128.16055	335	133.80482
291	128.30518	336	133.91208
292	128.44886	337	134.01862
293	128.59158	338	134.12446
294	128.73336	339	134.22959
295	128.87420	340	134.33403
296	129.01410	341	134.43778
297	129.15308	342	134.54084
298	129.29114	343	134.64322
299	129.42829	344	134.74492
300	129.56452	345	134.84595
301	129.69986	346	134.94630
302	129.83430	347	135.04600
303	129.96784	348	135.14503
304	130.10051	349	135.24341
305	130.23229	350	135.34113
306	130.36320	351	135.43821
307	130.49325	352	135.53465
308	130.62243	353	135.63045
309	130.75076	354	135.72561
310	130.87824	355	135.82014
311	131.00487	356	135.91405
312	131.13067	357	136.00733
313	131.25563	358	136.10000
314	131.37977	359	136.19205
315	131.50308	360	136.28349

yearly interest rate = 8.25%

term (months)	constant	term (months)	constant
1	0.9931719	46	39.321252
2	1.9795625	47	40.045936
3	2.9592178	48	40.765672
4	3.9321841	49	41.480494
5	4.8985068	50	42.190435
6	5.8582315	51	42.895528
7	6.8114031	52	43.595807
8	7.7580664	53	44.291304
9	8.6982658	54	44.982053
10	9.6320455	55	45.668084
11	10.559449	56	46.349432
12	11.480521	57	47.026128
13	12.395303	58	47.698202
14	13.303839	59	48.365688
15	14.206172	60	49.028617
16	15.102343	61	49.687018
17	15.992395	62	50.340924
18	16.876370	63	50.990366
19	17.754309	64	51.635372
20	18.626254	65	52.275975
21	19.492245	66	52.912204
22	20.352323	67	53.544088
23	21.206528	68	54.171658
24	22.054900	69	54.794943
25	22.897480	70	55.413972
26	23.734307	71	56.028774
27	24.565419	72	56.639378
28	25.390857	73	57.245813
29	26.210659	74	57.848107
30	27.024863	75	58.446289
31	27.833508	76	59.040387
32	28.636631	77	59.630427
33	29.434270	78	60.216439
34	30.226463	79	60.798450
35	31.013247	80	61.376487
36	31.794659	81	61.950576
37	32.570735	82	62.520746
38	33.341512	83	63.087023
39	34.107027	84	63.649433
40	34.867314	85	64.208003
41	35.622410	86	64.762759
42	36.372350	87	65.313727
43	37.117169	88	65.860933
44	37.856903	89	66.404403
45	38.591586	90	66.944162

yearly interest rate = 8.25%

term (months)	constant	term (months)	constant
91	67.480235	136	88.168157
92	68.012648	137	88.559312
93	68.541426	138	88.947796
94	69.066593	139	89.333627
95	69.588175	140	89.716824
96	70.106195	141	90.097404
97	70.620677	142	90.475386
98	71.131647	143	90.850787
99	71.639128	144	91.223625
100	72.143144	145	91.593916
101	72.643719	146	91.961680
102	73.140875	147	92.326932
103	73.634637	148	92.689691
104	74.125027	149	93.049972
105	74.612069	150	93.407793
106	75.095786	151	93.763172
107	75.576200	152	94.116123
108	76.053333	153	94.466665
109	76.527208	154	94.814813
110	76.997848	155	95.160584
111	77.465274	156	95.503994
112	77.929509	157	95.845059
113	78.390574	158	96.183796
114	78.848490	159	96.520219
115	79.303280	160	96.854346
116	79.754965	161	97.186191
117	80.203565	162	97.515770
118	80.649103	163	97.843098
119	81.091598	164	98.168192
120	81.531072	165	98.491066
121	81.967545	166	98.811735
122	82.401038	167	99.130215
123	82.831571	168	99.446520
124	83.259164	169	99.760666
125	83.683838	170	100.07267
126	84.105612	171	100.38254
127	84.524506	172	100.69029
128	84.940540	173	100.99594
129	85.353733	174	101.29951
130	85.764104	175	101.60100
131	86.171674	176	101.90044
132	86.576461	177	102.19783
133	86.978484	178	102.49319
134	87.377762	179	102.78653
135	87.774313	180	103.07787

yearly interest rate = 8.25%

term (months)	constant	term (months)	constant
181	103.36722	226	114.53371
182	103.65459	227	114.74484
183	103.94001	228	114.95453
184	104.22347	229	115.16278
185	104.50500	230	115.36962
186	104.78460	231	115.57504
187	105.06230	232	115.77906
188	105.33810	233	115.98168
189	105.61202	234	116.18292
190	105.88407	235	116.38279
191	106.15425	236	116.58130
192	106.42260	237	116.77844
193	106.68911	238	116.97425
194	106.95380	239	117.16871
195	107.21669	240	117.36185
196	107.47778	241	117.55367
197	107.73709	242	117.74418
198	107.99462	243	117.93338
199	108.25040	244	118.12130
200	108.50443	245	118.30793
201	108.75673	246	118.49329
202	109.00731	247	118.67738
203	109.25617	248	118.86022
204	109.50334	249	119.04181
205	109.74881	250	119.22216
206	109.99261	251	119.40127
207	110.23475	252	119.57917
208	110.47523	253	119.75584
209	110.71407	254	119.93132
210	110.95128	255	120.10559
211	111.18687	256	120.27867
212	111.42085	257	120.45058
213	111.65324	258	120.62131
214	111.88404	259	120.79087
215	112.11326	260	120.95927
216	112.34091	261	121.12653
217	112.56702	262	121.29264
218	112.79157	263	121.45762
219	113.01460	264	121.62147
220	113.23610	265	121.78421
221	113.45609	266	121.94583
222	113.67458	267	122.10635
223	113.89157	268	122.26577
224	114.10709	269	122.42410
225	114.32113	270	122.58136

yearly interest rate = 8.25%

term (months)	constant	term (months)	constant
271	122.73754	316	128.76475
272	122.89265	317	128.87871
273	123.04670	318	128.99189
274	123.19971	319	129.10430
275	123.35166	320	129.21594
276	123.50258	321	129.32682
277	123.65247	322	129.43694
278	123.80134	323	129.54631
279	123.94919	324	129.65493
280	124.09603	325	129.76281
281	124.24186	326	129.86995
282	124.38671	327	129.97636
283	124.53056	328	130.08205
284	124.67343	329	130.18702
285	124.81532	330	130.29126
286	124.95625	331	130.39480
287	125.09621	332	130.49763
288	125.23522	333	130.59975
289	125.37328	334	130.70118
290	125.51039	335	130.80192
291	125.64657	336	130.90197
292	125.78182	337	131.00133
293	125.91615	338	131.10002
294	126.04956	339	131.19804
295	126.18206	340	131.29538
296	126.31365	341	131.39206
297	126.44435	342	131.48808
298	126.57415	343	131.58344
299	126.70307	344	131.67816
300	126.83110	345	131.77222
301	126.95826	346	131.86565
302	127.08456	347	131.95843
303	127.20999	348	132.05058
304	127.33456	349	132.14211
305	127.45829	350	132.23300
306	127.58117	351	132.32328
307	127.70321	352	132.41294
308	127.82442	353	132.50199
309	127.94480	354	132.59043
310	128.06435	355	132.67827
311	128.18309	356	132.76551
312	128.30102	357	132.85215
313	128.41815	358	132.93820
314	128.53448	359	133.02366
315	128.65001	360	133.10854

yearly interest rate = 8.50%

term (months)	constant	term (months)	constant
1	0.9929665	46	39.140448
2	1.9789489	47	39.858120
3	2.9579965	48	40.570744
4	3.9301578	49	41.278355
5	4.8954815	50	41.980990
6	5.8540155	51	42.678683
7	6.8058078	52	43.371468
8	7.7509055	53	44.059381
9	8.6893559	54	44.742455
10	9.6212057	55	45.420725
11	10.546501	56	46.094224
12	11.465289	57	46.762986
13	12.377614	58	47.427045
14	13.283522	59	48.086433
15	14.183059	60	48.741182
16	15.076269	61	49.391327
17	15.963196	62	50.036899
18	16.843885	63	50.677931
19	17.718380	64	51.314453
20	18.586724	65	51.946499
21	19.448961	66	52.574099
22	20.305133	67	53.197285
23	21.155283	68	53.816088
24	21.999453	69	54.430538
25	22.837686	70	55.040666
26	23.670024	71	55.646504
27	24.496507	72	56.248080
28	25.317177	73	56.845425
29	26.132075	74	57.438568
30	26.941241	75	58.027540
31	27.744716	76	58.612369
32	28.542539	77	59.193085
33	29.334752	78	59.769716
34	30.121392	79	60.342291
35	30.902499	80	60.910839
36	31.678112	81	61.475389
37	32.448270	82	62.035967
38	33.213012	83	62.592603
39	33.972374	84	63.145324
40	34.726395	85	63.694157
41	35.475113	86	64.239130
42	36.218565	87	64.780269
43	36.956788	88	65.317603
44	37.689818	89	65.851157
45	38.417693	90	66.380959

yearly interest rate = 8.50%

term (months)	constant	term (months)	constant
91	66.907034	136	87.117629
92	67.429409	137	87.497852
93	67.948110	138	87.875401
94	68.463162	139	88.250295
95	68.974592	140	88.622552
96	69.482425	141	88.992191
97	69.986686	142	89.359229
98	70.487400	143	89.723687
99	70.984593	144	90.085580
100	71.478288	145	90.444929
101	71.968511	146	90.801750
102	72.455286	147	91.156061
103	72.938638	148	91.507880
104	73.418589	149	91.857225
105	73.895165	150	92.204112
106	74.368389	151	92.548560
107	74.838285	152	92.890585
108	75.304875	153	93.230204
109	75.768184	154	93.567435
110	76.228234	155	93.902294
111	76.685048	156	94.234797
112	77.138649	157	94.564962
113	77.589060	158	94.892805
114	78.036303	159	95.218342
115	78.480400	160	95.541589
116	78.921374	161	95.862562
117	79.359246	162	96.181278
118	79.794038	163	96.497752
119	80.225772	164	96.812001
120	80.654470	165	97.124039
121	81.080152	166	97.433882
122	81.502840	167	97.741546
123	81.922555	168	98.047046
124	82.339319	169	98.350398
125	82.753150	170	98.651615
126	83.164072	171	98.950714
127	83.572102	172	99.247710
128	83.977264	173	99.542616
129	84.379575	174	99.835449
130	84.779057	175	100.12622
131	85.175728	176	100.41495
132	85.569610	177	100.70165
133	85.960722	178	100.98633
134	86.349083	179	101.26900
135	86.734712	180	101.54969

yearly interest rate = 8.50%

term (months)	constant	term (months)	constant
181	101.82841	226	112.53601
182	102.10516	227	112.73746
183	102.37997	228	112.93748
184	102.65285	229	113.13610
185	102.92380	230	113.33332
186	103.19285	231	113.52916
187	103.46001	232	113.72362
188	103.72529	233	113.91671
189	103.98871	234	114.10844
190	104.25027	235	114.29882
191	104.50999	236	114.48787
192	104.76788	237	114.67558
193	105.02396	238	114.86197
194	105.27824	239	115.04706
195	105.53073	240	115.23084
196	105.78145	241	115.41333
197	106.03040	242	115.59453
198	106.27760	243	115.77446
199	106.52306	244	115.95313
200	106.76679	245	116.13054
201	107.00882	246	116.30670
202	107.24913	247	116.48162
203	107.48776	248	116.65531
204	107.72471	249	116.82778
205	107.96000	250	116.99904
206	108.19362	251	117.16909
207	108.42561	252	117.33795
208	108.65596	253	117.50562
209	108.88470	254	117.67211
210	109.11182	255	117.83742
211	109.33735	256	118.00158
212	109.56129	257	118.16458
213	109.78365	258	118.32644
214	110.00446	259	118.48715
215	110.22371	260	118.64674
216	110.44141	261	118.80520
217	110.65759	262	118.96255
218	110.87224	263	119.11879
219	111.08539	264	119.27393
220	111.29703	265	119.42779
221	111.50719	266	119.58095
222	111.71587	267	119.73285
223	111.92308	268	119.88367
224	112.12884	269	120.03343
225	112.33314	270	120.18214

yearly interest rate = 8.50%

term (months)	constant
271	120.32981
272	120.47643
273	120.62203
274	120.76660
275	120.91015
276	121.05269
277	121.19423
278	121.33478
279	121.47434
280	121.61291
281	121.75051
282	121.88714
283	122.02282
284	122.15753
285	122.29130
286	122.42413
287	122.55603
288	122.68699
289	122.81704
290	122.94617
291	123.07439
292	123.20172
293	123.32814
294	123.45368
295	123.57833
296	123.70211
297	123.82501
298	123.94706
299	124.06824
300	124.18857
301	124.30805
302	124.42670
303	124.54451
304	124.66149
305	124.77765
306	124.89299
307	125.00752
308	125.12124
309	125.23417
310	125.34630
311	125.45764
312	125.56820
313	125.67798
314	125.78699
315	125.89523
316	125.00271
317	126.10944
318	126.21541
319	126.32064
320	126.42513
321	126.52888
322	126.63191
323	126.73421
324	126.83579
325	126.93665
326	127.03681
327	127.13626
328	127.23501
329	127.33307
330	127.43044
331	127.52712
332	127.62312
333	127.71845
334	127.81311
335	127.90710
336	128.00043
337	128.09310
338	128.18512
339	128.27650
340	128.36723
341	128.45732
342	128.54678
343	128.63562
344	128.72382
345	128.81141
346	128.89838
347	128.98474
348	129.07049
349	129.15563
350	129.24018
351	129.32414
352	129.40750
353	129.49028
354	129.57247
355	129.65409
356	129.73513
357	129.81561
358	129.89551
359	129.97486
360	130.05364

yearly interest rate = 8.75%

term (months)	constant	term (months)	constant
1	0.9927611	46	38.960805
2	1.9783358	47	39.671534
3	2.9567759	48	40.377117
4	3.9281333	49	41.077593
5	4.8924591	50	41.772998
6	5.8498043	51	42.463370
7	6.8002194	52	43.148743
8	7.7437545	53	43.829156
9	8.6804595	54	44.504643
10	9.6103838	55	45.175240
11	10.533576	56	45.840983
12	11.450086	57	46.501906
13	12.359962	58	47.158046
14	13.263250	59	47.809435
15	14.160000	60	48.456109
16	15.050259	61	49.098102
17	15.934073	62	49.735448
18	16.811489	63	50.368180
19	17.682554	64	50.996332
20	18.547313	65	51.619936
21	19.405812	66	52.239027
22	20.258097	67	52.853636
23	21.104212	68	53.463796
24	21.944202	69	54.069539
25	22.778112	70	54.670897
26	23.605985	71	55.267902
27	24.427865	72	55.860585
28	25.243796	73	56.448978
29	26.053820	74	57.033111
30	26.857981	75	57.613016
31	27.656320	76	58.188724
32	28.448880	77	58.760263
33	29.235703	78	59.327666
34	30.016831	79	59.890961
35	30.792303	80	60.450178
36	31.562163	81	61.005348
37	32.326449	82	61.556498
38	33.085203	83	62.103659
39	33.838464	84	62.646859
40	34.586272	85	63.186127
41	35.328667	86	63.721491
42	36.065688	87	64.252980
43	36.797374	88	64.780621
44	37.523763	89	65.304443
45	38.244894	90	65.824473

yearly interest rate = 8.75%

term (months)	constant	term (months)	constant
91	66.340738	136	86.085256
92	66.853266	137	86.454856
93	67.362084	138	86.821780
94	67.867219	139	87.186049
95	68.368698	140	87.547680
96	68.866546	141	87.906694
97	69.360790	142	88.263109
98	69.851456	143	88.616944
99	70.338571	144	88.968217
100	70.822159	145	89.316948
101	71.302247	146	89.663154
102	71.778860	147	90.006854
103	72.252022	148	90.348066
104	72.721759	149	90.686808
105	73.188096	150	91.023098
106	73.651057	151	91.356953
107	74.110667	152	91.688392
108	74.566949	153	92.017432
109	75.019929	154	92.344089
110	75.469630	155	92.668382
111	75.916075	156	92.990328
112	76.359289	157	93.309943
113	76.799294	158	93.627244
114	77.236114	159	93.942249
115	77.669772	160	94.254973
116	78.100290	161	94.565433
117	78.527693	162	94.873646
118	78.952001	163	95.179628
119	79.373238	164	95.483395
120	79.791425	165	95.784963
121	80.206586	166	96.084348
122	80.618741	167	96.381566
123	81.027912	168	96.676632
124	81.434122	169	96.969562
125	81.837391	170	97.260372
126	82.237740	171	97.549077
127	82.635192	172	97.835691
128	83.029767	173	98.120231
129	83.421485	174	98.402712
130	83.810368	175	98.683147
131	84.196436	176	98.961552
132	84.579708	177	99.237942
133	84.960207	178	99.512332
134	85.337951	179	99.784735
135	85.712961	180	100.05517

yearly interest rate = 8.75%

term (months)	constant	term (months)	constant
181	100.32364	226	110.59138
182	100.59017	227	110.78358
183	100.85477	228	110.97439
184	101.11746	229	111.16382
185	101.37824	230	111.35188
186	101.63713	231	111.53858
187	101.89416	232	111.72393
188	102.14932	233	111.90793
189	102.40263	234	112.09060
190	102.65411	235	112.27195
191	102.90377	236	112.45199
192	103.15162	237	112.63073
193	103.39768	238	112.80817
194	103.64196	239	112.98432
195	103.88447	240	113.15920
196	104.12522	241	113.33282
197	104.36423	242	113.50518
198	104.60151	243	113.67629
199	104.83708	244	113.84616
200	105.07094	245	114.01480
201	105.30310	246	114.18222
202	105.53358	247	114.34843
203	105.76240	248	114.51344
204	105.98956	249	114.67725
205	106.21508	250	114.83988
206	106.43896	251	115.00132
207	106.66122	252	115.16160
208	106.88187	253	115.32072
209	107.10093	254	115.47869
210	107.31840	255	115.63552
211	107.53429	256	115.79121
212	107.74863	257	115.94577
213	107.96141	258	116.09921
214	108.17265	259	116.25154
215	108.38236	260	116.40277
216	108.59056	261	116.55291
217	108.79724	262	116.70196
218	109.00243	263	116.84993
219	109.20614	264	116.99682
220	109.40837	265	117.14266
221	109.60914	266	117.28744
222	109.80845	267	117.43117
223	110.00632	268	117.57386
224	110.20276	269	117.71552
225	110.39777	270	117.85615

yearly interest rate = 8.75%

term (months)	constant	term (months)	constant
271	117.99576	316	123.33529
272	118.13437	317	123.43525
273	118.27197	318	123.53447
274	118.40857	319	123.63298
275	118.54419	320	123.73078
276	118.67882	321	123.82787
277	118.81248	322	123.92425
278	118.94517	323	124.01994
279	119.07690	324	124.11494
280	119.20768	325	124.20924
281	119.33751	326	124.30287
282	119.46640	327	124.39582
283	119.59436	328	124.48809
284	119.72139	329	124.57970
285	119.84750	330	124.67064
286	119.97270	331	124.76093
287	120.09699	332	124.85056
288	120.22039	333	124.93954
289	120.34289	334	125.02788
290	120.46450	335	125.11558
291	120.58523	336	125.20264
292	120.70509	337	125.28907
293	120.82408	338	125.37488
294	120.94221	339	125.46007
295	121.05949	340	125.54464
296	121.17591	341	125.62860
297	121.29149	342	125.71195
298	121.40624	343	125.79470
299	121.52016	344	125.87684
300	121.63325	345	125.95840
301	121.74552	346	126.03936
302	121.85698	347	126.11974
303	121.96763	348	126.19953
304	122.07748	349	126.27875
305	122.18654	350	126.35739
306	122.29481	351	126.43547
307	122.40229	352	126.51298
308	122.50900	353	126.58993
309	122.61493	354	126.66632
310	122.72009	355	126.74216
311	122.82450	356	126.81745
312	122.92815	357	126.89219
313	123.03105	358	126.96639
314	123.13320	359	127.04006
315	123.23461	360	127.11319

yearly interest rate = 9.00%

term (months)	constant	term (months)	constant
1	0.9925558	46	38.782314
2	1.9777229	47	39.486168
3	2.9555562	48	40.184782
4	3.9261104	49	40.878195
5	4.8894396	50	41.566447
6	5.8455976	51	42.249575
7	6.7946379	52	42.927618
8	7.7366133	53	43.600614
9	8.6715764	54	44.268599
10	9.5995796	55	44.931612
11	10.520675	56	45.589689
12	11.434913	57	46.242868
13	12.342345	58	46.891184
14	13.243022	59	47.534674
15	14.136995	60	48.173374
16	15.024313	61	48.807319
17	15.905025	62	49.436545
18	16.779181	63	50.061086
19	17.646830	64	50.680979
20	18.508020	65	51.296257
21	19.362799	66	51.906955
22	20.211215	67	52.513107
23	21.053315	68	53.114746
24	21.889146	69	53.711907
25	22.718756	70	54.304622
26	23.542189	71	54.892925
27	24.359493	72	55.476849
28	25.170713	73	56.056426
29	25.975893	74	56.631688
30	26.775080	75	57.202668
31	27.568318	76	57.769398
32	28.355651	77	58.331908
33	29.137122	78	58.890232
34	29.912776	79	59.444399
35	30.682656	80	59.994440
36	31.446805	81	60.540387
37	32.205266	82	61.082270
38	32.958080	83	61.620119
39	33.705291	84	62.153965
40	34.446939	85	62.683836
41	35.183066	86	63.209763
42	35.913713	87	63.731774
43	36.638921	88	64.249900
44	37.358730	89	64.764169
45	38.073181	90	65.274609

yearly interest rate = 9.00%

term (months)	constant	term (months)	constant
91	65.781250	136	85.070670
92	66.284119	137	85.429946
93	66.783245	138	85.786547
94	67.278655	139	86.140493
95	67.770377	140	86.491804
96	68.258439	141	86.840501
97	68.742867	142	87.186601
98	69.223689	143	87.530125
99	69.700932	144	87.871092
100	70.174623	145	88.209521
101	70.644787	146	88.545430
102	71.111451	147	88.878839
103	71.574641	148	89.209765
104	72.034383	149	89.538229
105	72.490703	150	89.864247
106	72.943626	151	90.187838
107	73.393177	152	90.509020
108	73.839382	153	90.827812
109	74.282265	154	91.144230
110	74.721851	155	91.458293
111	75.158165	156	91.770018
112	75.591230	157	92.079422
113	76.021072	158	92.386523
114	76.447714	159	92.691338
115	76.871181	160	92.993884
116	77.291494	161	93.294178
117	77.708679	162	93.592236
118	78.122759	163	93.888075
119	78.533755	164	94.181712
120	78.941693	165	94.473164
121	79.346593	166	94.762445
122	79.748480	167	95.049574
123	80.147374	168	95.334564
124	80.543300	169	95.617434
125	80.936278	170	95.898197
126	81.326330	171	96.176871
127	81.713479	172	96.453470
128	82.097746	173	96.728010
129	82.479152	174	97.000506
130	82.857719	175	97.270973
131	83.233468	176	97.539428
132	83.606420	177	97.805884
133	83.976596	178	98.070356
134	84.344016	179	98.332860
135	84.708700	180	98.593409

yearly interest rate = 9.00%

term (months)	constant	term (months)	constant
181	98.852019	226	108.69812
182	99.108704	227	108.88151
183	99.363477	228	109.06353
184	99.616355	229	109.24420
185	99.867350	230	109.42352
186	100.11648	231	109.60151
187	100.36375	232	109.77818
188	100.60918	233	109.95352
189	100.85278	234	110.12757
190	101.09457	235	110.30031
191	101.33456	236	110.47178
192	101.57277	237	110.64196
193	101.80920	238	110.81088
194	102.04387	239	110.97854
195	102.27679	240	111.14495
196	102.50799	241	111.31013
197	102.73745	242	111.47407
198	102.96522	243	111.63680
199	103.19128	244	111.79831
200	103.41566	245	111.95862
201	103.63838	246	112.11774
202	103.85943	247	112.27567
203	104.07884	248	112.43243
204	104.29661	249	112.58802
205	104.51277	250	112.74245
206	104.72731	251	112.89573
207	104.94026	252	113.04787
208	105.15162	253	113.19888
209	105.36141	254	113.34876
210	105.56964	255	113.49753
211	105.77632	256	113.64519
212	105.98146	257	113.79175
213	106.18507	258	113.93723
214	106.38717	259	114.08161
215	106.58776	260	114.22493
216	106.78686	261	114.36717
217	106.98447	262	114.50836
218	107.18062	263	114.64850
219	107.37530	264	114.78759
220	107.56854	265	114.92565
221	107.76034	266	115.06268
222	107.95071	267	115.19869
223	108.13966	268	115.33368
224	108.32720	269	115.46768
225	108.51335	270	115.60067

yearly interest rate = 9.00%

term (months)	constant	term (months)	constant
271	115.73268	316	120.75852
272	115.86370	317	120.85213
273	115.99375	318	120.94505
274	116.12282	319	121.03727
275	116.25094	320	121.12880
276	116.37811	321	121.21965
277	116.50432	322	121.30983
278	116.62960	323	121.39933
279	116.75395	324	121.48817
280	116.87737	325	121.57635
281	116.99987	326	121.66387
282	117.12146	327	121.75074
283	117.24214	328	121.83696
284	117.36193	329	121.92254
285	117.48082	330	122.00749
286	117.59883	331	122.09180
287	117.71596	332	122.17548
288	117.83222	333	122.25854
289	117.94761	334	122.34099
290	118.06214	335	122.42282
291	118.17583	336	122.50404
292	118.28866	337	122.58465
293	118.40066	338	122.66467
294	118.51182	339	122.74408
295	118.62215	340	122.82291
296	118.73166	341	122.90115
297	118.84036	342	122.97881
298	118.94825	343	123.05589
299	119.05533	344	123.13240
300	119.16162	345	123.20834
301	119.26712	346	123.28371
302	119.37183	347	123.35852
303	119.47576	348	123.43278
304	119.57892	349	123.50648
305	119.68131	350	123.57963
306	119.78294	351	123.65224
307	119.88381	352	123.72431
308	119.98393	353	123.79584
309	120.08331	354	123.86684
310	120.18194	355	123.93731
311	120.27984	356	124.00725
312	120.37701	357	124.07668
313	120.47346	358	124.14558
314	120.56919	359	124.21398
315	120.66421	360	124.28187

yearly interest rate = 9.25%

term (months)	constant	term (months)	constant
1	0.9923506	46	38.604966
2	1.9771104	47	39.302013
3	2.9543374	48	39.993728
4	3.9240892	49	40.680152
5	4.8864230	50	41.361325
6	5.8413956	51	42.037288
7	6.7890632	52	42.708080
8	7.7294818	53	43.373741
9	8.6627068	54	44.034309
10	9.5887931	55	44.689825
11	10.507796	56	45.340327
12	11.419768	57	45.985853
13	12.324765	58	46.626441
14	13.222839	59	47.262128
15	14.114043	60	47.892953
16	14.998430	61	48.518953
17	15.876052	62	49.140164
18	16.746961	63	49.756624
19	17.611208	64	50.368368
20	18.468844	65	50.975432
21	19.319920	66	51.577853
22	20.164485	67	52.175665
23	21.002590	68	52.768905
24	21.834284	69	53.357607
25	22.659616	70	53.941805
26	23.478635	71	54.521535
27	24.291389	72	55.096830
28	25.097926	73	55.667725
29	25.898293	74	56.234253
30	26.692538	75	56.796447
31	27.480708	76	57.354340
32	28.262848	77	57.907966
33	29.039006	78	58.457358
34	29.809226	79	59.002546
35	30.573555	80	59.543565
36	31.332037	81	60.080445
37	32.084718	82	60.613218
38	32.831640	83	61.141915
39	33.572850	84	61.666569
40	34.308389	85	62.187209
41	35.038302	86	62.703867
42	35.762632	87	63.216573
43	36.481421	88	63.725356
44	37.194712	89	64.230248
45	37.902546	90	64.731278

yearly interest rate = 9.25%

term (months)	constant	term (months)	constant
91	65.228475	136	84.073514
92	65.721869	137	84.422755
93	66.211489	138	84.769325
94	66.697363	139	85.113244
95	67.179521	140	85.454532
96	67.657991	141	85.793209
97	68.132800	142	86.129296
98	68.603978	143	86.462812
99	69.071551	144	86.793776
100	69.535548	145	87.122209
101	69.995996	146	87.448130
102	70.452921	147	87.771557
103	70.906351	148	88.092511
104	71.356313	149	88.411009
105	71.802833	150	88.727072
106	72.245937	151	89.040716
107	72.685652	152	89.351961
108	73.122003	153	89.660826
109	73.555017	154	89.967328
110	73.984718	155	90.271485
111	74.411132	156	90.573316
112	74.834284	157	90.872838
113	75.254200	158	91.170068
114	75.670903	159	91.465025
115	76.084419	160	91.757726
116	76.494772	161	92.048188
117	76.901986	162	92.336428
118	77.306085	163	92.622463
119	77.707093	164	92.906310
120	78.105033	165	93.187986
121	78.499929	166	93.467508
122	78.891805	167	93.744891
123	79.280683	168	94.020152
124	79.666587	169	94.293308
125	80.049538	170	94.564374
126	80.429560	171	94.833367
127	80.806675	172	95.100302
128	81.180906	173	95.365195
129	81.552274	174	95.628062
130	81.920801	175	95.888919
131	82.286509	176	96.147780
132	82.649420	177	96.404660
133	83.009555	178	96.659576
134	83.366934	179	96.912542
135	83.721581	180	97.163573

yearly interest rate = 9.25%

term (months)	constant	term (months)	constant
181	97.412683	226	106.85461
182	97.659888	227	107.02959
183	97.905202	228	107.20323
184	98.148640	229	107.37554
185	98.390215	230	107.54654
186	98.629943	231	107.71623
187	98.867837	232	107.88462
188	99.103911	233	108.05172
189	99.338179	234	108.21754
190	99.570655	235	108.38210
191	99.801353	236	108.54539
192	100.03029	237	108.70744
193	100.25747	238	108.86825
194	100.48291	239	109.02782
195	100.70663	240	109.18618
196	100.92864	241	109.34332
197	101.14895	242	109.49927
198	101.36758	243	109.65402
199	101.58453	244	109.80758
200	101.79982	245	109.95998
201	102.01347	246	110.11120
202	102.22548	247	110.26127
203	102.43587	248	110.41019
204	102.64465	249	110.55798
205	102.85183	250	110.70463
206	103.05743	251	110.85016
207	103.26146	252	110.99457
208	103.46392	253	111.13789
209	103.66484	254	111.28010
210	103.86422	255	111.42123
211	104.06208	256	111.56128
212	104.25842	257	111.70026
213	104.45326	258	111.83817
214	104.64661	259	111.97503
215	104.83848	260	112.11084
216	105.02888	261	112.24561
217	105.21782	262	112.37936
218	105.40533	263	112.51208
219	105.59139	264	112.64378
220	105.77603	265	112.77448
221	105.95927	266	112.90417
222	106.14109	267	113.03288
223	106.32153	268	113.16060
224	106.50059	269	113.28734
225	106.67828	270	113.41312

yearly interest rate = 9.25%

term (months)	constant	term (months)	constant
271	113.53793	316	118.26861
272	113.66179	317	118.35628
273	113.78470	318	118.44328
274	113.90666	319	118.52962
275	114.02770	320	118.61529
276	114.14781	321	118.70031
277	114.26700	322	118.78468
278	114.38528	323	118.86840
279	114.50266	324	118.95148
280	114.61914	325	119.03393
281	114.73472	326	119.11575
282	114.84943	327	119.19694
283	114.96325	328	119.27751
284	115.07620	329	119.35746
285	115.18829	330	119.43680
286	115.29953	331	119.51553
287	115.40991	332	119.59367
288	115.51945	333	119.67120
289	115.62815	334	119.74814
290	115.73602	335	119.82450
291	115.84306	336	119.90026
292	115.94928	337	119.97545
293	116.05469	338	120.05007
294	116.15930	339	120.12411
295	116.26310	340	120.19759
296	116.36612	341	120.27050
297	116.46834	342	120.34286
298	116.56978	343	120.41466
299	116.67045	344	120.48592
300	116.77034	345	120.55663
301	116.86947	346	120.62680
302	116.96785	347	120.69643
303	117.06547	348	120.76553
304	117.16234	349	120.83410
305	117.25847	350	120.90214
306	117.35387	351	120.96967
307	117.44854	352	121.03668
308	117.54248	353	121.10317
309	117.63570	354	121.16916
310	117.72822	355	121.23464
311	117.82002	356	121.29963
312	117.91112	357	121.36411
313	118.00153	358	121.42810
314	118.09124	359	121.49161
315	118.18027	360	121.55462

yearly interest rate = 9.50%

term (months)	constant	term (months)	constant
1	0.9921455	46	38.428754
2	1.9764982	47	39.119062
3	2.9531194	48	39.803947
4	3.9220697	49	40.483453
5	4.8834094	50	41.157622
6	5.8371982	51	41.826496
7	6.7834955	52	42.490116
8	7.7223602	53	43.148523
9	8.6538506	54	43.801759
10	9.5780245	55	44.449864
11	10.494940	56	45.092879
12	11.404653	57	45.730843
13	12.307221	58	46.363797
14	13.202699	59	46.991778
15	14.091144	60	47.614828
16	14.972611	61	48.232983
17	15.847155	62	48.846283
18	16.714829	63	49.454766
19	17.575688	64	50.058470
20	18.429786	65	50.657432
21	19.277175	66	51.251690
22	20.117908	67	51.841280
23	20.952037	68	52.426239
24	21.779616	69	53.006603
25	22.600693	70	53.582409
26	23.415322	71	54.153692
27	24.223552	72	54.720488
28	25.025434	73	55.282833
29	25.821018	74	55.840760
30	26.610353	75	56.394305
31	27.393488	76	56.943502
32	28.170471	77	57.488386
33	28.941352	78	58.028990
34	29.706178	79	58.565347
35	30.464997	80	59.097492
36	31.217856	81	59.625457
37	31.964801	82	60.149276
38	32.705880	83	60.668979
39	33.441137	84	61.184601
40	34.170620	85	61.696173
41	34.894373	86	62.203727
42	35.612441	87	62.707294
43	36.324869	88	63.206906
44	37.031701	89	63.702594
45	37.732982	90	64.194389

yearly interest rate = 9.50%

term (months)	constant	term (months)	constant
91	64.682320	136	83.093436
92	65.166419	137	83.432925
93	65.646716	138	83.769748
94	66.123241	139	84.103925
95	66.596022	140	84.435478
96	67.065090	141	84.764426
97	67.530474	142	85.090790
98	67.992202	143	85.414592
99	68.450304	144	85.735850
100	68.904808	145	86.054584
101	69.355741	146	86.370815
102	69.803133	147	86.684562
103	70.247011	148	86.995845
104	70.687403	149	87.304683
105	71.124335	150	87.611095
106	71.557835	151	87.915101
107	71.987931	152	88.216718
108	72.414648	153	88.515967
109	72.838014	154	88.812865
110	73.258054	155	89.107431
111	73.674796	156	89.399684
112	74.088264	157	89.689641
113	74.498484	158	89.977320
114	74.905482	159	90.262740
115	75.309284	160	90.545919
116	75.709913	161	90.826872
117	76.107397	162	91.105620
118	76.501758	163	91.382177
119	76.893021	164	91.656563
120	77.281212	165	91.928793
121	77.666353	166	92.198885
122	78.048469	167	92.466856
123	78.427584	168	92.732722
124	78.803721	169	92.996500
125	79.176904	170	93.258206
126	79.547156	171	93.517856
127	79.914500	172	93.775467
128	80.278958	173	94.031054
129	80.640553	174	94.284634
130	80.999309	175	94.536223
131	81.355247	176	94.785835
132	81.708388	177	95.033486
133	82.058757	178	95.279193
134	82.406373	179	95.522969
135	82.751259	180	95.764831

yearly interest rate = 9.50%

term (months)	constant	term (months)	constant
181	96.004793	226	105.05928
182	96.242870	227	105.22624
183	96.479078	228	105.39188
184	96.713430	229	105.55623
185	96.945941	230	105.71929
186	97.176626	231	105.88106
187	97.405499	232	106.04156
188	97.632575	233	106.20081
189	97.857866	234	106.35880
190	98.081389	235	106.51555
191	98.303155	236	106.67107
192	98.523180	237	106.82537
193	98.741477	238	106.97846
194	98.958059	239	107.13034
195	99.172940	240	107.28104
196	99.386133	241	107.43054
197	99.597652	242	107.57888
198	99.807509	243	107.72605
199	100.01572	244	107.87206
200	100.22229	245	108.01693
201	100.42724	246	108.16065
202	100.63058	247	108.30325
203	100.83233	248	108.44473
204	101.03249	249	108.58510
205	101.23107	250	108.72437
206	101.42810	251	108.86254
207	101.62358	252	108.99962
208	101.81753	253	109.13563
209	102.00995	254	109.27058
210	102.20086	255	109.40446
211	102.39027	256	109.53729
212	102.57819	257	109.66907
213	102.76464	258	109.79982
214	102.94962	259	109.92955
215	103.13315	260	110.05825
216	103.31524	261	110.18595
217	103.49589	262	110.31264
218	103.67513	263	110.43834
219	103.85296	264	110.56305
220	104.02940	265	110.68678
221	104.20445	266	110.80953
222	104.37812	267	110.93133
223	104.55043	268	111.05216
224	104.72138	269	111.17205
225	104.89100	270	111.29100

yearly interest rate = 9.50%

term (months)	constant	term (months)	constant
271	111.40901	316	115.86196
272	111.52610	317	115.94406
273	111.64226	318	116.02553
274	111.75751	319	116.10635
275	111.87186	320	116.18654
276	111.98531	321	116.26610
277	112.09787	322	116.34504
278	112.20954	323	116.42335
279	112.32034	324	116.50105
280	112.43027	325	116.57814
281	112.53933	326	116.65463
282	112.64754	327	116.73051
283	112.75490	328	116.80580
284	112.86141	329	116.88049
285	112.96709	330	116.95460
286	113.07193	331	117.02813
287	113.17596	332	117.10108
288	113.27916	333	117.17346
289	113.38156	334	117.24527
290	113.48315	335	117.31651
291	113.58395	336	117.38720
292	113.68395	337	117.45732
293	113.78317	338	117.52690
294	113.88160	339	117.59594
295	113.97927	340	117.66443
296	114.07616	341	117.73238
297	114.17230	342	117.79980
298	114.26768	343	117.86668
299	114.36231	344	117.93305
300	114.45620	345	117.99889
301	114.54935	346	118.06422
302	114.64177	347	118.12903
303	114.73346	348	118.19333
304	114.82444	349	118.25713
305	114.91470	350	118.32042
306	115.00425	351	118.38322
307	115.09309	352	118.44553
308	115.18124	353	118.50735
309	115.26870	354	118.56868
310	115.35547	355	118.62953
311	115.44155	356	118.68990
312	115.52697	357	118.74980
313	115.61171	358	118.80922
314	115.69578	359	118.86818
315	115.77920	360	118.92668

yearly interest rate = 9.75%

term (months)	constant	term (months)	constant
1	0.9919405	46	38.253668
2	1.9758864	47	38.937303
3	2.9519022	48	39.615427
4	3.9200518	49	40.288087
5	4.8803985	50	40.955325
6	5.8330054	51	41.617185
7	6.7779347	52	42.273711
8	7.7152483	53	42.924946
9	8.6450076	54	43.570932
10	9.5672735	55	44.211712
11	10.482106	56	44.847328
12	11.389566	57	45.477820
13	12.289712	58	46.103231
14	13.182604	59	46.723602
15	14.068299	60	47.338973
16	14.946855	61	47.949384
17	15.818332	62	48.554876
18	16.682784	63	49.155488
19	17.540269	64	49.751259
20	18.390844	65	50.342228
21	19.234563	66	50.928434
22	20.071482	67	51.509916
23	20.901656	68	52.086712
24	21.725139	69	52.658859
25	22.541986	70	53.226394
26	23.352249	71	53.789356
27	24.155981	72	54.347780
28	24.953236	73	54.901704
29	25.744066	74	55.451163
30	26.528521	75	55.996194
31	27.306655	76	56.536832
32	28.078517	77	57.073113
33	28.844158	78	57.605072
34	29.603629	79	58.132743
35	30.356978	80	58.656162
36	31.104256	81	59.175362
37	31.845511	82	59.690378
38	32.580792	83	60.201243
39	33.310148	84	60.707990
40	34.033624	85	61.210654
41	34.751270	86	61.709266
42	35.463132	87	62.203860
43	36.169257	88	62.694467
44	36.869691	89	63.181121
45	37.564479	90	63.663852

yearly interest rate = 9.75%

term (months)	constant	term (months)	constant
91	64.142692	136	82.130091
92	64.617674	137	82.460103
93	65.088827	138	82.787455
94	65.556183	139	83.112168
95	66.019772	140	83.434265
96	66.479625	141	83.753766
97	66.935772	142	84.070691
98	67.388243	143	84.385063
99	67.837067	144	84.696900
100	68.282273	145	85.006225
101	68.723892	146	85.313056
102	69.161951	147	85.617415
103	69.596479	148	85.919320
104	70.027506	149	86.218793
105	70.455058	150	86.515851
106	70.879165	151	86.810516
107	71.299854	152	87.102805
108	71.717152	153	87.392739
109	72.131087	154	87.680337
110	72.541686	155	87.965616
111	72.948975	156	88.248596
112	73.352982	157	88.529296
113	73.753733	158	88.807733
114	74.151254	159	89.083926
115	74.545572	160	89.357893
116	74.936711	161	89.629652
117	75.324698	162	89.899221
118	75.709558	163	90.166617
119	76.091316	164	90.431858
120	76.469997	165	90.694962
121	76.845626	166	90.955945
122	77.218228	167	91.214824
123	77.587827	168	91.471617
124	77.954447	169	91.726341
125	78.318112	170	91.979011
126	78.678847	171	92.229646
127	79.036674	172	92.478260
128	79.391617	173	92.724870
129	79.743699	174	92.969493
130	80.092944	175	93.212144
131	80.439374	176	93.452840
132	80.783012	177	93.691596
133	81.123881	178	93.928427
134	81.462002	179	94.163350
135	81.797398	180	94.396380

yearly interest rate = 9.75%

term (months)	constant	term (months)	constant
181	94.627531	226	103.31061
182	94.856819	227	103.46992
183	95.084260	228	103.62794
184	95.309867	229	103.78469
185	95.533656	230	103.94017
186	95.755641	231	104.09441
187	95.975838	232	104.24740
188	96.194259	233	104.39915
189	96.410921	234	104.54969
190	96.625836	235	104.69901
191	96.839019	236	104.84713
192	97.050484	237	104.99405
193	97.260244	238	105.13979
194	97.468314	239	105.28435
195	97.674707	240	105.42775
196	97.879437	241	105.57000
197	98.082516	242	105.71109
198	98.283959	243	105.85105
199	98.483778	244	105.98989
200	98.681987	245	106.12760
201	98.878598	246	106.26420
202	99.073625	247	106.39971
203	99.267080	248	106.53412
204	99.458976	249	106.66744
205	99.649325	250	106.79970
206	99.838140	251	106.93088
207	100.02543	252	107.06101
208	100.21122	253	107.19009
209	100.39550	254	107.31813
210	100.57831	255	107.44514
211	100.75963	256	107.57112
212	100.93950	257	107.69609
213	101.11792	258	107.82006
214	101.29490	259	107.94302
215	101.47045	260	108.06499
216	101.64459	261	108.18598
217	101.81732	262	108.30599
218	101.98866	263	108.42504
219	102.15862	264	108.54313
220	102.32722	265	108.66026
221	102.49445	266	108.77645
222	102.66033	267	108.89171
223	102.82488	268	109.00603
224	102.98810	269	109.11944
225	103.15001	270	109.23193

yearly interest rate = 9.75%

term (months)	constant	term (months)	constant
271	109.34351	316	113.53511
272	109.45420	317	113.61201
273	109.56399	318	113.68829
274	109.67290	319	113.76396
275	109.78093	320	113.83902
276	109.88809	321	113.91347
277	109.99438	322	113.98732
278	110.09982	323	114.06058
279	110.20441	324	114.13325
280	110.30816	325	114.20533
281	110.41107	326	114.27683
282	110.51315	327	114.34776
283	110.61441	328	114.41811
284	110.71485	329	114.48789
285	110.81448	330	114.55712
286	110.91331	331	114.62578
287	111.01134	332	114.69390
288	111.10859	333	114.76146
289	111.20504	334	114.82848
290	111.30073	335	114.89496
291	111.39564	336	114.96090
292	111.48978	337	115.02631
293	111.58317	338	115.09119
294	111.67580	339	115.15555
295	111.76769	340	115.21940
296	111.85884	341	115.28273
297	111.94925	342	115.34554
298	112.03893	343	115.40785
299	112.12789	344	115.46966
300	112.21614	345	115.53097
301	112.30367	346	115.59179
302	112.39050	347	115.65212
303	112.47663	348	115.71196
304	112.56206	349	115.77132
305	112.64680	350	115.83019
306	112.73087	351	115.88860
307	112.81425	352	115.94653
308	112.89696	353	116.00400
309	112.97901	354	116.06101
310	113.06039	355	116.11755
311	113.14112	356	116.17364
312	113.22120	357	116.22928
313	113.30063	358	116.28447
314	113.37942	359	116.33921
315	113.45758	360	116.39351

yearly interest rate = 10.00%

term (months)	constant	term (months)	constant
1	0.9917355	46	38.079701
2	1.9752749	47	38.756728
3	2.9506859	48	39.428160
4	3.9180356	49	40.094043
5	4.8773906	50	40.754423
6	5.8288172	51	41.409345
7	6.7723806	52	42.058854
8	7.7081461	53	42.702996
9	8.6361779	54	43.341814
10	9.5565401	55	43.975353
11	10.469296	56	44.603656
12	11.374508	57	45.226766
13	12.272240	58	45.844727
14	13.162552	59	46.457580
15	14.045506	60	47.065369
16	14.921163	61	47.668134
17	15.789583	62	48.265919
18	16.650826	63	48.858762
19	17.504952	64	49.446706
20	18.352018	65	50.029791
21	19.192084	66	50.608058
22	20.025207	67	51.181545
23	20.851445	68	51.750292
24	21.670855	69	52.314339
25	22.483492	70	52.873725
26	23.289414	71	53.428488
27	24.088675	72	53.978665
28	24.881331	73	54.524296
29	25.667435	74	55.065418
30	26.447043	75	55.602067
31	27.220208	76	56.134282
32	27.986983	77	56.662097
33	28.747421	78	57.185551
34	29.501575	79	57.704679
35	30.249496	80	58.219516
36	30.991236	81	58.730099
37	31.726845	82	59.236461
38	32.456375	83	59.738639
39	33.179876	84	60.236667
40	33.897398	85	60.730579
41	34.608990	86	61.220409
42	35.314701	87	61.706191
43	36.014579	88	62.187958
44	36.708674	89	62.665743
45	37.397032	90	63.139580

yearly interest rate = 10.00%

term (months)	constant	term (months)	constant
91	63.609501	136	81.183145
92	64.075538	137	81.503945
93	64.537724	138	81.822095
94	64.996090	139	82.137614
95	65.450667	140	82.450527
– 96	65.901488	141	82.760853
97	66.348583	142	83.068614
98	66.791984	143	83.373833
99	67.231719	144	83.676528
100	67.667821	145	83.976722
101	68.100318	146	84.274435
102	68.529241	147	84.569688
103	68.954619	148	84.862500
104	69.376482	149	85.152893
105	69.794858	150	85.440885
106	70.209777	151	85.726498
107	70.621266	152	86.009750
108	71.029355	153	86.290661
109	71.434071	154	86.569251
110	71.835442	155	86.845538
111	72.233496	156	87.119542
112	72.628261	157	87.391281
113	73.019763	158	87.660775
114	73.408029	159	87.928041
115	73.793087	160	88.193098
116	74.174962	161	88.455965
117	74.553682	162	88.716660
118	74.929271	163	88.975200
119	75.301756	164	89.231603
120	75.671163	165	89.485888
121	76.037517	166	89.738070
122	76.400844	167	89.988169
123	76.761167	168	90.236201
124	77.118513	169	90.482182
125	77.472905	170	90.726131
126	77.824369	171	90.968064
127	78.172928	172	91.207997
128	78.518606	173	91.445948
129	78.861428	174	91.681932
130	79.201416	175	91.915965
131	79.538594	176	92.148065
132	79.872986	177	92.378246
133	80.204614	178	92.606525
134	80.533502	179	92.832917
135	80.859671	180	93.057439

yearly interest rate = 10.00%

term (months)	constant	term (months)	constant
181	93.280105	226	101.60714
182	93.500930	227	101.75915
183	93.719931	228	101.90990
184	93.937121	229	102.05941
185	94.152517	230	102.20768
186	94.366133	231	102.35472
187	94.577983	232	102.50055
188	94.788082	233	102.64517
189	94.996445	234	102.78860
190	95.203086	235	102.93084
191	95.408019	236	103.07191
192	95.611259	237	103.21181
193	95.812818	238	103.35056
194	96.012713	239	103.48816
195	96.210955	240	103.62462
196	96.407558	241	103.75995
197	96.602537	242	103.89417
198	96.795905	243	104.02727
199	96.987674	244	104.15928
200	97.177858	245	104.29019
201	97.366471	246	104.42003
202	97.553525	247	104.54879
203	97.739033	248	104.67648
204	97.923008	249	104.80312
205	98.105463	250	104.92872
206	98.286409	251	105.05327
207	98.465860	252	105.17680
208	98.643828	253	105.29931
209	98.820326	254	105.42080
210	98.995364	255	105.54129
211	99.168956	256	105.66078
212	99.341114	257	105.77929
213	99.511848	258	105.89682
214	99.681172	259	106.01337
215	99.849096	260	106.12896
216	100.01563	261	106.24360
217	100.18079	262	106.35729
218	100.34459	263	106.47004
219	100.50703	264	106.58186
220	100.66813	265	106.69275
221	100.82790	266	106.80273
222	100.98634	267	106.91180
223	101.14348	268	107.01996
224	101.29932	269	107.12724
225	101.45387	270	107.23362

yearly interest rate = 10.00%

term (months)	constant	term (months)	constant
271	107.33913	316	111.28479
272	107.44376	317	111.35681
273	107.54754	318	111.42825
274	107.65045	319	111.49909
275	107.75251	320	111.56934
276	107.85373	321	111.63902
277	107.95411	322	111.70812
278	108.05366	323	111.77664
279	108.15239	324	111.84461
280	108.25031	325	111.91201
281	108.34741	326	111.97885
282	108.44372	327	112.04514
283	108.53922	328	112.11088
284	108.63394	329	112.17608
285	108.72787	330	112.24074
286	108.82103	331	112.30487
287	108.91342	332	112.36846
288	109.00504	333	112.43153
289	109.09591	334	112.49408
290	109.18603	335	112.55612
291	109.27540	336	112.61764
292	109.36403	337	112.67865
293	109.45193	338	112.73915
294	109.53911	339	112.79916
295	109.62556	340	112.85867
296	109.71130	341	112.91769
297	109.79633	342	112.97622
298	109.88066	343	113.03427
299	109.96429	344	113.09184
300	110.04723	345	113.14893
301	110.12948	346	113.20555
302	110.21106	347	113.26170
303	110.29196	348	113.31739
304	110.37219	349	113.37262
305	110.45176	350	113.42739
306	110.53067	351	113.48171
307	110.60893	352	113.53558
308	110.68654	353	113.58901
309	110.76351	354	113.64199
310	110.83985	355	113.69453
311	110.91555	356	113.74665
312	110.99063	357	113.79833
313	111.06509	358	113.84958
314	111.13893	359	113.90041
315	111.21216	360	113.95082

yearly interest rate = 10.25%

term (months)	constant	term (months)	constant
1	0.9915307	46	37.906843
2	1.9746638	47	38.577329
3	2.9494704	48	39.242136
4	3.9160210	49	39.901312
5	4.8743857	50	40.554905
6	5.8246336	51	41.202963
7	6.7668336	52	41.845533
8	7.7010537	53	42.482660
9	8.6273617	54	43.114391
10	9.5458244	55	43.740772
11	10.456508	56	44.361848
12	11.359480	57	44.977664
13	12.254803	58	45.588264
14	13.142544	59	46.193693
15	14.022766	60	46.793994
16	14.895533	61	47.389211
17	15.760909	62	47.979388
18	16.618955	63	48.564565
19	17.469735	64	49.144787
20	18.313309	65	49.720094
21	19.149738	66	50.290529
22	19.979083	67	50.856133
23	20.801405	68	51.416947
24	21.616761	69	51.973011
25	22.425213	70	52.524365
26	23.226817	71	53.071050
27	24.021632	72	53.613105
28	24.809716	73	54.150569
29	25.591125	74	54.683480
30	26.365916	75	55.211879
31	27.134145	76	55.735802
32	27.895868	77	56.255288
33	28.651140	78	56.770375
34	29.400015	79	57.281099
35	30.142547	80	57.787497
36	30.878791	81	58.289607
37	31.608799	82	58.787464
38	32.332624	83	59.281105
39	33.050320	84	59.770564
40	33.761936	85	60.255879
41	34.467526	86	60.737083
42	35.167140	87	61.214211
43	35.860829	88	61.687299
44	36.548643	89	62.156380
45	37.230631	90	62.621488

yearly interest rate = 10.25%

term (months)	constant	term (months)	constant
91	63.082657	136	80.252269
92	63.539920	137	80.564117
93	63.993311	138	80.873324
94	64.442861	139	81.179912
95	64.888604	140	81.483904
96	65.330572	141	81.785321
97	65.768797	142	82.084185
98	66.203311	143	82.380518
99	66.634144	144	82.674342
100	67.061329	145	82.965677
101	67.484895	146	83.254544
102	67.904874	147	83.540965
103	68.321297	148	83.824960
104	68.734192	149	84.106550
105	69.143590	150	84.385755
106	69.549522	151	84.662595
107	69.952015	152	84.937091
108	70.351099	153	85.209262
109	70.746804	154	85.479128
110	71.139157	155	85.746708
111	71.528187	156	86.012022
112	71.913922	157	86.275089
113	72.296390	158	86.535928
114	72.675619	159	86.794558
115	73.051637	160	87.050997
116	73.424469	161	87.305264
117	73.794144	162	87.557379
118	74.160688	163	87.807357
119	74.524128	164	88.055219
120	74.884490	165	88.300981
121	75.241799	166	88.544662
122	75.596083	167	88.786280
123	75.947366	168	89.025851
124	76.295674	169	89.263392
125	76.641032	170	89.498922
126	76.983464	171	89.732458
127	77.322997	172	89.964015
128	77.659654	173	90.193611
129	77.993460	174	90.421263
130	78.324439	175	90.646987
131	78.652614	176	90.870799
132	78.978011	177	91.092715
133	79.300651	178	91.312752
134	79.620559	179	91.530925
135	79.937757	180	91.747251

yearly interest rate = 10.25%

term (months)	constant	term (months)	constant
181	91.961744	226	99.947470
182	92.174421	227	100.09251
183	92.385297	228	100.23633
184	92.594386	229	100.37892
185	92.801705	230	100.52031
186	93.007268	231	100.66051
187	93.211090	232	100.79951
188	93.413186	233	100.93734
189	93.613570	234	101.07400
190	93.812257	235	101.20950
191	94.009261	236	101.34385
192	94.204597	237	101.47707
193	94.398278	238	101.60916
194	94.590319	239	101.74013
195	94.780734	240	101.86999
196	94.969536	241	101.99875
197	95.156738	242	102.12642
198	95.342356	243	102.25301
199	95.526401	244	102.37852
200	95.708888	245	102.50298
201	95.889829	246	102.62638
202	96.069237	247	102.74873
203	96.247126	248	102.87005
204	96.423509	249	102.99034
205	96.598398	250	103.10961
206	96.771805	251	103.22788
207	96.943744	252	103.34514
208	97.114227	253	103.46140
209	97.283265	254	103.57669
210	97.450873	255	103.69099
211	97.617060	256	103.80433
212	97.781840	257	103.91671
213	97.945225	258	104.02813
214	98.107226	259	104.13862
215	98.267854	260	104.24816
216	98.427123	261	104.35678
217	98.585042	262	104.46448
218	98.741624	263	104.57127
219	98.896880	264	104.67715
220	99.050821	265	104.78214
221	99.203458	266	104.88623
222	99.354802	267	104.98945
223	99.504865	268	105.09179
224	99.653657	269	105.19326
225	99.801188	270	105.29388

yearly interest rate = 10.25%

term (months)	constant	term (months)	constant
271	105.39364	316	109.10787
272	105.49256	317	109.17533
273	105.59064	318	109.24222
274	105.68789	319	109.30854
275	105.78431	320	109.37430
276	105.87992	321	109.43951
277	105.97472	322	109.50416
278	106.06872	323	109.56826
279	106.16192	324	109.63182
280	106.25433	325	109.69485
281	106.34596	326	109.75734
282	106.43681	327	109.81930
283	106.52689	328	109.88073
284	106.61621	329	109.94165
285	106.70478	330	110.00205
286	106.79259	331	110.06193
287	106.87966	332	110.12132
288	106.96599	333	110.18019
289	107.05159	334	110.23857
290	107.13647	335	110.29646
291	107.22063	336	110.35385
292	107.30407	337	110.41076
293	107.38681	338	110.46718
294	107.46885	339	110.52313
295	107.55019	340	110.57861
296	107.63084	341	110.63361
297	107.71081	342	110.68815
298	107.79010	343	110.74223
299	107.86873	344	110.79585
300	107.94668	345	110.84901
301	108.02398	346	110.90173
302	108.10062	347	110.95399
303	108.17661	348	111.00582
304	108.25196	349	111.05720
305	108.32667	350	111.10816
306	108.40074	351	111.15868
307	108.47419	352	111.20877
308	108.54702	353	111.25843
309	108.61923	354	111.30768
310	108.69083	355	111.35651
311	108.76182	356	111.40493
312	108.83221	357	111.45293
313	108.90201	358	111.50053
314	108.97121	359	111.54773
315	109.03983	360	111.59453

yearly interest rate = 10.50%

term (months)	constant	term (months)	constant
1	0.9913259	46	37.735087
2	1.9740529	47	38.399095
3	2.9482557	48	39.057344
4	3.9140081	49	39.709882
5	4.8713835	50	40.356761
6	5.8204546	51	40.998028
7	6.7612932	52	41.633733
8	7.6939710	53	42.263923
9	8.6185586	54	42.888648
10	9.5351263	55	43.507953
11	10.443743	56	44.121887
12	11.344479	57	44.730495
13	12.237402	58	45.333824
14	13.122579	59	45.931919
15	14.000079	60	46.524827
16	14.869967	61	47.112592
17	15.732309	62	47.695259
18	16.587171	63	48.272871
19	17.434618	64	48.845473
20	18.274714	65	49.413108
21	19.107524	66	49.975820
22	19.933109	67	50.533650
23	20.751533	68	51.086642
24	21.562858	69	51.634838
25	22.367145	70	52.178278
26	23.164457	71	52.717004
27	23.954852	72	53.251057
28	24.738391	73	53.780478
29	25.515133	74	54.305306
30	26.285138	75	54.825583
31	27.048464	76	55.341346
32	27.805169	77	55.852635
33	28.555310	78	56.359490
34	29.298944	79	56.861948
35	30.036128	80	57.360047
36	30.766918	81	57.853826
37	31.491368	82	58.343322
38	32.209535	83	58.828572
39	32.921472	84	59.309613
40	33.627234	85	59.786481
41	34.326873	86	60.259213
42	35.020445	87	60.727845
43	35.708000	88	61.192411
44	36.389591	89	61.652948
45	37.065269	90	62.109490

yearly interest rate = 10.50%

term (months)	constant	term (months)	constant
91	62.562072	136	79.337141
92	63.010728	137	79.640288
93	63.455492	138	79.940806
94	63.896399	139	80.238717
95	64.333481	140	80.534044
96	64.766771	141	80.826810
97	65.196304	142	81.117036
98	65.622110	143	81.404744
99	66.044223	144	81.689957
100	66.462675	145	81.972696
101	66.877497	146	82.252982
102	67.288721	147	82.530838
103	67.696377	148	82.806283
104	68.100498	149	83.079338
105	68.501113	150	83.350026
106	68.898253	151	83.618365
107	69.291949	152	83.884377
108	69.682229	153	84.148081
109	70.069125	154	84.409498
110	70.452664	155	84.668647
111	70.832876	156	84.925549
112	71.209790	157	85.180222
113	71.583435	158	85.432686
114	71.953839	159	85.682960
115	72.321030	160	85.931063
116	72.685036	161	86.177014
117	73.045885	162	86.420832
118	73.403603	163	86.662535
119	73.758219	164	86.902141
120	74.109758	165	87.139669
121	74.458249	166	87.375136
122	74.803716	167	87.608562
123	75.146187	168	87.839962
124	75.485687	169	88.069355
125	75.822243	170	88.296758
126	76.155879	171	88.522189
127	76.486621	172	88.745665
128	76.814494	173	88.967202
129	77.139523	174	89.186817
130	77.461733	175	89.404527
131	77.781148	176	89.620349
132	78.097792	177	89.834299
133	78.411690	178	90.046393
134	78.722865	179	90.256648
135	79.031341	180	90.465078

yearly interest rate = 10.50%

term (months)	constant	term (months)	constant
181	90.671701	226	98.330224
182	90.876531	227	98.468623
183	91.079585	228	98.605822
184	91.280877	229	98.741831
185	91.480423	230	98.876661
186	91.678239	231	99.010320
187	91.874338	232	99.142821
188	92.068737	233	99.274172
189	92.261449	234	99.404383
190	92.452490	235	99.533465
191	92.641874	236	99.661428
192	92.829614	237	99.788281
193	93.015727	238	99.914033
194	93.200225	239	100.03869
195	93.383123	240	100.16227
196	93.564434	241	100.28478
197	93.744172	242	100.40623
198	93.922352	243	100.52662
199	94.098986	244	100.64597
200	94.274087	245	100.76428
201	94.447670	246	100.88157
202	94.619747	247	100.99784
203	94.790332	248	101.11310
204	94.959437	249	101.22736
205	95.127075	250	101.34063
206	95.293259	251	101.45291
207	95.458001	252	101.56423
208	95.621315	253	101.67457
209	95.783212	254	101.78396
210	95.943704	255	101.89241
211	96.102805	256	101.99991
212	96.260525	257	102.10647
213	96.416878	258	102.21212
214	96.571874	259	102.31685
215	96.725525	260	102.42067
216	96.877844	261	102.52358
217	97.028842	262	102.62561
218	97.178530	263	102.72675
219	97.326919	264	102.82701
220	97.474022	265	102.92641
221	97.619848	266	103.02494
222	97.764409	267	103.12262
223	97.907717	268	103.21945
224	98.049781	269	103.31544
225	98.190613	270	103.41059

yearly interest rate = 10.50%

term (months)	constant	term (months)	constant
271	103.50493	316	107.00136
272	103.59844	317	107.06455
273	103.69114	318	107.12719
274	103.78304	319	107.18928
275	103.87414	320	107.25083
276	103.96445	321	107.31186
277	104.05398	322	107.37235
278	104.14273	323	107.43232
279	104.23071	324	107.49176
280	104.31793	325	107.55069
281	104.40439	326	107.60911
282	104.49010	327	107.66703
283	104.57507	328	107.72444
284	104.65930	329	107.78135
285	104.74280	330	107.83777
286	104.82558	331	107.89370
287	104.90764	332	107.94915
288	104.98898	333	108.00411
289	105.06963	334	108.05860
290	105.14957	335	108.11261
291	105.22881	336	108.16616
292	105.30738	337	108.21924
293	105.38525	338	108.27186
294	105.46246	339	108.32403
295	105.53899	340	108.37574
296	105.61486	341	108.42700
297	105.69007	342	108.47782
298	105.76463	343	108.52820
299	105.83855	344	108.57814
300	105.91182	345	108.62765
301	105.98445	346	108.67673
302	106.05646	347	108.72538
303	106.12784	348	108.77361
304	106.19860	349	108.82142
305	106.26875	350	108.86882
306	106.33829	351	108.91581
307	106.40723	352	108.96239
308	106.47557	353	109.00856
309	106.54331	354	109.05434
310	106.61047	355	109.09971
311	106.67705	356	109.14470
312	106.74305	357	109.18929
313	106.80847	358	109.23350
314	106.87333	359	109.27732
315	106.93763	360	109.32077

yearly interest rate = 10.75%

term (months)	constant	term (months)	constant
1	0.9911212	46	37.564425
2	1.9734425	47	38.222019
3	2.9470419	48	38.873775
4	3.9119969	49	39.519744
5	4.8683843	50	40.159978
6	5.8162801	51	40.794527
7	6.7557597	52	41.423442
8	7.6868979	53	42.046773
9	8.6097688	54	42.664569
10	9.5244456	55	43.276881
11	10.431001	56	43.883755
12	11.329508	57	44.485242
13	12.220037	58	45.081388
14	13.102659	59	45.672240
15	13.977444	60	46.257847
16	14.844462	61	46.838255
17	15.703783	62	47.413508
18	16.555473	63	47.983655
19	17.399602	64	48.548739
20	18.236235	65	49.108806
21	19.065441	66	49.663900
22	19.887284	67	50.214066
23	20.701830	68	50.759347
24	21.509144	69	51.299786
25	22.309290	70	51.835427
26	23.102332	71	52.366312
27	23.888332	72	52.892484
28	24.667353	73	53.413984
29	25.439458	74	53.930853
30	26.204708	75	54.443133
31	26.963163	76	54.950865
32	27.714884	77	55.454089
33	28.459930	78	55.952845
34	29.198361	79	56.447172
35	29.930236	80	56.937110
36	30.655613	81	57.422699
37	31.374550	82	57.903976
38	32.087103	83	58.380979
39	32.793329	84	58.853748
40	33.493285	85	59.322319
41	34.187026	86	59.786729
42	34.874608	87	60.247016
43	35.556085	88	60.703217
44	36.231511	89	61.155367
45	36.900940	90	61.603502

yearly interest rate = 10.75%

term (months)	constant	term (months)	constant
91	62.047658	136	78.437447
92	62.487871	137	78.732138
93	62.924175	138	79.024213
94	63.356606	139	79.313694
95	63.785197	140	79.600605
96	64.209982	141	79.884969
97	64.630996	142	80.166808
98	65.048272	143	80.446145
99	65.461843	144	80.723001
100	65.871742	145	80.997400
101	66.278002	146	81.269362
102	66.680654	147	81.538909
103	67.079732	148	81.806063
104	67.475266	149	82.070845
105	67.867288	150	82.333276
106	68.255829	151	82.593377
107	68.640921	152	82.851169
108	69.022594	153	83.106671
109	69.400878	154	83.359905
110	69.775803	155	83.610891
111	70.147399	156	83.859649
112	70.515696	157	84.106197
113	70.880723	158	84.350557
114	71.242509	159	84.592747
115	71.601082	160	84.832786
116	71.956472	161	85.070695
117	72.308707	162	85.306491
118	72.657814	163	85.540193
119	73.003821	164	85.771821
120	73.346756	165	86.001392
121	73.686647	166	86.228924
122	74.023520	167	86.454436
123	74.357401	168	86.677946
124	74.688318	169	86.899472
125	75.016297	170	87.119031
126	75.341364	171	87.336640
127	75.663545	172	87.552317
128	75.982865	173	87.766079
129	76.299350	174	87.977944
130	76.613025	175	88.187927
131	76.923915	176	88.396046
132	77.232045	177	88.602316
133	77.537438	178	88.806756
134	77.840121	179	89.009380
135	78.140115	180	89.210205

yearly interest rate = 10.75%

term (months)	constant	term (months)	constant
181	89.409248	226	96.754090
182	89.606523	227	96.886152
183	89.802046	228	97.017041
184	89.995833	229	97.146768
185	90.187900	230	97.275343
186	90.378261	231	97.402776
187	90.566933	232	97.529078
188	90.753929	233	97.654259
189	90.939264	234	97.778328
190	91.122955	235	97.901296
191	91.305014	236	98.023171
192	91.485457	237	98.143965
193	91.664297	238	98.263686
194	91.841550	239	98.382344
195	92.017229	240	98.499949
196	92.191348	241	98.616509
197	92.363921	242	98.732035
198	92.534962	243	98.846535
199	92.704485	244	98.960018
200	92.872502	245	99.072493
201	93.039027	246	99.183970
202	93.204074	247	99.294457
203	93.367655	248	99.403964
204	93.529785	249	99.512497
205	93.690474	250	99.620068
206	93.849737	251	99.726683
207	94.007585	252	99.832351
208	94.164033	253	99.937082
209	94.319091	254	100.04088
210	94.472772	255	100.14376
211	94.625089	256	100.24573
212	94.776054	257	100.34679
213	94.925678	258	100.44695
214	95.073973	259	100.54622
215	95.220952	260	100.64461
216	95.366626	261	100.74213
217	95.511007	262	100.83879
218	95.654106	263	100.93458
219	95.795934	264	101.02952
220	95.936503	265	101.12362
221	96.075823	266	101.21689
222	96.213907	267	101.30933
223	96.350765	268	101.40094
224	96.486407	269	101.49175
225	96.620846	270	101.58174

yearly interest rate = 10.75%

term (months)	constant	term (months)	constant
271	101.67094	316	104.96242
272	101.75935	317	105.02161
273	101.84697	318	105.08026
274	101.93381	319	105.13840
275	102.01988	320	105.19602
276	102.10519	321	105.25312
277	102.18974	322	105.30972
278	102.27354	323	105.36582
279	102.35660	324	105.42142
280	102.43891	325	105.47653
281	102.52050	326	105.53114
282	102.60136	327	105.58528
283	102.68151	328	105.63893
284	102.76094	329	105.69210
285	102.83967	330	105.74481
286	102.91770	331	105.79704
287	102.99504	332	105.84881
288	103.07168	333	105.90012
289	103.14765	334	105.95098
290	103.22295	335	106.00138
291	103.29757	336	106.05134
292	103.37154	337	106.10085
293	103.44484	338	106.14993
294	103.51750	339	106.19856
295	103.58951	340	106.24677
296	103.66088	341	106.29455
297	103.73162	342	106.34190
298	103.80173	343	106.38884
299	103.87122	344	106.43535
300	103.94009	345	106.48146
301	104.00834	346	106.52715
302	104.07600	347	106.57244
303	104.14305	348	106.61733
304	104.20951	349	106.66181
305	104.27537	350	106.70591
306	104.34065	351	106.74961
307	104.40536	352	106.79292
308	104.46948	353	106.83585
309	104.53304	354	106.87840
310	104.59603	355	106.92057
311	104.65847	356	106.96236
312	104.72035	357	107.00379
313	104.78168	358	107.04484
314	104.84247	359	107.08554
315	104.90271	360	107.12587

yearly interest rate = 11.00%

term (months)	constant	term (months)	constant
1	0.9909166	46	37.394848
2	1.9728323	47	38.046093
3	2.9458289	48	38.691421
4	3.9099873	49	39.330888
5	4.8653880	50	39.964546
6	5.8121103	51	40.592449
7	6.7502331	52	41.214648
8	7.6798347	53	41.831195
9	8.6009922	54	42.442142
10	9.5137826	55	43.047540
11	10.418282	56	43.647439
12	11.314565	57	44.241888
13	12.202707	58	44.830938
14	13.082781	59	45.414637
15	13.954862	60	45.993034
16	14.819021	61	46.566177
17	15.675330	62	47.134115
18	16.523861	63	47.696893
19	17.364685	64	48.254560
20	18.197871	65	48.807161
21	19.023489	66	49.354742
22	19.841608	67	49.897350
23	20.652295	68	50.435029
24	21.455619	69	50.967824
25	22.251645	70	51.495779
26	23.040441	71	52.018939
27	23.822072	72	52.537346
28	24.596603	73	53.051045
29	25.364099	74	53.560078
30	26.124623	75	54.064487
31	26.878240	76	54.564314
32	27.625010	77	55.059601
33	28.364998	78	55.550389
34	29.098264	79	56.036719
35	29.824869	80	56.518632
36	30.544874	81	56.996167
37	31.258340	82	57.469364
38	31.965324	83	57.938263
39	32.665887	84	58.402904
40	33.360086	85	58.863323
41	34.047980	86	59.319560
42	34.729625	87	59.771654
43	35.405078	88	60.219640
44	36.074396	89	60.663558
45	36.737635	90	61.103443

yearly interest rate = 11.00%

term (months)	constant	term (months)	constant
91	61.539332	136	77.552880
92	61.971262	137	77.839352
93	62.399269	138	78.123223
94	62.823388	139	78.404515
95	63.243654	140	78.683252
96	63.660104	141	78.959457
97	64.072770	142	79.233153
98	64.481688	143	79.504363
99	64.886891	144	79.773109
100	65.288414	145	80.039415
101	65.686290	146	80.303301
102	66.080551	147	80.564790
103	66.471232	148	80.823905
104	66.858363	149	81.080665
105	67.241979	150	81.335093
106	67.622109	151	81.587211
107	67.998787	152	81.837038
108	68.372043	153	82.084596
109	68.741909	154	82.329905
110	69.108415	155	82.572986
111	69.471592	156	82.813859
112	69.831471	157	83.052544
113	70.188080	158	83.289061
114	70.541450	159	83.523429
115	70.891610	160	83.755669
116	71.238590	161	83.985799
117	71.582418	162	84.213839
118	71.923122	163	84.439808
119	72.260732	164	84.663723
120	72.595276	165	84.885605
121	72.926780	166	85.105472
122	73.255273	167	85.323341
123	73.580783	168	85.539232
124	73.903336	169	85.753161
125	74.222959	170	85.965147
126	74.539678	171	86.175208
127	74.853521	172	86.383360
128	75.164513	173	86.589622
129	75.472680	174	86.794010
130	75.778048	175	86.996542
131	76.080642	176	87.197234
132	76.380487	177	87.396103
133	76.677609	178	87.593166
134	76.972032	179	87.788438
135	77.263781	180	87.981937

yearly interest rate = 11.00%

term (months)	constant	term (months)	constant
181	88.173679	226	95.217800
182	88.363678	227	95.343815
183	88.551952	228	95.468685
184	88.738516	229	95.592421
185	88.923385	230	95.715033
186	89.106574	231	95.836532
187	89.288100	232	95.956927
188	89.467977	233	96.076228
189	89.646220	234	96.194446
190	89.822844	235	96.311589
191	89.997863	236	96.427669
192	90.171293	237	96.542694
193	90.343148	238	96.656675
194	90.513441	239	96.769620
195	90.682188	240	96.881539
196	90.849402	241	96.992442
197	91.015097	242	97.102337
198	91.179286	243	97.211234
199	91.341985	244	97.319142
200	91.503205	245	97.426070
201	91.662962	246	97.532026
202	91.821267	247	97.637020
203	91.978134	248	97.741060
204	92.133576	249	97.844156
205	92.287606	250	97.946314
206	92.440237	251	98.047545
207	92.591482	252	98.147856
208	92.741353	253	98.247257
209	92.889863	254	98.345754
210	93.037023	255	98.443356
211	93.182847	256	98.540072
212	93.327347	257	98.635910
213	93.470533	258	98.730877
214	93.612420	259	98.824981
215	93.753017	260	98.918231
216	93.892337	261	99.010633
217	94.030392	262	99.102197
218	94.167193	263	99.192928
219	94.302751	264	99.282835
220	94.437078	265	99.371926
221	94.570184	266	99.460207
222	94.702082	267	99.547687
223	94.832781	268	99.634372
224	94.962294	269	99.720269
225	95.090629	270	99.805387

yearly interest rate = 11.00%

term (months)	constant	term (months)	constant
271	99.889731	316	102.98838
272	99.973309	317	103.04377
273	100.05613	318	103.09870
274	100.13819	319	103.15313
275	100.21952	320	103.20706
276	100.30010	321	103.26051
277	100.37995	322	103.31347
278	100.45907	323	103.36594
279	100.53748	324	103.41795
280	100.61517	325	103.46948
281	100.69216	326	103.52054
282	100.76845	327	103.57114
283	100.84405	328	103.62127
284	100.91896	329	103.67096
285	100.99319	330	103.72019
286	101.06674	331	103.76897
287	101.13963	332	103.81731
288	101.21185	333	103.86522
289	101.28342	334	103.91268
290	101.35434	335	103.95972
291	101.42461	336	104.00633
292	101.49425	337	104.05251
293	101.56325	338	104.09828
294	101.63163	339	104.14363
295	101.69939	340	104.18857
296	101.76653	341	104.23310
297	101.83306	342	104.27722
298	101.89898	343	104.32095
299	101.96431	344	104.36428
300	102.02904	345	104.40721
301	102.09319	346	104.44975
302	102.15675	347	104.49191
303	102.21974	348	104.53369
304	102.28215	349	104.57508
305	102.34400	350	104.61610
306	102.40528	351	104.65675
307	102.46601	352	104.69702
308	102.52619	353	104.73693
309	102.58582	354	104.77648
310	102.64491	355	104.81567
311	102.70346	356	104.85451
312	102.76148	357	104.89299
313	102.81897	358	104.93112
314	102.87594	359	104.96890
315	102.93239	360	105.00635

yearly interest rate = 11.25%

term (months)	constant	term (months)	constant
1	0.9907121	46	37.226349
2	1.9722225	47	37.871306
3	2.9446167	48	38.510272
4	3.9079794	49	39.143303
5	4.8623945	50	39.770455
6	5.8079450	51	40.391782
7	6.7447133	52	41.007338
8	7.6727810	53	41.617177
9	8.5922288	54	42.221352
10	9.5031369	55	42.819916
11	10.405585	56	43.412919
12	11.299650	57	44.000416
13	12.185412	58	44.582455
14	13.062947	59	45.159089
15	13.932331	60	45.730366
16	14.793641	61	46.296338
17	15.646951	62	46.857053
18	16.492335	63	47.412561
19	17.329868	64	47.962908
20	18.159621	65	48.508144
21	18.981668	66	49.048317
22	19.796080	67	49.583471
23	20.602927	68	50.113656
24	21.402281	69	50.638916
25	22.194210	70	51.159298
26	22.978784	71	51.674846
27	23.756071	72	52.185606
28	24.526138	73	52.691622
29	25.289054	74	53.192938
30	26.044883	75	53.689598
31	26.793692	76	54.181645
32	27.535546	77	54.669122
33	28.270510	78	55.152072
34	28.998648	79	55.630535
35	29.720023	80	56.104555
36	30.434697	81	56.574172
37	31.142734	82	57.039428
38	31.844195	83	57.500362
39	32.539140	84	57.957015
40	33.227631	85	58.409426
41	33.909728	86	58.857636
42	34.585489	87	59.301683
43	35.254973	88	59.741605
44	35.918240	89	60.177442
45	36.575346	90	60.609230

yearly interest rate = 11.25%

term (months)	constant	term (months)	constant
91	61.037008	136	76.683138
92	61.460813	137	76.961623
93	61.880682	138	77.237521
94	62.296651	139	77.510857
95	62.708756	140	77.781654
96	63.117034	141	78.049936
97	63.521520	142	78.315726
98	63.922249	143	78.579047
99	64.319255	144	78.839923
100	64.712575	145	79.098376
101	65.102242	146	79.354428
102	65.488289	147	79.608102
103	65.870751	148	79.859420
104	66.249660	149	80.108404
105	66.625050	150	80.355075
106	66.996954	151	80.599455
107	67.365403	152	80.841565
108	67.730430	153	81.081427
109	68.092067	154	81.319061
110	68.450345	155	81.554488
111	68.805296	156	81.787728
112	69.156949	157	82.018801
113	69.505337	158	82.247729
114	69.850488	159	82.474530
115	70.192434	160	82.699225
116	70.531204	161	82.921833
117	70.866828	162	83.142373
118	71.199334	163	83.360865
119	71.528752	164	83.577327
120	71.855110	165	83.791779
121	72.178437	166	84.004240
122	72.498761	167	84.214727
123	72.816110	168	84.423259
124	73.130512	169	84.629854
125	73.441993	170	84.834530
126	73.750582	171	85.037305
127	74.056304	172	85.238197
128	74.359186	173	85.437223
129	74.659256	174	85.634401
130	74.956538	175	85.829747
131	75.251060	176	86.023279
132	75.542845	177	86.215013
133	75.831921	178	86.404966
134	76.118312	179	86.593155
135	76.402043	180	86.779597

yearly interest rate = 11.25%

term (months)	constant	term (months)	constant
181	86.964306	226	93.720125
182	87.147300	227	93.840371
183	87.328595	228	93.959501
184	87.508205	229	94.077524
185	87.686148	230	94.194451
186	87.862437	231	94.310292
187	88.037090	232	94.425057
188	88.210120	233	94.538757
189	88.381543	234	94.651400
190	88.551374	235	94.762997
191	88.719627	236	94.873557
192	88.886318	237	94.983091
193	89.051461	238	95.091607
194	89.215069	239	95.199115
195	89.377158	240	95.305625
196	89.537742	241	95.411145
197	89.696834	242	95.515686
198	89.854449	243	95.619255
199	90.010599	244	95.721863
200	90.165300	245	95.823517
201	90.318563	246	95.924228
202	90.470403	247	96.024003
203	90.620833	248	96.122851
204	90.769865	249	96.220781
205	90.917514	250	96.317802
206	91.063791	251	96.413921
207	91.208709	252	96.509148
208	91.352281	253	96.603490
209	91.494520	254	96.696956
210	91.635438	255	96.789554
211	91.775047	256	96.881292
212	91.913359	257	96.972178
213	92.050387	258	97.062220
214	92.186142	259	97.151425
215	92.320636	260	97.239802
216	92.453881	261	97.327358
217	92.585888	262	97.414101
218	92.716669	263	97.500038
219	92.846236	264	97.585177
220	92.974599	265	97.669525
221	93.101770	266	97.753090
222	93.227760	267	97.835878
223	93.352579	268	97.917898
224	93.476239	269	97.999156
225	93.598751	270	98.079659

yearly interest rate = 11.25%

term (months)	constant	term (months)	constant
271	98.159415	316	101.07650
272	98.238429	317	101.12842
273	98.316710	318	101.17986
274	98.394264	319	101.23082
275	98.471098	320	101.28131
276	98.547217	321	101.33133
277	98.622630	322	101.38088
278	98.697343	323	101.42997
279	98.771361	324	101.47861
280	98.844692	325	101.52680
281	98.917342	326	101.57454
282	98.989317	327	101.62183
283	99.060624	328	101.66869
284	99.131268	329	101.71511
285	99.201256	330	101.76110
286	99.270595	331	101.80666
287	99.339289	332	101.85180
288	99.407345	333	101.89652
289	99.474769	334	101.94083
290	99.541567	335	101.98472
291	99.607744	336	102.02821
292	99.673307	337	102.07129
293	99.738261	338	102.11397
294	99.802611	339	102.15625
295	99.866364	340	102.19815
296	99.929525	341	102.23965
297	99.992099	342	102.28077
298	100.05409	343	102.32150
299	100.11551	344	102.36186
300	100.17636	345	102.40184
301	100.23664	346	102.44145
302	100.29636	347	102.48070
303	100.35553	348	102.51958
304	100.41414	349	102.55810
305	100.47222	350	102.59626
306	100.52975	351	102.63406
307	100.58675	352	102.67152
308	100.64322	353	102.70862
309	100.69916	354	102.74538
310	100.75459	355	102.78180
311	100.80950	356	102.81789
312	100.86390	357	102.85363
313	100.91780	358	102.88905
314	100.97119	359	102.92414
315	101.02409	360	102.95890

yearly interest rate = 11.50%

term (months)	constant	term (months)	constant
1	0.9905076	46	37.058919
2	1.9716130	47	37.697650
3	2.9434054	48	38.330318
4	3.9059731	49	38.956980
5	4.8594038	50	39.577694
6	5.8037842	51	40.192515
7	6.7392002	52	40.801501
8	7.6657369	53	41.404706
9	8.5834786	54	42.002185
10	9.4925087	55	42.593993
11	10.392910	56	43.180182
12	11.284764	57	43.760808
13	12.168153	58	44.335922
14	13.043156	59	44.905577
15	13.909853	60	45.469825
16	14.768323	61	46.028716
17	15.618645	62	46.582302
18	16.460894	63	47.130634
19	17.295149	64	47.673760
20	18.121485	65	48.211731
21	18.939977	66	48.744595
22	19.750699	67	49.272402
23	20.553726	68	49.795198
24	21.349130	69	50.313031
25	22.136984	70	50.825949
26	22.917360	71	51.333998
27	23.690327	72	51.837225
28	24.455958	73	52.335675
29	25.214320	74	52.829393
30	25.965485	75	53.318425
31	26.709518	76	53.802814
32	27.446489	77	54.282606
33	28.176465	78	54.757843
34	28.899511	79	55.228570
35	29.615694	80	55.694827
36	30.325079	81	56.156659
37	31.027730	82	56.614108
38	31.723711	83	57.067213
39	32.413086	84	57.516018
40	33.095916	85	57.960563
41	33.772265	86	58.400888
42	34.442194	87	58.837033
43	35.105764	88	59.269038
44	35.763035	89	59.696942
45	36.414067	90	60.120785

yearly interest rate = 11.50%

term (months)	constant	term (months)	constant
91	60.540604	136	75.827929
92	60.956438	137	76.098650
93	61.368325	138	76.366802
94	61.776302	139	76.632408
95	62.180406	140	76.895493
96	62.580675	141	77.156080
97	62.977144	142	77.414194
98	63.369850	143	77.669858
99	63.758828	144	77.923095
100	64.144113	145	78.173928
101	64.525741	146	78.422380
102	64.903747	147	78.668474
103	65.278165	148	78.912232
104	65.649028	149	79.153676
105	66.016371	150	79.392828
106	66.380227	151	79.629710
107	66.740630	152	79.864343
108	67.097611	153	80.096749
109	67.451204	154	80.326949
110	67.801440	155	80.554964
111	68.148351	156	80.780815
112	68.491970	157	81.004522
113	68.832327	158	81.226105
114	69.169453	159	81.445585
115	69.503379	160	81.662981
116	69.834135	161	81.878314
117	70.161752	162	82.091603
118	70.486258	163	82.302867
119	70.807685	164	82.512126
120	71.126060	165	82.719398
121	71.441413	166	82.924703
122	71.753773	167	83.128059
123	72.063167	168	83.329485
124	72.369625	169	83.528999
125	72.673174	170	83.726618
126	72.973841	171	83.922362
127	73.271655	172	84.116248
128	73.566641	173	84.308294
129	73.858827	174	84.498517
130	74.148240	175	84.686933
131	74.434905	176	84.873562
132	74.718850	177	85.058419
133	75.000099	178	85.241521
134	75.278678	179	85.422885
135	75.554613	180	85.602527

yearly interest rate = 11.50%

term (months)	constant	term (months)	constant
181	85.780464	226	92.259882
182	85.956713	227	92.374625
183	86.131288	228	92.488279
184	86.304206	229	92.600854
185	86.475482	230	92.712361
186	86.645133	231	92.822809
187	86.813174	232	92.932209
188	86.979619	233	93.040570
189	87.144484	234	93.147902
190	87.307785	235	93.254216
191	87.469535	236	93.359521
192	87.629750	237	93.463826
193	87.788444	238	93.567141
194	87.945632	239	93.669475
195	88.101327	240	93.770838
196	88.255545	241	93.871238
197	88.408299	242	93.970686
198	88.559603	243	94.069190
199	88.709470	244	94.166758
200	88.857915	245	94.263401
201	89.004951	246	94.359126
202	89.150591	247	94.453942
203	89.294849	248	94.547858
204	89.437737	249	94.640883
205	89.579269	250	94.733025
206	89.719458	251	94.824292
207	89.858316	252	94.914693
208	89.995855	253	95.004236
209	90.132089	254	95.092929
210	90.267030	255	95.180779
211	90.400690	256	95.267796
212	90.533082	257	95.353987
213	90.664216	258	95.439360
214	90.794106	259	95.523923
215	90.922763	260	95.607682
216	91.050199	261	95.690647
217	91.176425	262	95.772824
218	91.301452	263	95.854221
219	91.425293	264	95.934845
220	91.547959	265	96.014705
221	91.669460	266	96.093806
222	91.789807	267	96.172156
223	91.909013	268	96.249762
224	92.027086	269	96.326632
225	92.144039	270	96.402772

yearly interest rate = 11.50%

term (months)	constant	term (months)	constant
271	96.478189	316	99.224442
272	96.552891	317	99.273075
273	96.626883	318	99.321246
274	96.700173	319	99.368960
275	96.772768	320	99.416222
276	96.844673	321	99.463034
277	96.915895	322	99.509402
278	96.986442	323	99.555331
279	97.056319	324	99.600823
280	97.125533	325	99.645883
281	97.194089	326	99.690516
282	97.261995	327	99.734724
283	97.329256	328	99.778514
284	97.395879	329	99.821887
285	97.461870	330	99.864849
286	97.527234	331	99.907403
287	97.591977	332	99.949553
288	97.656106	333	99.991303
289	97.719627	334	100.03266
290	97.782544	335	100.07362
291	97.844864	336	100.11419
292	97.906592	337	100.15438
293	97.967735	338	100.19418
294	98.028297	339	100.23361
295	98.088284	340	100.27266
296	98.147702	341	100.31135
297	98.206556	342	100.34966
298	98.264851	343	100.38762
299	98.322593	344	100.42521
300	98.379787	345	100.46244
301	98.436438	346	100.49932
302	98.492551	347	100.53586
303	98.548131	348	100.57204
304	98.603184	349	100.60788
305	98.657714	350	100.64338
306	98.711727	351	100.67855
307	98.765227	352	100.71338
308	98.818219	353	100.74788
309	98.870708	354	100.78205
310	98.922698	355	100.81590
311	98.974196	356	100.84942
312	99.025204	357	100.88263
313	99.075729	358	100.91552
314	99.125773	359	100.94810
315	99.175343	360	100.98037

yearly interest rate = 11.75%

term (months)	constant	term (months)	constant
1	0.9903033	46	36.892551
2	1.9710039	47	37.525117
3	2.9421949	48	38.151550
4	3.9039685	49	38.771909
5	4.8564161	50	39.386251
6	5.7996281	51	39.994637
7	6.7336940	52	40.597124
8	7.6587026	53	41.193768
9	8.5747416	54	41.784627
10	9.4818980	55	42.369757
11	10.380258	56	42.949212
12	11.269907	57	43.523049
13	12.150929	58	44.091321
14	13.023408	59	44.654084
15	13.887427	60	45.211389
16	14.743068	61	45.763290
17	15.590412	62	46.309839
18	16.429539	63	46.851089
19	17.260530	64	47.387090
20	18.083463	65	47.917894
21	18.898416	66	48.443551
22	19.705466	67	48.964111
23	20.504691	68	49.479623
24	21.296166	69	49.990136
25	22.079967	70	50.495699
26	22.856167	71	50.996360
27	23.624840	72	51.492166
28	24.386060	73	51.983164
29	25.139898	74	52.469401
30	25.886427	75	52.950923
31	26.625717	76	53.427776
32	27.357838	77	53.900005
33	28.082860	78	54.367656
34	28.800852	79	54.830771
35	29.511881	80	55.289396
36	30.216016	81	55.743573
37	30.913323	82	56.193347
38	31.603869	83	56.638759
39	32.287718	84	57.079852
40	32.964936	85	57.516668
41	33.635588	86	57.949248
42	34.299736	87	58.377634
43	34.957445	88	58.801866
44	35.608775	89	59.221984
45	36.253790	90	59.638028

yearly interest rate = 11.75%

term (months)	constant	term (months)	constant
91	60.050038	136	74.986964
92	60.458053	137	75.250139
93	60.862111	138	75.510763
94	61.262252	139	75.768860
95	61.658512	140	76.024454
96	62.050930	141	76.277569
97	62.439543	142	76.528230
98	62.824388	143	76.776461
99	63.205500	144	77.022284
100	63.582918	145	77.265724
101	63.956675	146	77.506803
102	64.326808	147	77.745545
103	64.693353	148	77.981971
104	65.056343	149	78.216105
105	65.415813	150	78.447969
106	65.771797	151	78.677584
107	66.124330	152	78.904973
108	66.473444	153	79.130157
109	66.819173	154	79.353157
110	67.161550	155	79.573995
111	67.500606	156	79.792692
112	67.836375	157	80.009268
113	68.168888	158	80.223744
114	68.498177	159	80.436140
115	68.824272	160	80.646476
116	69.147206	161	80.854773
117	69.467008	162	81.061051
118	69.783709	163	81.265328
119	70.097340	164	81.467624
120	70.407929	165	81.667958
121	70.715506	166	81.866350
122	71.020101	167	82.062819
123	71.321742	168	82.257382
124	71.620458	169	82.450058
125	71.916278	170	82.640866
126	72.209229	171	82.829824
127	72.499340	172	83.016950
128	72.786638	173	83.202261
129	73.071149	174	83.385775
130	73.352902	175	83.567510
131	73.631923	176	83.747483
132	73.908238	177	83.925710
133	74.181874	178	84.102209
134	74.452856	179	84.276997
135	74.721211	180	84.450090

yearly interest rate = 11.75%

term (months)	constant	term (months)	constant
181	84.621505	226	90.835928
182	84.791257	227	90.945420
183	84.959363	228	91.053851
184	85.125839	229	91.161231
185	85.290701	230	91.267569
186	85.453964	231	91.372877
187	85.615644	232	91.477163
188	85.775757	233	91.580438
189	85.934317	234	91.682711
190	86.091339	235	91.783993
191	86.246839	236	91.884292
192	86.400831	237	91.983619
193	86.553329	238	92.081983
194	86.704349	239	92.179393
195	86.853905	240	92.275859
196	87.002010	241	92.371389
197	87.148679	242	92.465993
198	87.293926	243	92.559679
199	87.437765	244	92.652457
200	87.580208	245	92.744336
201	87.721271	246	92.835323
202	87.860966	247	92.925428
203	87.999306	248	93.014660
204	88.136305	249	93.103026
205	88.271975	250	93.190535
206	88.406329	251	93.277196
207	88.539381	252	93.363017
208	88.671143	253	93.448005
209	88.801627	254	93.532169
210	88.930846	255	93.615517
211	89.058812	256	93.698057
212	89.185537	257	93.779797
213	89.311033	258	93.860743
214	89.435312	259	93.940905
215	89.558386	260	94.020290
216	89.680267	261	94.098905
217	89.800966	262	94.176758
218	89.920494	263	94.253855
219	90.038864	264	94.330205
220	90.156085	265	94.405815
221	90.272170	266	94.480692
222	90.387130	267	94.554842
223	90.500974	268	94.628274
224	90.613715	269	94.700993
225	90.725363	270	94.773007

yearly interest rate = 11.75%

term (months)	constant	term (months)	constant
271	94.844323	316	97.429799
272	94.914948	317	97.475353
273	94.984887	318	97.520465
274	95.054149	319	97.565139
275	95.122739	320	97.609381
276	95.190664	321	97.653193
277	95.257930	322	97.696581
278	95.324543	323	97.739548
279	95.390511	324	97.782098
280	95.455840	325	97.824236
281	95.520534	326	97.865965
282	95.584602	327	97.907289
283	95.648048	328	97.948213
284	95.710879	329	97.988740
285	95.773101	330	98.028874
286	95.834719	331	98.068619
287	95.895740	332	98.107978
288	95.956169	333	98.146956
289	96.016012	334	98.185556
290	96.075275	335	98.223781
291	96.133964	336	98.261636
292	96.192083	337	98.299124
293	96.249638	338	98.336248
294	96.306636	339	98.373012
295	96.363081	340	98.409420
296	96.418978	341	98.445475
297	96.474334	342	98.481180
298	96.529152	343	98.516539
299	96.583440	344	98.551555
300	96.637200	345	98.586231
301	96.690440	346	98.620571
302	96.743163	347	98.654579
303	96.795375	348	98.688256
304	96.847081	349	98.721607
305	96.898285	350	98.754635
306	96.948993	351	98.787342
307	96.999209	352	98.819732
308	97.048938	353	98.851808
309	97.098185	354	98.883573
310	97.146954	355	98.915030
311	97.195251	356	98.946182
312	97.243079	357	98.977032
313	97.290443	358	99.007583
314	97.337349	359	99.037837
315	97.383799	360	99.067798

yearly interest rate = 12.00%

term (months)	constant	term (months)	constant
1	0.9900990	46	36.727236
2	1.9703951	47	37.353699
3	2.9409852	48	37.973960
4	3.9019656	49	38.588079
5	4.8534313	50	39.196118
6	5.7954765	51	39.798136
7	6.7281945	52	40.394194
8	7.6516778	53	40.984351
9	8.5660176	54	41.568664
10	9.4713045	55	42.147192
11	10.367628	56	42.719992
12	11.255077	57	43.287121
13	12.133740	58	43.848635
14	13.003703	59	44.404589
15	13.865053	60	44.955038
16	14.717874	61	45.500038
17	15.562251	62	46.039642
18	16.398269	63	46.573903
19	17.226009	64	47.102874
20	18.045553	65	47.626608
21	18.856983	66	48.145156
22	19.660379	67	48.658571
23	20.455821	68	49.166902
24	21.243387	69	49.670200
25	22.023156	70	50.168514
26	22.795204	71	50.661895
27	23.559608	72	51.150392
28	24.316443	73	51.634051
29	25.065785	74	52.112922
30	25.807708	75	52.587051
31	26.542285	76	53.056486
32	27.269590	77	53.521274
33	27.989693	78	53.981459
34	28.702666	79	54.437088
35	29.408580	80	54.888206
36	30.107505	81	55.334858
37	30.799510	82	55.777087
38	31.484663	83	56.214937
39	32.163033	84	56.648453
40	32.834686	85	57.077676
41	33.499689	86	57.502650
42	34.158108	87	57.923415
43	34.810008	88	58.340015
44	35.455454	89	58.752490
45	36.094508	90	59.160882

yearly interest rate = 12.00%

term (months)	constant	term (months)	constant
91	59.565229	136	74.159961
92	59.965574	137	74.415803
93	60.361954	138	74.669112
94	60.754410	139	74.919913
95	61.142980	140	75.168230
96	61.527703	141	75.414090
97	61.908617	142	75.657514
98	62.285759	143	75.898529
99	62.659168	144	76.137158
100	63.028879	145	76.373423
101	63.394930	146	76.607350
102	63.757356	147	76.838960
103	64.116194	148	77.068277
104	64.471479	149	77.295324
105	64.823247	150	77.520123
106	65.171531	151	77.742696
107	65.516368	152	77.963065
108	65.857790	153	78.181253
109	66.195832	154	78.397280
110	66.530526	155	78.611168
111	66.861907	156	78.822939
112	67.190007	157	79.032613
113	67.514859	158	79.240211
114	67.836494	159	79.445753
115	68.154944	160	79.649261
116	68.470242	161	79.850753
117	68.782418	162	80.050251
118	69.091503	163	80.247773
119	69.397527	164	80.443339
120	69.700522	165	80.636970
121	70.000517	166	80.828683
122	70.297542	167	81.018498
123	70.591625	168	81.206434
124	70.882797	169	81.392508
125	71.171086	170	81.576741
126	71.456521	171	81.759150
127	71.739130	172	81.939752
128	72.018941	173	82.118566
129	72.295981	174	82.295610
130	72.570278	175	82.470901
131	72.841859	176	82.644457
132	73.110752	177	82.816294
133	73.376982	178	82.986429
134	73.640576	179	83.154881
135	73.901561	180	83.321664

yearly interest rate = 12.00%

term (months)	constant	term (months)	constant
181	83.486796	226	89.447156
182	83.650293	227	89.551639
183	83.812171	228	89.655089
184	83.972447	229	89.757513
185	84.131136	230	89.858924
186	84.288253	231	89.959331
187	84.443815	232	90.058743
188	84.597837	233	90.157172
189	84.750333	234	90.254625
190	84.901320	235	90.351114
191	85.050812	236	90.446648
192	85.198824	237	90.541236
193	85.345370	238	90.634887
194	85.490465	239	90.727611
195	85.634124	240	90.819416
196	85.776360	241	90.910313
197	85.917189	242	91.000310
198	86.056622	243	91.089416
199	86.194676	244	91.177640
200	86.331362	245	91.264990
201	86.466695	246	91.351475
202	86.600688	247	91.437104
203	86.733355	248	91.521885
204	86.864708	249	91.605827
205	86.994760	250	91.688937
206	87.123525	251	91.771225
207	87.251015	252	91.852698
208	87.377242	253	91.933365
209	87.502220	254	92.013232
210	87.625960	255	92.092309
211	87.748476	256	92.170603
212	87.869778	257	92.248122
213	87.989879	258	92.324873
214	88.108791	259	92.400864
215	88.226526	260	92.476103
216	88.343095	261	92.550597
217	88.458510	262	92.624354
218	88.572782	263	92.697380
219	88.685923	264	92.769683
220	88.797943	265	92.841271
221	88.908855	266	92.912149
222	89.018668	267	92.982326
223	89.127394	268	93.051808
224	89.235044	269	93.120602
225	89.341627	270	93.188715

yearly interest rate = 12.00%

term (months)	constant	term (months)	constant
271	93.256153	316	95.690311
272	93.322924	317	95.732982
273	93.389034	318	95.775229
274	93.454489	319	95.817059
275	93.519296	320	95.858474
276	93.583461	321	95.899479
277	93.646991	322	95.940078
278	93.709892	323	95.980276
279	93.772171	324	96.020075
280	93.833832	325	96.059480
281	93.894883	326	96.098495
282	93.955330	327	96.137124
283	94.015178	328	96.175370
284	94.074434	329	96.213238
285	94.133103	330	96.250731
286	94.191191	331	96.287852
287	94.248704	332	96.324606
288	94.305647	333	96.360996
289	94.362027	334	96.397026
290	94.417849	335	96.432699
291	94.473118	336	96.468019
292	94.527839	337	96.502989
293	94.582019	338	96.537613
294	94.635662	339	96.571894
295	94.688775	340	96.605835
296	94.741361	341	96.639441
297	94.793427	342	96.672714
298	94.844977	343	96.705657
299	94.896017	344	96.738274
300	94.946551	345	96.770569
301	94.996585	346	96.802543
302	95.046124	347	96.834201
303	95.095172	348	96.865546
304	95.143735	349	96.896580
305	95.191817	350	96.927307
306	95.239423	351	96.957730
307	95.286557	352	96.987851
308	95.333225	353	97.017674
309	95.379431	354	97.047202
310	95.425179	355	97.076438
311	95.470474	356	97.105384
312	95.515321	357	97.134044
313	95.559724	358	97.162420
314	95.603687	359	97.190514
315	95.647215	360	97.218331

yearly interest rate = 12.25%

term (months)	constant	term (months)	constant
1	0.9898948	46	36.562967
2	1.9697866	47	37.183387
3	2.9397764	48	37.797537
4	3.8999642	49	38.405481
5	4.8504492	50	39.007282
6	5.7913294	51	39.603001
7	6.7227018	52	40.192701
8	7.6446625	53	40.776441
9	8.5573067	54	41.354283
10	9.4607284	55	41.926285
11	10.355021	56	42.492508
12	11.240276	57	43.053008
13	12.116586	58	43.607845
14	12.984041	59	44.157075
15	13.842730	60	44.700754
16	14.692741	61	45.238940
17	15.534163	62	45.771688
18	16.367083	63	46.299051
19	17.191585	64	46.821086
20	18.007756	65	47.337846
21	18.815679	66	47.849383
22	19.615438	67	48.355752
23	20.407116	68	48.857003
24	21.190793	69	49.353189
25	21.966551	70	49.844361
26	22.734470	71	50.330570
27	23.494629	72	50.811866
28	24.247107	73	51.288298
29	24.991980	74	51.759915
30	25.729327	75	52.226767
31	26.459222	76	52.688901
32	27.181742	77	53.146365
33	27.896960	78	53.599207
34	28.604951	79	54.047472
35	29.305788	80	54.491208
36	29.999543	81	54.930459
37	30.686287	82	55.365272
38	31.366091	83	55.795691
39	32.039026	84	56.221761
40	32.705161	85	56.643525
41	33.364565	86	57.061027
42	34.017305	87	57.474310
43	34.663449	88	57.883416
44	35.303063	89	58.288389
45	35.936214	90	58.689270

yearly interest rate = 12.25%

term (months)	constant	term (months)	constant
91	59.086099	136	73.346646
92	59.478918	137	73.595360
93	59.867768	138	73.841560
94	60.252689	139	74.085273
95	60.633719	140	74.326523
96	61.010900	141	74.565335
97	61.384269	142	74.801734
98	61.753865	143	75.035745
99	62.119726	144	75.267390
100	62.481890	145	75.496694
101	62.840394	146	75.723682
102	63.195276	147	75.948376
103	63.546571	148	76.170799
104	63.894317	149	76.390974
105	64.238548	150	76.608925
106	64.579301	151	76.824673
107	64.916611	152	77.038241
108	65.250512	153	77.249651
109	65.581039	154	77.458924
110	65.908226	155	77.666083
111	66.232106	156	77.871148
112	66.552714	157	78.074141
113	66.870082	158	78.275083
114	67.184243	159	78.473994
115	67.495229	160	78.670896
116	67.803072	161	78.865807
117	68.107805	162	79.058749
118	68.409459	163	79.249741
119	68.708064	164	79.438804
120	69.003652	165	79.625955
121	69.296252	166	79.811216
122	69.585896	167	79.994604
123	69.872613	168	80.176140
124	70.156433	169	80.355840
125	70.437385	170	80.533725
126	70.715497	171	80.709813
127	70.990800	172	80.884120
128	71.263320	173	81.056667
129	71.533086	174	81.227470
130	71.800127	175	81.396547
131	72.064469	176	81.563915
132	72.326139	177	81.729592
133	72.585166	178	81.893595
134	72.841575	179	82.055941
135	73.095393	180	82.216646

yearly interest rate = 12.25%

term (months)	constant	term (months)	constant
181	82.375727	226	88.092500
182	82.533201	227	88.192205
183	82.689083	228	88.290902
184	82.843390	229	88.388602
185	82.996138	230	88.485314
186	83.147342	231	88.581049
187	83.297018	232	88.675817
188	83.445182	233	88.769627
189	83.591848	234	88.862489
190	83.737033	235	88.954413
191	83.880750	236	89.045407
192	84.023015	237	89.135483
193	84.163843	238	89.224648
194	84.303247	239	89.312912
195	84.441243	240	89.400284
196	84.577844	241	89.486773
197	84.713065	242	89.572388
198	84.846919	243	89.657138
199	84.979421	244	89.741032
200	85.110584	245	89.824078
201	85.240421	246	89.906285
202	85.368946	247	89.987660
203	85.496173	248	90.068214
204	85.622114	249	90.147954
205	85.746782	250	90.226888
206	85.870191	251	90.305024
207	85.992352	252	90.382370
208	86.113279	253	90.458935
209	86.232984	254	90.534727
210	86.351479	255	90.609752
211	86.468777	256	90.684020
212	86.584890	257	90.757536
213	86.699829	258	90.830310
214	86.813607	259	90.902349
215	86.926235	260	90.973659
216	87.037725	261	91.044249
217	87.148088	262	91.114126
218	87.257336	263	91.183296
219	87.365480	264	91.251768
220	87.472531	265	91.319548
221	87.578501	266	91.386642
222	87.683399	267	91.453059
223	87.787238	268	91.518805
224	87.890027	269	91.583886
225	87.991778	270	91.648309

yearly interest rate = 12.25%

term (months)	constant	term (months)	constant
271	91.712082	316	94.003824
272	91.775210	317	94.043794
273	91.837700	318	94.083359
274	91.899559	319	94.122525
275	91.960792	320	94.161295
276	92.021407	321	94.199674
277	92.081409	322	94.237664
278	92.140805	323	94.275271
279	92.199601	324	94.312497
280	92.257803	325	94.349348
281	92.315416	326	94.385826
282	92.372447	327	94.421935
283	92.428902	328	94.457680
284	92.484787	329	94.493063
285	92.540106	330	94.528089
286	92.594867	331	94.562761
287	92.649075	332	94.597082
288	92.702734	333	94.631057
289	92.755852	334	94.664688
290	92.808432	335	94.697979
291	92.860481	336	94.730934
292	92.912005	337	94.763556
293	92.963007	338	94.795849
294	93.013495	339	94.827815
295	93.063472	340	94.859458
296	93.112944	341	94.890781
297	93.161916	342	94.921788
298	93.210393	343	94.952481
299	93.258380	344	94.982865
300	93.305883	345	95.012941
301	93.352905	346	95.042713
302	93.399452	347	95.072185
303	93.445529	348	95.101358
304	93.491141	349	95.130237
305	93.536291	350	95.158824
306	93.580985	351	95.187122
307	93.625228	352	95.215134
308	93.669023	353	95.242863
309	93.712376	354	95.270312
310	93.755291	355	95.297484
311	93.797772	356	95.324381
312	93.839823	357	95.351006
313	93.881450	358	95.377362
314	93.922656	359	95.403452
315	93.963446	360	95.429278

yearly interest rate = 12.50%

term (months)	constant	term (months)	constant
1	0.9896907	46	36.399737
2	1.9691785	47	37.014173
3	2.9385684	48	37.622274
4	3.8979646	49	38.224106
5	4.8474701	50	38.819734
6	5.7871869	51	39.409221
7	6.7172159	52	39.992631
8	7.6376570	53	40.570027
9	8.5486090	54	41.141470
10	9.4501697	55	41.707022
11	10.342436	56	42.266743
12	11.225504	57	42.820694
13	12.099468	58	43.368935
14	12.964422	59	43.911523
15	13.820458	60	44.448518
16	14.667670	61	44.979976
17	15.506148	62	45.505956
18	16.335981	63	46.026513
19	17.157260	64	46.541704
20	17.970072	65	47.051583
21	18.774504	66	47.556206
22	19.570643	67	48.055626
23	20.358575	68	48.549898
24	21.138383	69	49.039075
25	21.910152	70	49.523208
26	22.673965	71	50.002350
27	23.429904	72	50.476553
28	24.178049	73	50.945866
29	24.918482	74	51.410342
30	25.651281	75	51.870029
31	26.376525	76	52.324977
32	27.094293	77	52.775235
33	27.804661	78	53.220852
34	28.507706	79	53.661874
35	29.203503	80	54.098349
36	29.892126	81	54.530325
37	30.573651	82	54.957847
38	31.248149	83	55.380962
39	31.915694	84	55.799715
40	32.576357	85	56.214151
41	33.230209	86	56.624315
42	33.877320	87	57.030250
43	34.517760	88	57.432000
44	35.151598	89	57.829608
45	35.778901	90	58.223117

yearly interest rate = 12.50%

term (months)	constant	term (months)	constant
91	58.612569	136	72.546748
92	58.998007	137	72.788534
93	59.379471	138	73.027828
94	59.757002	139	73.264654
95	60.130641	140	73.499039
96	60.500428	141	73.731008
97	60.866403	142	73.960585
98	61.228605	143	74.187796
99	61.587073	144	74.412664
100	61.941846	145	74.635214
101	62.292961	146	74.855469
102	62.640456	147	75.073454
103	62.984369	148	75.289192
104	63.324736	149	75.502705
105	63.661595	150	75.714018
106	63.994980	151	75.923151
107	64.324929	152	76.130129
108	64.651476	153	76.334973
109	64.974657	154	76.537705
110	65.294506	155	76.738348
111	65.611057	156	76.936921
112	65.924345	157	77.133448
113	66.234403	158	77.327949
114	66.541265	159	77.520444
115	66.844964	160	77.710955
116	67.145531	161	77.899502
117	67.443000	162	78.086105
118	67.737402	163	78.270784
119	68.028769	164	78.453559
120	68.317132	165	78.634451
121	68.602522	166	78.813477
122	68.884971	167	78.990658
123	69.164507	168	79.166012
124	69.441161	169	79.339558
125	69.714964	170	79.511315
126	69.985944	171	79.681301
127	70.254130	172	79.849535
128	70.519551	173	80.016035
129	70.782236	174	80.180818
130	71.042213	175	80.343903
131	71.299510	176	80.505306
132	71.554154	177	80.665045
133	71.806173	178	80.823137
134	72.055594	179	80.979600
135	72.302444	180	81.134449

yearly interest rate = 12.50%

term (months)	constant	term (months)	constant
181	81.287702	226	86.770930
182	81.439375	227	86.866075
183	81.589485	228	86.960239
184	81.738047	229	87.053432
185	81.885077	230	87.145665
186	82.030592	231	87.236947
187	82.174607	232	87.327288
188	82.317136	233	87.416697
189	82.458197	234	87.505185
190	82.597803	235	87.592760
191	82.735970	236	87.679433
192	82.872713	237	87.765212
193	83.008045	238	87.850106
194	83.141983	239	87.934126
195	83.274540	240	88.017279
196	83.405730	241	88.099575
197	83.535568	242	88.181023
198	83.664067	243	88.261631
199	83.791242	244	88.341408
200	83.917106	245	88.420363
201	84.041671	246	88.498503
202	84.164953	247	88.575838
203	84.286964	248	88.652376
204	84.407717	249	88.728125
205	84.527225	250	88.803093
206	84.645501	251	88.877287
207	84.762558	252	88.950717
208	84.878408	253	89.023390
209	84.993063	254	89.095314
210	85.106537	255	89.166497
211	85.218841	256	89.236945
212	85.329987	257	89.306667
213	85.439987	258	89.375671
214	85.548853	259	89.443963
215	85.656597	260	89.511551
216	85.763230	261	89.578442
217	85.868763	262	89.644644
218	85.973209	263	89.710163
219	86.076578	264	89.775006
220	86.178881	265	89.839182
221	86.280130	266	89.902695
222	86.380335	267	89.965554
223	86.479507	268	90.027765
224	86.577656	269	90.089334
225	86.674794	270	90.150269

yearly interest rate = 12.50%

term (months)	constant	term (months)	constant
271	90.210575	316	92.368276
272	90.270260	317	92.405716
273	90.329330	318	92.442771
274	90.387790	319	92.479443
275	90.445648	320	92.515738
276	90.502909	321	92.551658
277	90.559581	322	92.587208
278	90.615667	323	92.622391
279	90.671176	324	92.657212
280	90.726112	325	92.691674
281	90.780482	326	92.725780
282	90.834292	327	92.759535
283	90.887546	328	92.792942
284	90.940252	329	92.826004
285	90.992414	330	92.858726
286	91.044039	331	92.891110
287	91.095131	332	92.923161
288	91.145697	333	92.954881
289	91.195741	334	92.986274
290	91.245270	335	93.017343
291	91.294288	336	93.048092
292	91.342800	337	93.078524
293	91.390813	338	93.108642
294	91.438330	339	93.138450
295	91.485358	340	93.167951
296	91.531900	341	93.197147
297	91.577963	342	93.226042
298	91.623551	343	93.254640
299	91.668669	344	93.282943
300	91.713322	345	93.310954
301	91.757515	346	93.338676
302	91.801252	347	93.366112
303	91.844538	348	93.393266
304	91.887377	349	93.420139
305	91.929776	350	93.446736
306	91.971737	351	93.473058
307	92.013265	352	93.499109
308	92.054366	353	93.524891
309	92.095042	354	93.550408
310	92.135299	355	93.575661
311	92.175142	356	93.600655
312	92.214573	357	93.625390
313	92.253598	358	93.649871
314	92.292221	359	93.674099
315	92.330446	360	93.698077

yearly interest rate = 12.75%

term (months)	constant	term (months)	constant
1	0.9894867	46	36.237537
2	1.9685706	47	36.846048
3	2.9373612	48	37.448161
4	3.8959665	49	38.043944
5	4.8444938	50	38.633464
6	5.7830489	51	39.216785
7	6.7117367	52	39.793974
8	7.6306609	53	40.365095
9	8.5399242	54	40.930212
10	9.4396282	55	41.489387
11	10.329873	56	42.042683
12	11.210759	57	42.590163
13	12.082384	58	43.131887
14	12.944845	59	43.667915
15	13.798238	60	44.198308
16	14.642660	61	44.723125
17	15.478204	62	45.242424
18	16.304964	63	45.756264
19	17.123032	64	46.264701
20	17.932499	65	46.767794
21	18.733456	66	47.265597
22	19.525992	67	47.758166
23	20.310196	68	48.245557
24	21.086156	69	48.727824
25	21.853958	70	49.205021
26	22.613687	71	49.677200
27	23.365430	72	50.144416
28	24.109269	73	50.606720
29	24.845288	74	51.064163
30	25.573568	75	51.516797
31	26.294193	76	51.964672
32	27.007241	77	52.407839
33	27.712792	78	52.846346
34	28.410926	79	53.280244
35	29.101720	80	53.709580
36	29.785252	81	54.134402
37	30.461598	82	54.554757
38	31.130832	83	54.970694
39	31.793032	84	55.382257
40	32.448269	85	55.789494
41	33.096617	86	56.192449
42	33.738149	87	56.591168
43	34.372937	88	56.985695
44	35.001051	89	57.376074
45	35.622561	90	57.762349

yearly interest rate = 12.75%

term (months)	constant	term (months)	constant
91	58.144563	136	71.760005
92	58.522759	137	71.995058
93	58.896978	138	72.227639
94	59.267264	139	72.457775
95	59.633656	140	72.685492
96	59.996197	141	72.910814
97	60.354925	142	73.133768
98	60.709883	143	73.354378
99	61.061109	144	73.572668
100	61.408642	145	73.788664
101	61.752521	146	74.002388
102	62.092785	147	74.213866
103	62.429472	148	74.423120
104	62.762620	149	74.630175
105	63.092264	150	74.835052
106	63.418443	151	75.037776
107	63.741193	152	75.238368
108	64.060550	153	75.436852
109	64.376549	154	75.633249
110	64.689226	155	75.827580
111	64.998616	156	76.019869
112	65.304753	157	76.210137
113	65.607671	158	76.398404
114	65.907405	159	76.584691
115	66.203988	160	76.769020
116	66.497452	161	76.951412
117	66.787831	162	77.131885
118	67.075158	163	77.310462
119	67.359464	164	77.487161
120	67.640780	165	77.662002
121	67.919139	166	77.835005
122	68.194572	167	78.006189
123	68.467109	168	78.175574
124	68.736781	169	78.343177
125	69.003617	170	78.509019
126	69.267649	171	78.673117
127	69.528904	172	78.835490
128	69.787413	173	78.996156
129	70.043204	174	79.155133
130	70.296305	175	79.312438
131	70.546746	176	79.468090
132	70.794554	177	79.622105
133	71.039757	178	79.774501
134	71.282381	179	79.925294
135	71.522455	180	80.074503

yearly interest rate = 12.75%

term (months)	constant	term (months)	constant
181	80.222143	226	85.481448
182	80.368230	227	85.572243
183	80.512782	228	85.662083
184	80.655814	229	85.750979
185	80.797342	230	85.838940
186	80.937382	231	85.925977
187	81.075950	232	86.012098
188	81.213062	233	86.097314
189	81.348731	234	86.181635
190	81.482975	235	86.265068
191	81.615807	236	86.347625
192	81.747242	237	86.429313
193	81.877296	238	86.510143
194	82.005983	239	86.590123
195	82.133316	240	86.669262
196	82.259311	241	86.747569
197	82.383981	242	86.825053
198	82.507341	243	86.901722
199	82.629403	244	86.977585
200	82.750182	245	87.052651
201	82.869692	246	87.126927
202	82.987945	247	87.200423
203	83.104955	248	87.273146
204	83.220735	249	87.345104
205	83.335297	250	87.416306
206	83.448655	251	87.486759
207	83.560821	252	87.556471
208	83.671808	253	87.625451
209	83.781629	254	87.693705
210	83.890294	255	87.761242
211	83.997817	256	87.828069
212	84.104210	257	87.894193
213	84.209484	258	87.959622
214	84.313652	259	88.024363
215	84.416724	260	88.088424
216	84.518713	261	88.151811
217	84.619629	262	88.214531
218	84.719485	263	88.276592
219	84.818290	264	88.338001
220	84.916057	265	88.398764
221	85.012796	266	88.458889
222	85.108518	267	88.518381
223	85.203234	268	88.577248
224	85.296954	269	88.635495
225	85.389688	270	88.693131

yearly interest rate = 12.75%

term (months)	constant	term (months)	constant
271	88.750161	316	90.781699
272	88.806590	317	90.816771
273	88.862427	318	90.851474
274	88.917677	319	90.885812
275	88.972346	320	90.919789
276	89.026440	321	90.953409
277	89.079965	322	90.986676
278	89.132928	323	91.019593
279	89.185334	324	91.052164
280	89.237188	325	91.084392
281	89.288498	326	91.116281
282	89.339268	327	91.147836
283	89.389505	328	91.179058
284	89.439213	329	91.209952
285	89.488399	330	91.240522
286	89.537068	331	91.270770
287	89.585225	332	91.300700
288	89.632875	333	91.330315
289	89.680025	334	91.359619
290	89.726679	335	91.388615
291	89.772843	336	91.417306
292	89.818521	337	91.445696
293	89.863719	338	91.473787
294	89.908442	339	91.501583
295	89.952694	340	91.529086
296	89.996482	341	91.556300
297	90.039809	342	91.583229
298	90.082680	343	91.609874
299	90.125101	344	91.636239
300	90.167076	345	91.662326
301	90.208609	346	91.688140
302	90.249706	347	91.713682
303	90.290371	348	91.738956
304	90.330608	349	91.763964
305	90.370423	350	91.788709
306	90.409818	351	91.813193
307	90.448800	352	91.837421
308	90.487372	353	91.861393
309	90.525538	354	91.885114
310	90.563303	355	91.908585
311	90.600670	356	91.931810
312	90.637646	357	91.954790
313	90.674232	358	91.977529
314	90.710433	359	92.000029
315	90.746254	360	92.022292

yearly interest rate = 13.00%

term (months)	constant	term (months)	constant
1	0.9892828	46	36.076360
2	1.9679632	47	36.679004
3	2.9361548	48	37.275190
4	3.8939701	49	37.864986
5	4.8415203	50	38.448461
6	5.7789154	51	39.025682
7	6.7062642	52	39.596718
8	7.6236744	53	40.161634
9	8.5312525	54	40.720495
10	9.4291039	55	41.273367
11	10.317333	56	41.820313
12	11.196042	57	42.361398
13	12.065335	58	42.896684
14	12.925310	59	43.426233
15	13.776070	60	43.950107
16	14.617711	61	44.468367
17	15.450332	62	44.981072
18	16.274030	63	45.488282
19	17.088901	64	45.990056
20	17.895038	65	46.486453
21	18.692535	66	46.977530
22	19.481486	67	47.463344
23	20.261981	68	47.943951
24	21.034112	69	48.419407
25	21.797967	70	48.889768
26	22.553636	71	49.355088
27	23.301206	72	49.815421
28	24.040764	73	50.270820
29	24.772397	74	50.721339
30	25.496188	75	51.167030
31	26.212222	76	51.607944
32	26.920583	77	52.044132
33	27.621351	78	52.475646
34	28.314610	79	52.902535
35	29.000438	80	53.324849
36	29.678917	81	53.742637
37	30.350124	82	54.155948
38	31.014137	83	54.564829
39	31.671034	84	54.969328
40	32.320891	85	55.369492
41	32.963784	86	55.765367
42	33.599786	87	56.156999
43	34.228972	88	56.544435
44	34.851415	89	56.927718
45	35.467187	90	57.306893

yearly interest rate = 13.00%

term (months)	constant	term (months)	constant
91	57.682005	136	70.986159
92	58.053096	137	71.214666
93	58.420211	138	71.440725
94	58.783391	139	71.664361
95	59.142678	140	71.885601
96	59.498115	141	72.104469
97	59.849743	142	72.320992
98	60.197602	143	72.535194
99	60.541734	144	72.747100
100	60.882177	145	72.956735
101	61.218971	146	73.164124
102	61.552156	147	73.369290
103	61.881770	148	73.572257
104	62.207852	149	73.773049
105	62.530439	150	73.971689
106	62.849568	151	74.168200
107	63.165278	152	74.362606
108	63.477604	153	74.554927
109	63.786583	154	74.745188
110	64.092250	155	74.933409
111	64.394641	156	75.119613
112	64.693792	157	75.303822
113	64.989736	158	75.486056
114	65.282509	159	75.666338
115	65.572144	160	75.844687
116	65.858675	161	76.021125
117	66.142135	162	76.195671
118	66.422558	163	76.368348
119	66.699975	164	76.539173
120	66.974419	165	76.708168
121	67.245921	166	76.875352
122	67.514514	167	77.040744
123	67.780228	168	77.204363
124	68.043094	169	77.366229
125	68.303144	170	77.526360
126	68.560406	171	77.684775
127	68.814911	172	77.841492
128	69.066689	173	77.996530
129	69.315768	174	78.149906
130	69.562178	175	78.301638
131	69.805947	176	78.451744
132	70.047103	177	78.600242
133	70.285675	178	78.747148
134	70.521690	179	78.892479
135	70.755175	180	79.036253

yearly interest rate = 13.00%

term (months)	constant	term (months)	constant
181	79.178486	226	84.223093
182	79.319195	227	84.309737
183	79.458395	228	84.395453
184	79.596104	229	84.480251
185	79.732337	230	84.564139
186	79.867110	231	84.647129
187	80.000439	232	84.729229
188	80.132339	233	84.810449
189	80.262825	234	84.890798
190	80.391912	235	84.970287
191	80.519616	236	85.048924
192	80.645952	237	85.126717
193	80.770933	238	85.203678
194	80.894576	239	85.279813
195	81.016893	240	85.355132
196	81.137899	241	85.429645
197	81.257608	242	85.503358
198	81.376034	243	85.576282
199	81.493191	244	85.648424
200	81.609093	245	85.719793
201	81.723752	246	85.790397
202	81.837183	247	85.860244
203	81.949397	248	85.929343
204	82.060410	249	85.997701
205	82.170232	250	86.065327
206	82.278878	251	86.132228
207	82.386359	252	86.198412
208	82.492688	253	86.263886
209	82.597878	254	86.328659
210	82.701940	255	86.392738
211	82.804887	256	86.456130
212	82.906731	257	86.518842
213	83.007483	258	86.580883
214	83.107156	259	86.642258
215	83.205760	260	86.702976
216	83.303307	261	86.763043
217	83.399809	262	86.822466
218	83.495277	263	86.881253
219	83.589722	264	86.939409
220	83.683154	265	86.996942
221	83.775586	266	87.053859
222	83.867026	267	87.110165
223	83.957487	268	87.165868
224	84.046978	269	87.220974
225	84.135510	270	87.275490

yearly interest rate = 13.00%

term (months)	constant	term (months)	constant
271	87.329421	316	89.242212
272	87.382775	317	89.275065
273	87.435556	318	89.307567
274	87.487772	319	89.339720
275	87.539428	320	89.371528
276	87.590531	321	89.402996
277	87.641085	322	89.434126
278	87.691099	323	89.464923
279	87.740576	324	89.495389
280	87.789523	325	89.525529
281	87.837945	326	89.555346
282	87.885848	327	89.584844
283	87.933238	328	89.614025
284	87.980120	329	89.642894
285	88.026500	330	89.671453
286	88.072382	331	89.699706
287	88.117773	332	89.727657
288	88.162677	333	89.755308
289	88.207100	334	89.782662
290	88.251047	335	89.809723
291	88.294523	336	89.836495
292	88.337533	337	89.862979
293	88.380083	338	89.889180
294	88.422176	339	89.915099
295	88.463818	340	89.940741
296	88.505013	341	89.966109
297	88.545767	342	89.991204
298	88.586085	343	90.016030
299	88.625970	344	90.040590
300	88.665428	345	90.064887
301	88.704463	346	90.088924
302	88.743080	347	90.112703
303	88.781282	348	90.136227
304	88.819076	349	90.159499
305	88.856464	350	90.182522
306	88.893452	351	90.205298
307	88.930043	352	90.227830
308	88.966242	353	90.250120
309	89.002053	354	90.272172
310	89.037480	355	90.293987
311	89.072528	356	90.315568
312	89.107200	357	90.336918
313	89.141500	358	90.358040
314	89.175433	359	90.378934
315	89.209002	360	90.399605

yearly interest rate = 13.25%

term (months)	constant	term (months)	constant
1	0.9890789	46	35.916199
2	1.9673560	47	36.513034
3	2.9349493	48	37.103351
4	3.8919754	49	37.687222
5	4.8385498	50	38.264715
6	5.7747865	51	38.835902
7	6.7007985	52	39.400851
8	7.6166975	53	39.959630
9	8.5225939	54	40.512307
10	9.4185969	55	41.058948
11	10.304815	56	41.599619
12	11.181354	57	42.134385
13	12.048320	58	42.663311
14	12.905818	59	43.186460
15	13.753952	60	43.703896
16	14.592823	61	44.215682
17	15.422532	62	44.721877
18	16.243181	63	45.222545
19	17.054866	64	45.717745
20	17.857688	65	46.207537
21	18.651742	66	46.691980
22	19.437123	67	47.171132
23	20.213928	68	47.645051
24	20.982249	69	48.113794
25	21.742179	70	48.577419
26	22.493810	71	49.035980
27	23.237232	72	49.489533
28	23.972535	73	49.938133
29	24.699808	74	50.381833
30	25.419139	75	50.820688
31	26.130613	76	51.254750
32	26.834318	77	51.684072
33	27.530337	78	52.108705
34	28.218755	79	52.528701
35	28.899654	80	52.944109
36	29.573118	81	53.354982
37	30.239226	82	53.761366
38	30.898060	83	54.163313
39	31.549699	84	54.560870
40	32.194221	85	54.954086
41	32.831704	86	55.343007
42	33.462226	87	55.727680
43	34.085861	88	56.108153
44	34.702685	89	56.484470
45	35.312774	90	56.856677

yearly interest rate = 13.25%

term (months)	constant	term (months)	constant
91	57.224820	136	70.224957
92	57.588942	137	70.447103
93	57.949088	138	70.666824
94	58.305300	139	70.884145
95	58.657622	140	71.099092
96	59.006096	141	71.311692
97	59.350765	142	71.521971
98	59.691669	143	71.729952
99	60.028851	144	71.935663
100	60.362350	145	72.139127
101	60.692207	146	72.340368
102	61.018461	147	72.539412
103	61.341153	148	72.736282
104	61.660320	149	72.931003
105	61.976002	150	73.123596
106	62.288236	151	73.314087
107	62.597060	152	73.502497
108	62.902511	153	73.688849
109	63.204627	154	73.873166
110	63.503443	155	74.055470
111	63.798996	156	74.235783
112	64.091321	157	74.414127
113	64.380453	158	74.590524
114	64.666428	159	74.764994
115	64.949280	160	74.937558
116	65.229043	161	75.108238
117	65.505750	162	75.277054
118	65.779435	163	75.444026
119	66.050132	164	75.609175
120	66.317872	165	75.772520
121	66.582688	166	75.934081
122	66.844612	167	76.093878
123	67.103676	168	76.251929
124	67.359910	169	76.408255
125	67.613346	170	76.562873
126	67.864014	171	76.715803
127	68.111945	172	76.867062
128	68.357168	173	77.016670
129	68.599713	174	77.164644
130	68.839609	175	77.311001
131	69.076885	176	77.455761
132	69.311569	177	77.598939
133	69.543691	178	77.740554
134	69.773278	179	77.880622
135	70.000357	180	78.019160

yearly interest rate = 13.25%

term (months)	constant	term (months)	constant
181	78.156186	226	82.994934
182	78.291715	227	83.077619
183	78.425764	228	83.159401
184	78.558349	229	83.240289
185	78.689485	230	83.320294
186	78.819190	231	83.399426
187	78.947478	232	83.477693
188	79.074366	233	83.555105
189	79.199867	234	83.631672
190	79.323998	235	83.707403
191	79.446773	236	83.782307
192	79.568208	237	83.856392
193	79.688316	238	83.929669
194	79.807112	239	84.002145
195	79.924611	240	84.073830
196	80.040827	241	84.144732
197	80.155774	242	84.214859
198	80.269465	243	84.284221
199	80.381915	244	84.352825
200	80.493136	245	84.420680
201	80.603143	246	84.487794
202	80.711949	247	84.554175
203	80.819566	248	84.619831
204	80.926008	249	84.684770
205	81.031288	250	84.749000
206	81.135418	251	84.812528
207	81.238410	252	84.875363
208	81.340278	253	84.937511
209	81.441033	254	84.998981
210	81.540688	255	85.059779
211	81.639255	256	85.119913
212	81.736745	257	85.179391
213	81.833170	258	85.238219
214	81.928543	259	85.296404
215	82.022873	260	85.353955
216	82.116174	261	85.410876
217	82.208456	262	85.467176
218	82.299729	263	85.522861
219	82.390006	264	85.577938
220	82.479297	265	85.632414
221	82.567613	266	85.686294
222	82.654965	267	85.739586
223	82.741362	268	85.792296
224	82.826816	269	85.844431
225	82.911337	270	85.895996

yearly interest rate = 13.25%

term (months)	constant	term (months)	constant
271	85.946998	316	87.748016
272	85.997442	317	87.778792
273	86.047336	318	87.809232
274	86.096686	319	87.839339
275	86.145496	320	87.869118
276	86.193773	321	87.898571
277	86.241523	322	87.927702
278	86.288751	323	87.956516
279	86.335464	324	87.985015
280	86.381666	325	88.013202
281	86.427364	326	88.041082
282	86.472563	327	88.068657
283	86.517268	328	88.095931
284	86.561485	329	88.122908
285	86.605219	330	88.149589
286	86.648475	331	88.175979
287	86.691259	332	88.202081
288	86.733576	333	88.227898
289	86.775431	334	88.253433
290	86.816828	335	88.278689
291	86.857774	336	88.303670
292	86.898272	337	88.328377
293	86.938328	338	88.352815
294	86.977946	339	88.376986
295	87.017132	340	88.400893
296	87.055890	341	88.424538
297	87.094225	342	88.447926
298	87.132141	343	88.471058
299	87.169642	344	88.493937
300	87.206735	345	88.516567
301	87.243422	346	88.538949
302	87.279708	347	88.561087
303	87.315599	348	88.582984
304	87.351097	349	88.604641
305	87.386208	350	88.626061
306	87.420935	351	88.647248
307	87.455283	352	88.668203
308	87.489256	353	88.688929
309	87.522857	354	88.709430
310	87.556092	355	88.729706
311	87.588964	356	88.749760
312	87.621477	357	88.769596
313	87.653635	358	88.789215
314	87.685441	359	88.808620
315	87.716900	360	88.827813

yearly interest rate = 13.50%

term (months)	constant	term (months)	constant
1	0.9888752	46	35.757045
2	1.9667492	47	36.348129
3	2.9337446	48	36.932637
4	3.8899823	49	37.510642
5	4.8355820	50	38.082217
6	5.7706621	51	38.647433
7	6.6953395	52	39.206362
8	7.6097300	53	39.759072
9	8.5139481	54	40.305634
10	9.4081069	55	40.846115
11	10.292318	56	41.380584
12	11.166693	57	41.909106
13	12.031340	58	42.431749
14	12.886369	59	42.948578
15	13.731885	60	43.459656
16	14.567995	61	43.965050
17	15.394804	62	44.464820
18	16.212414	63	44.959031
19	17.020929	64	45.447744
20	17.820448	65	45.931020
21	18.611074	66	46.408920
22	19.392904	67	46.881503
23	20.166036	68	47.348829
24	20.930567	69	47.810955
25	21.686593	70	48.267941
26	22.434208	71	48.719843
27	23.173506	72	49.166717
28	23.904579	73	49.608620
29	24.627520	74	50.045607
30	25.342418	75	50.477733
31	26.049362	76	50.905051
32	26.748442	77	51.327615
33	27.439745	78	51.745479
34	28.123357	79	52.158693
35	28.799365	80	52.567311
36	29.467851	81	52.971383
37	30.128901	82	53.370960
38	30.782597	83	53.766091
39	31.429020	84	54.156827
40	32.068253	85	54.543216
41	32.700373	86	54.925306
42	33.325462	87	55.303146
43	33.943597	88	55.676782
44	34.554854	89	56.046261
45	35.159312	90	56.411630

yearly interest rate = 13.50%

term (months)	constant	term (months)	constant
91	56.772935	136	69.476152
92	57.130220	137	69.692116
93	57.483530	138	69.905677
94	57.832910	139	70.116862
95	58.178403	140	70.325698
96	58.520052	141	70.532211
97	58.857901	142	70.736426
98	59.191991	143	70.938369
99	59.522365	144	71.138066
100	59.849063	145	71.335541
101	60.172126	146	71.530819
102	60.491596	147	71.723925
103	60.807511	148	71.914883
104	61.119912	149	72.103716
105	61.428838	150	72.290448
106	61.734327	151	72.475104
107	62.036417	152	72.657704
108	62.335146	153	72.838274
109	62.630553	154	73.016834
110	62.922673	155	73.193409
111	63.211543	156	73.368018
112	63.497199	157	73.540686
113	63.779678	158	73.711432
114	64.059014	159	73.880279
115	64.335243	160	74.047247
116	64.608398	161	74.212358
117	64.878515	162	74.375632
118	65.145627	163	74.537090
119	65.409767	164	74.696752
120	65.670968	165	74.854637
121	65.929264	166	75.010766
122	66.184686	167	75.165158
123	66.437267	168	75.317832
124	66.687038	169	75.468808
125	66.934030	170	75.618105
126	67.178274	171	75.765740
127	67.419802	172	75.911733
128	67.658642	173	76.056102
129	67.894825	174	76.198865
130	68.128381	175	76.340039
131	68.359338	176	76.479643
132	68.587726	177	76.617694
133	68.813574	178	76.754209
134	69.036908	179	76.889206
135	69.257759	180	77.022700

yearly interest rate = 13.50%

term (months)	constant	term (months)	constant
181	77.154710	226	81.796074
182	77.285251	227	81.874980
183	77.414339	228	81.953009
184	77.541992	229	82.030169
185	77.668225	230	82.106471
186	77.793053	231	82.181925
187	77.916492	232	82.256539
188	78.038558	233	82.330323
189	78.159267	234	82.403286
190	78.278632	235	82.475437
191	78.396669	236	82.546786
192	78.513394	237	82.617341
193	78.628820	238	82.687111
194	78.742961	239	82.756104
195	78.855833	240	82.824331
196	78.967449	241	82.891798
197	79.077824	242	82.958515
198	79.186970	243	83.024489
199	79.294903	244	83.089730
200	79.401634	245	83.154244
201	79.507179	246	83.218042
202	79.611549	247	83.281129
203	79.714758	248	83.343514
204	79.816818	249	83.405206
205	79.917744	250	83.466211
206	80.017546	251	83.526537
207	80.116239	252	83.586193
208	80.213833	253	83.645184
209	80.310342	254	83.703520
210	80.405777	255	83.761206
211	80.500150	256	83.818251
212	80.593474	257	83.874661
213	80.685759	258	83.930443
214	80.777017	259	83.985605
215	80.867261	260	84.040154
216	80.956500	261	84.094095
217	81.044747	262	84.147436
218	81.132011	263	84.200184
219	81.218306	264	84.252345
220	81.303640	265	84.303926
221	81.388024	266	84.354933
222	81.471470	267	84.405373
223	81.553988	268	84.455251
224	81.635588	269	84.504575
225	81.716279	270	84.553350

yearly interest rate = 13.50%

term (months)	constant	term (months)	constant
271	84.601582	316	86.297393
272	84.649277	317	86.326223
273	84.696442	318	86.354732
274	84.743083	319	86.382924
275	84.789204	320	86.410803
276	84.834813	321	86.438371
277	84.879914	322	86.465633
278	84.924513	323	86.492591
279	84.968616	324	86.519250
280	85.012228	325	86.545611
281	85.055356	326	86.571680
282	85.098003	327	86.597459
283	85.140176	328	86.622950
284	85.181880	329	86.648159
285	85.223120	330	86.673086
286	85.263901	331	86.697737
287	85.304228	332	86.722113
288	85.344107	333	86.746218
289	85.383542	334	86.770055
290	85.422539	335	86.793627
291	85.461101	336	86.816936
292	85.499235	337	86.839986
293	85.536944	338	86.862780
294	85.574234	339	86.885320
295	85.611109	340	86.907610
296	85.647574	341	86.929651
297	85.683633	342	86.951447
298	85.719291	343	86.973001
299	85.754552	344	86.994315
300	85.789421	345	87.015392
301	85.823902	346	87.036234
302	85.858000	347	87.056845
303	85.891718	348	87.077226
304	85.925061	349	87.097380
305	85.958033	350	87.117311
306	85.990639	351	87.137019
307	86.022881	352	87.156508
308	86.054765	353	87.175781
309	86.086294	354	87.194839
310	86.117473	355	87.213685
311	86.148304	356	87.232321
312	86.178793	357	87.250750
313	86.208942	358	87.268974
314	86.238756	359	87.286996
315	86.268239	360	87.304817

yearly interest rate = 13.75%

term (months)	constant	term (months)	constant
1	0.9886715	46	35.598892
2	1.9661427	47	36.184281
3	2.9325407	48	36.763038
4	3.8879908	49	37.335238
5	4.8326171	50	37.900956
6	5.7665421	51	38.460266
7	6.6898872	52	39.013239
8	7.6027721	53	39.559948
9	8.5053153	54	40.100464
10	9.3976341	55	40.634856
11	10.279844	56	41.163194
12	11.152060	57	41.685547
13	12.014395	58	42.201983
14	12.866961	59	42.712568
15	13.709869	60	43.217369
16	14.543228	61	43.716451
17	15.367146	62	44.209880
18	16.181730	63	44.697719
19	16.987087	64	45.180031
20	17.783319	65	45.656879
21	18.570532	66	46.128325
22	19.348827	67	46.594431
23	20.118305	68	47.055256
24	20.879065	69	47.510861
25	21.631208	70	47.961304
26	22.374829	71	48.406645
27	23.110027	72	48.846940
28	23.836896	73	49.282248
29	24.555530	74	49.712624
30	25.266024	75	50.138124
31	25.968469	76	50.558805
32	26.662956	77	50.974719
33	27.349575	78	51.385922
34	28.028416	79	51.792467
35	28.699567	80	52.194406
36	29.363114	81	52.591792
37	30.019145	82	52.984676
38	30.667744	83	53.373109
39	31.308995	84	53.757142
40	31.942982	85	54.136824
41	32.569786	86	54.512205
42	33.189490	87	54.883333
43	33.802173	88	55.250258
44	34.407916	89	55.613025
45	35.006796	90	55.971683

yearly interest rate = 13.75%

term (months)	constant	term (months)	constant
91	56.326277	136	68.739503
92	56.676855	137	68.949457
93	57.023461	138	69.157033
94	57.366141	139	69.362257
95	57.704939	140	69.565156
96	58.039898	141	69.765757
97	58.371063	142	69.964085
98	58.698476	143	70.160167
99	59.022180	144	70.354027
100	59.342218	145	70.545691
101	59.658629	146	70.735184
102	59.971456	147	70.922530
103	60.280739	148	71.107753
104	60.586519	149	71.290879
105	60.888834	150	71.471929
106	61.187725	151	71.650929
107	61.483230	152	71.827901
108	61.775387	153	72.002868
109	62.064234	154	72.175853
110	62.349809	155	72.346879
111	62.632149	156	72.515966
112	62.911290	157	72.683139
113	63.187270	158	72.848417
114	63.460122	159	73.011824
115	63.729884	160	73.173379
116	63.996590	161	73.333103
117	64.260274	162	73.491019
118	64.520971	163	73.647145
119	64.778715	164	73.801503
120	65.033539	165	73.954112
121	65.285477	166	74.104993
122	65.534560	167	74.254164
123	65.780821	168	74.401645
124	66.024293	169	74.547455
125	66.265006	170	74.691614
126	66.502993	171	74.834139
127	66.738283	172	74.975050
128	66.970908	173	75.114365
129	67.200898	174	75.252101
130	67.428282	175	75.388277
131	67.653091	176	75.522910
132	67.875352	177	75.656018
133	68.095096	178	75.787619
134	68.312350	179	75.917728
135	68.527143	180	76.046363

yearly interest rate = 13.75%

term (months)	constant	term (months)	constant
181	76.173542	226	80.625642
182	76.299279	227	80.700944
183	76.423592	228	80.775392
184	76.546497	229	80.848997
185	76.668009	230	80.921769
186	76.788145	231	80.993716
187	76.906920	232	81.064848
188	77.024349	233	81.135174
189	77.140448	234	81.204703
190	77.255232	235	81.273445
191	77.368716	236	81.341408
192	77.480913	237	81.408601
193	77.591840	238	81.475033
194	77.701510	239	81.540713
195	77.809938	240	81.605648
196	77.917138	241	81.669847
197	78.023123	242	81.733320
198	78.127907	243	81.796073
199	78.231504	244	81.858116
200	78.333928	245	81.919455
201	78.435192	246	81.980100
202	78.535308	247	82.040058
203	78.634290	248	82.099336
204	78.732151	249	82.157943
205	78.828903	250	82.215886
206	78.924559	251	82.273172
207	79.019131	252	82.329810
208	79.112633	253	82.385806
209	79.205074	254	82.441168
210	79.296469	255	82.495902
211	79.386828	256	82.550016
212	79.476164	257	82.603518
213	79.564487	258	82.656413
214	79.651810	259	82.708709
215	79.738144	260	82.760413
216	79.823500	261	82.811531
217	79.907889	262	82.862069
218	79.991322	263	82.912036
219	80.073809	264	82.961436
220	80.155362	265	83.010276
221	80.235992	266	83.058564
222	80.315707	267	83.106304
223	80.394520	268	83.153503
224	80.472440	269	83.200168
225	80.549477	270	83.246304

yearly interest rate = 13.75%

term (months)	constant	term (months)	constant
271	83.291918	316	84.888698
272	83.337014	317	84.915706
273	83.381600	318	84.942407
274	83.425681	319	84.968806
275	83.469262	320	84.994906
276	83.512350	321	85.020711
277	83.554950	322	85.046223
278	83.597067	323	85.071446
279	83.638706	324	85.096383
280	83.679874	325	85.121038
281	83.720576	326	85.145413
282	83.760817	327	85.169513
283	83.800602	328	85.193339
284	83.839936	329	85.216895
285	83.878824	330	85.240185
286	83.917272	331	85.263211
287	83.955284	332	85.285976
288	83.992866	333	85.308483
289	84.030022	334	85.330735
290	84.066757	335	85.352734
291	84.103076	336	85.374485
292	84.138984	337	85.395989
293	84.174484	338	85.417250
294	84.209583	339	85.438270
295	84.244284	340	85.459052
296	84.278592	341	85.479598
297	84.312511	342	85.499911
298	84.346046	343	85.519995
299	84.379201	344	85.539851
300	84.411980	345	85.559482
301	84.444388	346	85.578890
302	84.476429	347	85.598079
303	84.508107	348	85.617050
304	84.539426	349	85.635807
305	84.570390	350	85.654350
306	84.601004	351	85.672684
307	84.631270	352	85.690810
308	84.661194	353	85.708731
309	84.690779	354	85.726449
310	84.720029	355	85.743966
311	84.748947	356	85.761285
312	84.777538	357	85.778407
313	84.805805	358	85.795336
314	84.833751	359	85.812072
315	84.861381	360	85.828619

yearly interest rate = 14.00%

term (months)	constant	term (months)	constant
1	0.9884679	46	35.441733
2	1.9655366	47	36.021482
3	2.9313377	48	36.594546
4	3.8860010	49	37.161001
5	4.8296550	50	37.720924
6	5.7624267	51	38.274389
7	6.6844416	52	38.821472
8	7.5958236	53	39.362246
9	8.4966955	54	39.896783
10	9.3871785	55	40.425156
11	10.267392	56	40.947436
12	11.137455	57	41.463693
13	11.997485	58	41.973997
14	12.847596	59	42.478415
15	13.687904	60	42.977017
16	14.518521	61	43.469868
17	15.339560	62	43.957036
18	16.151130	63	44.438586
19	16.953341	64	44.914582
20	17.746301	65	45.385090
21	18.530116	66	45.850171
22	19.304892	67	46.309889
23	20.070734	68	46.764305
24	20.827743	69	47.213482
25	21.576023	70	47.657478
26	22.315673	71	48.096353
27	23.046794	72	48.530168
28	23.769484	73	48.958980
29	24.483839	74	49.382847
30	25.189956	75	49.801826
31	25.887930	76	50.215973
32	26.577855	77	50.625344
33	27.259824	78	51.029994
34	27.933928	79	51.429977
35	28.600258	80	51.825348
36	29.258904	81	52.216160
37	29.909955	82	52.602464
38	30.553498	83	52.984314
39	31.189619	84	53.361760
40	31.818404	85	53.734853
41	32.439938	86	54.103644
42	33.054304	87	54.468182
43	33.661586	88	54.828516
44	34.261864	89	55.184695
45	34.855220	90	55.536766

yearly interest rate = 14.00%

term (months)	constant	term (months)	constant
91	55.884777	136	68.014774
92	56.228774	137	68.218887
93	56.568805	138	68.420647
94	56.904914	139	68.620079
95	57.237148	140	68.817212
96	57.565549	141	69.012071
97	57.890164	142	69.204683
98	58.211035	143	69.395074
99	58.528206	144	69.583269
100	58.841720	145	69.769294
101	59.151617	146	69.953173
102	59.457941	147	70.134932
103	59.760733	148	70.314595
104	60.060033	149	70.492187
105	60.355881	150	70.667730
106	60.648317	151	70.841249
107	60.937381	152	71.012766
108	61.223111	153	71.182306
109	61.505546	154	71.349891
110	61.784725	155	71.515543
111	62.060683	156	71.679284
112	62.333460	157	71.841138
113	62.603090	158	72.001125
114	62.869611	159	72.159267
115	63.133059	160	72.315585
116	63.393469	161	72.470100
117	63.650875	162	72.622834
118	63.905313	163	72.773806
119	64.156817	164	72.923037
120	64.405420	165	73.070548
121	64.651157	166	73.216357
122	64.894060	167	73.360484
123	65.134161	168	73.502950
124	65.371494	169	73.643773
125	65.606089	170	73.782971
126	65.837979	171	73.920565
127	66.067195	172	74.056571
128	66.293768	173	74.191010
129	66.517728	174	74.323897
130	66.739105	175	74.455253
131	66.957929	176	74.585093
132	67.174230	177	74.713437
133	67.388036	178	74.840300
134	67.599377	179	74.965700
135	67.808280	180	75.089654

yearly interest rate = 14.00%

term (months)	constant	term (months)	constant
181	75.212179	226	79.482800
182	75.333290	227	79.554662
183	75.453005	228	79.625696
184	75.571340	229	79.695910
185	75.688309	230	79.765315
186	75.803930	231	79.833919
187	75.918218	232	79.901732
188	76.031187	233	79.968763
189	76.142854	234	80.035021
190	76.253233	235	80.100515
191	76.362339	236	80.165254
192	76.470187	237	80.229246
193	76.576791	238	80.292500
194	76.682165	239	80.355025
195	76.786325	240	80.416829
196	76.889283	241	80.477920
197	76.991054	242	80.538306
198	77.091652	243	80.597996
199	77.191089	244	80.656998
200	77.289380	245	80.715319
201	77.386537	246	80.772968
202	77.482573	247	80.829952
203	77.577502	248	80.886278
204	77.671337	249	80.941956
205	77.764089	250	80.996991
206	77.855772	251	81.051391
207	77.946397	252	81.105164
208	78.035977	253	81.158317
209	78.124525	254	81.210857
210	78.212051	255	81.262791
211	78.298567	256	81.314127
212	78.384086	257	81.364870
213	78.468619	258	81.415028
214	78.552177	259	81.464607
215	78.634772	260	81.513615
216	78.716413	261	81.562058
217	78.797114	262	81.609942
218	78.876883	263	81.657274
219	78.955733	264	81.704060
220	79.033674	265	81.750306
221	79.110715	266	81.796019
222	79.186869	267	81.841205
223	79.262143	268	81.885870
224	79.336550	269	81.930020
225	79.410099	270	81.973660

yearly interest rate = 14.00%

term (months)	constant	term (months)	constant
271	82.016798	316	83.520360
272	82.059438	317	83.545660
273	82.101586	318	83.570669
274	82.143248	319	83.595390
275	82.184430	320	83.619825
276	82.225136	321	83.643979
277	82.265374	322	83.667854
278	82.305147	323	83.691454
279	82.344461	324	83.714781
280	82.383323	325	83.737840
281	82.421736	326	83.760632
282	82.459706	327	83.783162
283	82.497238	328	83.805432
284	82.534337	329	83.827445
285	82.571009	330	83.849204
286	82.607258	331	83.870713
287	82.643088	332	83.891973
288	82.678506	333	83.912988
289	82.713515	334	83.933761
290	82.748120	335	83.954294
291	82.782326	336	83.974591
292	82.816138	337	83.994653
293	82.849560	338	84.014484
294	82.882596	339	84.034086
295	82.915252	340	84.053463
296	82.947530	341	84.072615
297	82.979437	342	84.091547
298	83.010976	343	84.110261
299	83.042150	344	84.128759
300	83.072966	345	84.147043
301	83.103426	346	84.165117
302	83.133535	347	84.182982
303	83.163296	348	84.200641
304	83.192715	349	84.218097
305	83.221794	350	84.235351
306	83.250537	351	84.252406
307	83.278950	352	84.269265
308	83.307034	353	84.285929
309	83.334795	354	84.302401
310	83.362236	355	84.318683
311	83.389360	356	84.334777
312	83.416171	357	84.350686
313	83.442673	358	84.366411
314	83.468870	359	84.381955
315	83.494764	360	84.397320

yearly interest rate = 14.25%

term (months)	constant	term (months)	constant
1	0.9882644	46	35.285559
2	1.9649308	47	35.859725
3	2.9301355	48	36.427153
4	3.8840128	49	36.987921
5	4.8266958	50	37.542109
6	5.7583158	51	38.089792
7	6.6790026	52	38.631049
8	7.5888846	53	39.165953
9	8.4880886	54	39.694580
10	9.3767398	55	40.217003
11	10.254962	56	40.733295
12	11.122878	57	41.243528
13	11.980608	58	41.747773
14	12.828272	59	42.246101
15	13.665989	60	42.738580
16	14.493874	61	43.225280
17	15.312044	62	43.706268
18	16.120611	63	44.181611
19	16.919690	64	44.651376
20	17.709391	65	45.115628
21	18.489824	66	45.574432
22	19.261099	67	46.027851
23	20.023322	68	46.475949
24	20.776600	69	46.918789
25	21.521037	70	47.356431
26	22.256739	71	47.788937
27	22.983806	72	48.216368
28	23.702341	73	48.638782
29	24.412443	74	49.056240
30	25.114212	75	49.468798
31	25.807745	76	49.876514
32	26.493139	77	50.279446
33	27.170489	78	50.677649
34	27.839890	79	51.071178
35	28.501436	80	51.460090
36	29.155218	81	51.844437
37	29.801327	82	52.224274
38	30.439854	83	52.599653
39	31.070887	84	52.970627
40	31.694514	85	53.337247
41	32.310823	86	53.699565
42	32.919900	87	54.057630
43	33.521828	88	54.411494
44	34.116692	89	54.761204
45	34.704575	90	55.106811

yearly interest rate = 14.25%

term (months)	constant	term (months)	constant
91	55.448362	136	67.301734
92	55.785904	137	67.500169
93	56.119485	138	67.696276
94	56.449152	139	67.890081
95	56.774949	140	68.081612
96	57.096923	141	68.270895
97	57.415119	142	68.457957
98	57.729580	143	68.642824
99	58.040351	144	68.825521
100	58.347474	145	69.006073
101	58.650994	146	69.184507
102	58.950951	147	69.360847
103	59.247389	148	69.535118
104	59.540347	149	69.707343
105	59.829867	150	69.877547
106	60.115990	151	70.045754
107	60.398755	152	70.211987
108	60.678201	153	70.376268
109	60.954368	154	70.538622
110	61.227294	155	70.699071
111	61.497017	156	70.857636
112	61.763574	157	71.014341
113	62.027004	158	71.169207
114	62.287341	159	71.322255
115	62.544624	160	71.473507
116	62.798887	161	71.622984
117	63.050167	162	71.770707
118	63.298497	163	71.916696
119	63.543913	164	72.060972
120	63.786449	165	72.203555
121	64.026138	166	72.344464
122	64.263015	167	72.483720
123	64.497112	168	72.621342
124	64.728461	169	72.757348
125	64.957096	170	72.891759
126	65.183047	171	73.024592
127	65.406347	172	73.155866
128	65.627026	173	73.285599
129	65.845115	174	73.413810
130	66.060645	175	73.540517
131	66.273646	176	73.665736
132	66.484146	177	73.789486
133	66.692177	178	73.911783
134	66.897766	179	74.032646
135	67.100942	180	74.152090

yearly interest rate = 14.25%

term (months)	constant	term (months)	constant
181	74.270132	226	78.366736
182	74.386789	227	78.435316
183	74.502077	228	78.503092
184	74.616011	229	78.570073
185	74.728609	230	78.636267
186	74.839886	231	78.701684
187	74.949856	232	78.766334
188	75.058536	233	78.830225
189	75.165940	234	78.893367
190	75.272084	235	78.955767
191	75.376983	236	79.017435
192	75.480650	237	79.078379
193	75.583101	238	79.138608
194	75.684349	239	79.198130
195	75.784409	240	79.256954
196	75.883295	241	79.315087
197	75.981020	242	79.372538
198	76.077599	243	79.429315
199	76.173044	244	79.485426
200	76.267369	245	79.540878
201	76.360587	246	79.595679
202	76.452711	247	79.649837
203	76.543754	248	79.703360
204	76.633729	249	79.756254
205	76.722647	250	79.808528
206	76.810522	251	79.860188
207	76.897366	252	79.911242
208	76.983191	253	79.961697
209	77.068008	254	80.011560
210	77.151830	255	80.060838
211	77.234668	256	80.109537
212	77.316534	257	80.157665
213	77.397440	258	80.205227
214	77.477396	259	80.252232
215	77.556413	260	80.298685
216	77.634504	261	80.344593
217	77.711677	262	80.389962
218	77.787946	263	80.434799
219	77.863319	264	80.479110
220	77.937807	265	80.522900
221	78.011422	266	80.566177
222	78.084172	267	80.608946
223	78.156069	268	80.651213
224	78.227122	269	80.692983
225	78.297341	270	80.734264

yearly interest rate = 14.25%

term (months)	constant	term (months)	constant
271	80.775060	316	82.190874
272	80.815378	317	82.214576
273	80.855222	318	82.237999
274	80.894598	319	82.261148
275	80.933513	320	82.284025
276	80.971971	321	82.306634
277	81.009977	322	82.328977
278	81.047538	323	82.351059
279	81.084658	324	82.372881
280	81.121342	325	82.394447
281	81.157595	326	82.415759
282	81.193423	327	82.436822
283	81.228831	328	82.457638
284	81.263823	329	82.478209
285	81.298404	330	82.498539
286	81.332580	331	82.518630
287	81.366355	332	82.538486
288	81.399733	333	82.558108
289	81.432719	334	82.577500
290	81.465319	335	82.596665
291	81.497535	336	82.615605
292	81.529374	337	82.634322
293	81.560839	338	82.652820
294	81.591935	339	82.671100
295	81.622666	340	82.689167
296	81.653036	341	82.707021
297	81.683050	342	82.724665
298	81.712711	343	82.742103
299	81.742025	344	82.759336
300	81.770994	345	82.776366
301	81.799624	346	82.793197
302	81.827917	347	82.809830
303	81.855879	348	82.826269
304	81.883512	349	82.842514
305	81.910821	350	82.858568
306	81.937809	351	82.874434
307	81.964481	352	82.890114
308	81.990840	353	82.905610
309	82.016889	354	82.920924
310	82.042633	355	82.936058
311	82.068075	356	82.951015
312	82.093218	357	82.965796
313	82.118066	358	82.980404
314	82.142622	359	82.994840
315	82.166890	360	83.009107

yearly interest rate = 14.50%

term (months)	constant	term (months)	constant
1	0.9880609	46	35.130364
2	1.9643253	47	35.699001
3	2.9289340	48	36.260850
4	3.8820262	49	36.815990
5	4.8237394	50	37.364502
6	5.7542093	51	37.906465
7	6.6735704	52	38.441958
8	7.5819551	53	38.971058
9	8.4794945	54	39.493841
10	9.3663182	55	40.010382
11	10.242554	56	40.520756
12	11.108328	57	41.025037
13	11.963766	58	41.523297
14	12.808991	59	42.015609
15	13.644124	60	42.502042
16	14.469287	61	42.982668
17	15.284598	62	43.457556
18	16.090175	63	43.926774
19	16.886134	64	44.390391
20	17.672591	65	44.848472
21	18.449657	66	45.301083
22	19.217447	67	45.748292
23	19.976069	68	46.190160
24	20.725634	69	46.626754
25	21.466250	70	47.058135
26	22.198024	71	47.484365
27	22.921061	72	47.905507
28	23.635466	73	48.321621
29	24.341342	74	48.732767
30	25.038790	75	49.139004
31	25.727911	76	49.540391
32	26.408804	77	49.936985
33	27.081569	78	50.328845
34	27.746301	79	50.716026
35	28.403097	80	51.098585
36	29.052051	81	51.476577
37	29.693258	82	51.850055
38	30.326809	83	52.219075
39	30.952796	84	52.583688
40	31.571309	85	52.943949
41	32.182438	86	53.299908
42	32.786271	87	53.651618
43	33.382894	88	53.999129
44	33.972394	89	54.342490
45	34.554856	90	54.681752

yearly interest rate = 14.50%

term (months)	constant	term (months)	constant
91	55.016964	136	66.600156
92	55.348174	137	66.793073
93	55.675429	138	66.983686
94	55.998777	139	67.172024
95	56.318265	140	67.358114
96	56.633938	141	67.541982
97	56.945842	142	67.723654
98	57.254023	143	67.903158
99	57.558524	144	68.080518
100	57.859390	145	68.255761
101	58.156663	146	68.428912
102	58.450388	147	68.599995
103	58.740605	148	68.769036
104	59.027358	149	68.936058
105	59.310687	150	69.101087
106	59.590634	151	69.264145
107	59.867238	152	69.425257
108	60.140540	153	69.584445
109	60.410579	154	69.741732
110	60.677394	155	69.897142
111	60.941023	156	70.050696
112	61.201505	157	70.202417
113	61.458877	158	70.352326
114	61.713176	159	70.500446
115	61.964439	160	70.646797
116	62.212702	161	70.791401
117	62.458001	162	70.934278
118	62.700372	163	71.075450
119	62.939848	164	71.214936
120	63.176466	165	71.352757
121	63.410259	166	71.488932
122	63.641260	167	71.623482
123	63.869504	168	71.756425
124	64.095022	169	71.887781
125	64.317848	170	72.017569
126	64.538014	171	72.145807
127	64.755551	172	72.272514
128	64.970491	173	72.397708
129	65.182865	174	72.521408
130	65.392703	175	72.643631
131	65.600036	176	72.764394
132	65.804893	177	72.883716
133	66.007305	178	73.001613
134	66.207300	179	73.118103
135	66.404907	180	73.233202

yearly interest rate = 14.50%

term (months)	constant	term (months)	constant
181	73.346926	226	77.276665
182	73.459293	227	77.342114
183	73.570319	228	77.406782
184	73.680018	229	77.470678
185	73.788408	230	77.533812
186	73.895504	231	77.596191
187	74.001322	232	77.657825
188	74.105876	233	77.718724
189	74.209181	234	77.778896
190	74.311254	235	77.838349
191	74.412107	236	77.897093
192	74.511757	237	77.955135
193	74.610217	238	78.012484
194	74.707501	239	78.069148
195	74.803624	240	78.125136
196	74.898599	241	78.180456
197	74.992441	242	78.235115
198	75.085162	243	78.289121
199	75.176776	244	78.342483
200	75.267296	245	78.395208
201	75.356735	246	78.447303
202	75.445107	247	78.498776
203	75.532424	248	78.549634
204	75.618698	249	78.599886
205	75.703942	250	78.649537
206	75.788168	251	78.698596
207	75.871389	252	78.747069
208	75.953616	253	78.794963
209	76.034861	254	78.842285
210	76.115137	255	78.889043
211	76.194454	256	78.935242
212	76.272824	257	78.980889
213	76.350258	258	79.025992
214	76.426768	259	79.070556
215	76.502364	260	79.114588
216	76.577058	261	79.158095
217	76.650860	262	79.201081
218	76.723781	263	79.243555
219	76.795832	264	79.285522
220	76.867022	265	79.326987
221	76.937362	266	79.367958
222	77.006863	267	79.408439
223	77.075533	268	79.448437
224	77.143384	269	79.487958
225	77.210425	270	79.527006

yearly interest rate = 14.50%

term (months)	constant	term (months)	constant
271	79.565589	316	80.898801
272	79.603711	317	80.921005
273	79.641377	318	80.942944
274	79.678594	319	80.964622
275	79.715367	320	80.986041
276	79.751701	321	81.007204
277	79.787601	322	81.028114
278	79.823072	323	81.048775
279	79.858119	324	81.069189
280	79.892749	325	81.089359
281	79.926965	326	81.109288
282	79.960772	327	81.128980
283	79.994176	328	81.148436
284	80.027181	329	81.167660
285	80.059791	330	81.186655
286	80.092013	331	81.205423
287	80.123850	332	81.223966
288	80.155306	333	81.242289
289	80.186388	334	81.260392
290	80.217098	335	81.278280
291	80.247441	336	81.295954
292	80.277422	337	81.313416
293	80.307045	338	81.330671
294	80.336315	339	81.347719
295	80.365235	340	81.364564
296	80.393810	341	81.381208
297	80.422043	342	81.397653
298	80.449940	343	81.413902
299	80.477504	344	81.429956
300	80.504738	345	81.445819
301	80.531647	346	81.461493
302	80.558235	347	81.476979
303	80.584506	348	81.492281
304	80.610463	349	81.507400
305	80.636110	350	81.522338
306	80.661450	351	81.537098
307	80.686489	352	81.551682
308	80.711228	353	81.566092
309	80.735672	354	81.580330
310	80.759824	355	81.594397
311	80.783688	356	81.608297
312	80.807267	357	81.622031
313	80.830564	358	81.635601
314	80.853583	359	81.649009
315	80.876328	360	81.662256

yearly interest rate = 14.75%

term (months)	constant	term (months)	constant
1	0.9878576	46	34.976141
2	1.9637202	47	35.539304
3	2.9277335	48	36.095629
4	3.8800413	49	36.645198
5	4.8207858	50	37.188094
6	5.7501074	51	37.724399
7	6.6681448	52	38.254191
8	7.5750350	53	38.777550
9	8.4709134	54	39.294555
10	9.3559136	55	39.805281
11	10.230168	56	40.309807
12	11.093806	57	40.808206
13	11.946958	58	41.300553
14	12.789751	59	41.786922
15	13.622310	60	42.267386
16	14.444760	61	42.742015
17	15.257223	62	43.210881
18	16.059821	63	43.674054
19	16.852674	64	44.131603
20	17.635899	65	44.583597
21	18.409614	66	45.030102
22	19.173935	67	45.471185
23	19.928975	68	45.906913
24	20.674846	69	46.337349
25	21.411661	70	46.762559
26	22.139529	71	47.182607
27	22.858560	72	47.597553
28	23.568859	73	48.007462
29	24.270534	74	48.412393
30	24.963688	75	48.812407
31	25.648427	76	49.207564
32	26.324850	77	49.597923
33	26.993061	78	49.983542
34	27.653157	79	50.364478
35	28.305239	80	50.740789
36	28.949402	81	51.112531
37	29.585744	82	51.479759
38	30.214359	83	51.842528
39	30.835342	84	52.200892
40	31.448784	85	52.554905
41	32.054777	86	52.904619
42	32.653412	87	53.250087
43	33.244778	88	53.591359
44	33.828964	89	53.928488
45	34.406056	90	54.261524

yearly interest rate = 14.75%

term (months)	constant	term (months)	constant
91	54.590515	136	65.909818
92	54.915512	137	66.097371
93	55.236563	138	66.282647
94	55.553715	139	66.465673
95	55.867016	140	66.646477
96	56.176513	141	66.825085
97	56.482252	142	67.001525
98	56.784279	143	67.175822
99	57.082638	144	67.348003
100	57.377375	145	67.518093
101	57.668532	146	67.686118
102	57.956155	147	67.852102
103	58.240284	148	68.016072
104	58.520964	149	68.178050
105	58.798236	150	68.338061
106	59.072141	151	68.496129
107	59.342720	152	68.652279
108	59.610013	153	68.806532
109	59.874061	154	68.958912
110	60.134903	155	69.109441
111	60.392578	156	69.258143
112	60.647124	157	69.405040
113	60.898579	158	69.550152
114	61.146980	159	69.693503
115	61.392366	160	69.835113
116	61.634772	161	69.975004
117	61.874234	162	70.113196
118	62.110789	163	70.249710
119	62.344472	164	70.384566
120	62.575317	165	70.517785
121	62.803359	166	70.649386
122	63.028632	167	70.779390
123	63.251170	168	70.907814
124	63.471005	169	71.034680
125	63.688171	170	71.160005
126	63.902701	171	71.283808
127	64.114625	172	71.406108
128	64.323976	173	71.526923
129	64.530785	174	71.646271
130	64.735083	175	71.764169
131	64.936900	176	71.880637
132	65.136267	177	71.995690
133	65.333213	178	72.109346
134	65.527768	179	72.221621
135	65.719960	180	72.332534

yearly interest rate = 14.75%

term (months)	constant	term (months)	constant
181	72.442100	226	76.211829
182	72.550335	227	76.274291
183	72.657257	228	76.335994
184	72.762880	229	76.396948
185	72.867220	230	76.457162
186	72.970293	231	76.516645
187	73.072115	232	76.575406
188	73.172701	233	76.633453
189	73.272065	234	76.690795
190	73.370223	235	76.747441
191	73.467189	236	76.803400
192	73.562977	237	76.858678
193	73.657602	238	76.913286
194	73.751079	239	76.967230
195	73.843420	240	77.020520
196	73.934640	241	77.073162
197	74.024752	242	77.125165
198	74.113771	243	77.176537
199	74.201708	244	77.227285
200	74.288578	245	77.277417
201	74.374392	246	77.326940
202	74.459165	247	77.375862
203	74.542909	248	77.424189
204	74.625635	249	77.471930
205	74.707357	250	77.519091
206	74.788087	251	77.565680
207	74.867836	252	77.611703
208	74.946618	253	77.657167
209	75.024442	254	77.702079
210	75.101322	255	77.746445
211	75.177268	256	77.790273
212	75.252292	257	77.833569
213	75.326405	258	77.876339
214	75.399618	259	77.918589
215	75.471942	260	77.960327
216	75.543388	261	78.001558
217	75.613966	262	78.042288
218	75.683687	263	78.082524
219	75.752562	264	78.122271
220	75.820601	265	78.161535
221	75.887813	266	78.200323
222	75.954209	267	78.238640
223	76.019799	268	78.276491
224	76.084593	269	78.313883
225	76.148599	270	78.350821

yearly interest rate = 14.75%

term (months)	constant	term (months)	constant
271	78.387310	316	79.642764
272	78.423356	317	79.663566
273	78.458965	318	79.684115
274	78.494141	319	79.704415
275	78.528890	320	79.724468
276	78.563217	321	79.744278
277	78.597128	322	79.763848
278	78.630626	323	79.783179
279	78.663718	324	79.802276
280	78.696408	325	79.821141
281	78.728701	326	79.839778
282	78.760602	327	79.858187
283	78.792116	328	79.876374
284	78.823246	329	79.894339
285	78.853999	330	79.912086
286	78.884379	331	79.929618
287	78.914390	332	79.946937
288	78.944036	333	79.964046
289	78.973322	334	79.980946
290	79.002253	335	79.997642
291	79.030832	336	80.014135
292	79.059064	337	80.030428
293	79.086954	338	80.046522
294	79.114505	339	80.062422
295	79.141721	340	80.078128
296	79.168607	341	80.093644
297	79.195166	342	80.108971
298	79.221403	343	80.124112
299	79.247322	344	80.139069
300	79.272925	345	80.153845
301	79.298218	346	80.168441
302	79.323204	347	80.182860
303	79.347886	348	80.197104
304	79.372268	349	80.211175
305	79.396355	350	80.225075
306	79.420149	351	80.238807
307	79.443654	352	80.252371
308	79.466874	353	80.265771
309	79.489811	354	80.279008
310	79.512471	355	80.292085
311	79.534855	356	80.305003
312	79.556967	357	80.317763
313	79.578811	358	80.330369
314	79.600389	359	80.342822
315	79.621706	360	80.355124

yearly interest rate = 15.00%

term (months)	constant	term (months)	constant
1	0.9876543	46	34.822882
2	1.9631151	47	35.380624
3	2.9265337	48	35.931481
4	3.8780580	49	36.475537
5	4.8178350	50	37.012876
6	5.7460099	51	37.543581
7	6.6627259	52	38.067734
8	7.5681243	53	38.585417
9	8.4623450	54	39.096708
10	9.3455259	55	39.601687
11	10.217803	56	40.100431
12	11.079312	57	40.593019
13	11.930185	58	41.079525
14	12.770553	59	41.560024
15	13.600546	60	42.034592
16	14.420292	61	42.503301
17	15.229918	62	42.966223
18	16.029549	63	43.423430
19	16.819308	64	43.874993
20	17.599316	65	44.320980
21	18.369695	66	44.761462
22	19.130563	67	45.196506
23	19.882037	68	45.626178
24	20.624235	69	46.050547
25	21.357269	70	46.469676
26	22.081253	71	46.883630
27	22.796299	72	47.292474
28	23.502518	73	47.696271
29	24.200018	74	48.095082
30	24.888906	75	48.488970
31	25.569290	76	48.877995
32	26.241274	77	49.262218
33	26.904962	78	49.641696
34	27.560456	79	50.016490
35	28.207858	80	50.386657
36	28.847267	81	50.752254
37	29.478783	82	51.113337
38	30.102501	83	51.469963
39	30.718520	84	51.822185
40	31.326933	85	52.170060
41	31.927835	86	52.513639
42	32.521319	87	52.852977
43	33.107475	88	53.188125
44	33.686395	89	53.519136
45	34.258168	90	53.846060

yearly interest rate = 15.00%

term (months)	constant	term (months)	constant
91	54.168949	136	65.230505
92	54.487850	137	65.412844
93	54.802815	138	65.592933
94	55.113892	139	65.770798
95	55.421127	140	65.946467
96	55.724570	141	66.119967
97	56.024267	142	66.291326
98	56.320264	143	66.460569
99	56.612606	144	66.627722
100	56.901339	145	66.792812
101	57.186508	146	66.955864
102	57.468156	147	67.116902
103	57.746327	148	67.275953
104	58.021064	149	67.433040
105	58.292409	150	67.588188
106	58.560404	151	67.741420
107	58.825090	152	67.892760
108	59.086509	153	68.042232
109	59.344700	154	68.189859
110	59.599704	155	68.335663
111	59.851559	156	68.479668
112	60.100305	157	68.621894
113	60.345980	158	68.762364
114	60.588623	159	68.901101
115	60.828269	160	69.038124
116	61.064957	161	69.173456
117	61.298723	162	69.307117
118	61.529603	163	69.439128
119	61.757633	164	69.569509
120	61.982847	165	69.698280
121	62.205281	166	69.825462
122	62.424969	167	69.951074
123	62.641945	168	70.075135
124	62.856242	169	70.197664
125	63.067893	170	70.318680
126	63.276932	171	70.438203
127	63.483389	172	70.556250
128	63.687298	173	70.672839
129	63.888689	174	70.787989
130	64.087594	175	70.901718
131	64.284044	176	71.014042
132	64.478068	177	71.124980
133	64.669697	178	71.234548
134	64.858960	179	71.342764
135	65.045886	180	71.449643

yearly interest rate = 15.00%

term (months)	constant	term (months)	constant
181	71.555203	226	75.171494
182	71.659460	227	75.231105
183	71.762429	228	75.289980
184	71.864128	229	75.348129
185	71.964571	230	75.405559
186	72.063773	231	75.462281
187	72.161752	232	75.518302
188	72.258520	233	75.573632
189	72.354094	234	75.628278
190	72.448488	235	75.682250
191	72.541716	236	75.735556
192	72.633794	237	75.788203
193	72.724735	238	75.840201
194	72.814553	239	75.891556
195	72.903262	240	75.942278
196	72.990876	241	75.992373
197	73.077409	242	76.041850
198	73.162873	243	76.090716
199	73.247282	244	76.138979
200	73.330648	245	76.186646
201	73.412986	246	76.233724
202	73.494307	247	76.280221
203	73.574625	248	76.326144
204	73.653950	249	76.371501
205	73.732296	250	76.416297
206	73.809675	251	76.460540
207	73.886099	252	76.504237
208	73.961579	253	76.547395
209	74.036128	254	76.590020
210	74.109756	255	76.632118
211	74.182475	256	76.673697
212	74.254296	257	76.714762
213	74.325231	258	76.755321
214	74.395290	259	76.795379
215	74.464484	260	76.834942
216	74.532823	261	76.874017
217	74.600319	262	76.912609
218	74.666982	263	76.950725
219	74.732822	264	76.988370
220	74.797849	265	77.025551
221	74.862073	266	77.062273
222	74.925504	267	77.098541
223	74.988152	268	77.134361
224	75.050027	269	77.169740
225	75.111138	270	77.204681

yearly interest rate = 15.00%

term (months)	constant	term (months)	constant
271	77.239191	316	78.421444
272	77.273275	317	78.440933
273	77.306938	318	78.460180
274	77.340186	319	78.479191
275	77.373023	320	78.497966
276	77.405455	321	78.516510
277	77.437487	322	78.534824
278	77.469123	323	78.552913
279	77.500368	324	78.570778
280	77.531228	325	78.588423
281	77.561706	326	78.605850
282	77.591809	327	78.623061
283	77.621539	328	78.640061
284	77.650903	329	78.656850
285	77.679904	330	78.673432
286	77.708547	331	78.689810
287	77.736837	332	78.705985
288	77.764777	333	78.721960
289	77.792373	334	78.737739
290	77.819627	335	78.753322
291	77.846545	336	78.768713
292	77.873131	337	78.783914
293	77.899389	338	78.798928
294	77.925322	339	78.813756
295	77.950936	340	78.828401
296	77.976233	341	78.842865
297	78.001218	342	78.857150
298	78.025894	343	78.871260
299	78.050266	344	78.885195
300	78.074336	345	78.898958
301	78.098110	346	78.912551
302	78.121590	347	78.925976
303	78.144780	348	78.939236
304	78.167684	349	78.952332
305	78.190306	350	78.965266
306	78.212647	351	78.978040
307	78.234714	352	78.990657
308	78.256507	353	79.003118
309	78.278032	354	79.015425
310	78.299291	355	79.027580
311	78.320287	356	79.039586
312	78.341024	357	79.051443
313	78.361505	358	79.063153
314	78.381734	359	79.074719
315	78.401712	360	79.086142

yearly interest rate = 15.25%

term (months)	constant	term (months)	constant
1	0.9874511	46	34.670581
2	1.9625109	47	35.222956
3	2.9253348	48	35.768399
4	3.8760763	49	36.306997
5	4.8148871	50	36.838837
6	5.7419169	51	37.364003
7	6.6573136	52	37.882579
8	7.5612230	53	38.394647
9	8.4537894	54	38.900289
10	9.3351552	55	39.399586
11	10.205461	56	39.892617
12	11.064845	57	40.379461
13	11.913445	58	40.860196
14	12.751396	59	41.334899
15	13.578832	60	41.803644
16	14.395884	61	42.266507
17	15.202683	62	42.723562
18	15.999358	63	43.174881
19	16.786036	64	43.620537
20	17.562841	65	44.060600
21	18.329899	66	44.495141
22	19.087330	67	44.924229
23	19.835257	68	45.347932
24	20.573799	69	45.766319
25	21.303072	70	46.179455
26	22.023194	71	46.587406
27	22.734279	72	46.990239
28	23.436441	73	47.388016
29	24.129792	74	47.780802
30	24.814442	75	48.168658
31	25.490500	76	48.551648
32	26.158074	77	48.929831
33	26.817271	78	49.303269
34	27.468196	79	49.672020
35	28.110953	80	50.036144
36	28.745644	81	50.395699
37	29.372370	82	50.750742
38	29.991231	83	51.101329
39	30.602327	84	51.447517
40	31.205754	85	51.789360
41	31.801608	86	52.126914
42	32.389986	87	52.460232
43	32.970979	88	52.789367
44	33.544682	89	53.114372
45	34.111186	90	53.435298

yearly interest rate = 15.25%

term (months)	constant	term (months)	constant
91	53.752197	136	64.562004
92	54.065120	137	64.739275
93	54.374116	138	64.914322
94	54.679234	139	65.087173
95	54.980523	140	65.257854
96	55.278031	141	65.426394
97	55.571806	142	65.592819
98	55.861895	143	65.757155
99	56.148343	144	65.919429
100	56.431196	145	66.079666
101	56.710500	146	66.237893
102	56.986299	147	66.394134
103	57.258638	148	66.548415
104	57.527558	149	66.700759
105	57.793104	150	66.851192
106	58.055318	151	66.999737
107	58.314241	152	67.146418
108	58.569915	153	67.291258
109	58.822381	154	67.434281
110	59.071678	155	67.575509
111	59.317847	156	67.714964
112	59.560927	157	67.852670
113	59.800956	158	67.988648
114	60.037974	159	68.122919
115	60.272017	160	68.255505
116	60.503123	161	68.386428
117	60.731329	162	68.515707
118	60.956671	163	68.643365
119	61.179186	164	68.769420
120	61.398908	165	68.893893
121	61.615873	166	69.016805
122	61.830115	167	69.138174
123	62.041669	168	69.258020
124	62.250568	169	69.376362
125	62.456846	170	69.493219
126	62.660535	171	69.608609
127	62.861668	172	69.722552
128	63.060277	173	69.835065
129	63.256393	174	69.946166
130	63.450049	175	70.055872
131	63.641275	176	70.164202
132	63.830100	177	70.271173
133	64.016557	178	70.376801
134	64.200673	179	70.481103
135	64.382479	180	70.584097

yearly interest rate = 15.25%

term (months)	constant	term (months)	constant
181	70.685798	226	74.154951
182	70.786224	227	74.211842
183	70.885388	228	74.268019
184	70.983309	229	74.323492
185	71.080001	230	74.378268
186	71.175479	231	74.432357
187	71.269759	232	74.485767
188	71.362856	233	74.538506
189	71.454785	234	74.590584
190	71.545560	235	74.642009
191	71.635196	236	74.692788
192	71.723707	237	74.742930
193	71.811108	238	74.792443
194	71.897411	239	74.841334
195	71.982632	240	74.889612
196	72.066783	241	74.937284
197	72.149879	242	74.984358
198	72.231931	243	75.030841
199	72.312954	244	75.076740
200	72.392960	245	75.122064
201	72.471962	246	75.166819
202	72.549973	247	75.211013
203	72.627005	248	75.254651
204	72.703070	249	75.297743
205	72.778181	250	75.340293
206	72.852349	251	75.382310
207	72.925586	252	75.423799
208	72.997904	253	75.464767
209	73.069315	254	75.505222
210	73.139830	255	75.545169
211	73.209460	256	75.584614
212	73.278216	257	75.623565
213	73.346109	258	75.662026
214	73.413150	259	75.700006
215	73.479350	260	75.737508
216	73.544719	261	75.774540
217	73.609268	262	75.811107
218	73.673007	263	75.847215
219	73.735946	264	75.882871
220	73.798095	265	75.918078
221	73.859465	266	75.952844
222	73.920064	267	75.987174
223	73.979902	268	76.021073
224	74.038990	269	76.054546
225	74.097337	270	76.087600

yearly interest rate = 15.25%

term (months)	constant	term (months)	constant
271	76.120238	316	77.233581
272	76.152467	317	77.251839
273	76.184292	318	77.269868
274	76.215717	319	77.287670
275	76.246748	320	77.305249
276	76.277390	321	77.322608
277	76.307647	322	77.339749
278	76.337524	323	77.356674
279	76.367026	324	77.373387
280	76.396159	325	77.389891
281	76.424925	326	77.406187
282	76.453331	327	77.422279
283	76.481380	328	77.438169
284	76.509077	329	77.453860
285	76.536427	330	77.469353
286	76.563433	331	77.484652
287	76.590100	332	77.499760
288	76.616433	333	77.514677
289	76.642436	334	77.529408
290	76.668112	335	77.543953
291	76.693466	336	77.558316
292	76.718501	337	77.572499
293	76.743223	338	77.586504
294	76.767634	339	77.600333
295	76.791739	340	77.613989
296	76.815542	341	77.627473
297	76.839045	342	77.640788
298	76.862254	343	77.653936
299	76.885172	344	77.666919
300	76.907802	345	77.679739
301	76.930148	346	77.692398
302	76.952214	347	77.704898
303	76.974002	348	77.717241
304	76.995518	349	77.729430
305	77.016763	350	77.741465
306	77.037742	351	77.753350
307	77.058457	352	77.765085
308	77.078913	353	77.776673
309	77.099111	354	77.788116
310	77.119057	355	77.799415
311	77.138752	356	77.810573
312	77.158200	357	77.821590
313	77.177403	358	77.832469
314	77.196366	359	77.843211
315	77.215091	360	77.853819

yearly interest rate = 15.50%

term (months)	constant	term (months)	constant
1	0.9872480	46	34.519230
2	1.9619068	47	35.066290
3	2.9241367	48	35.606374
4	3.8740963	49	36.139572
5	4.8119420	50	36.665970
6	5.7378284	51	37.185655
7	6.6519079	52	37.698713
8	7.5543311	53	38.205229
9	8.4452467	54	38.705286
10	9.3248014	55	39.198966
11	10.193140	56	39.686350
12	11.050406	57	40.167520
13	11.896739	58	40.642554
14	12.732281	59	41.111530
15	13.557167	60	41.574525
16	14.371535	61	42.031617
17	15.175518	62	42.482880
18	15.969248	63	42.928388
19	16.752857	64	43.368215
20	17.526474	65	43.802434
21	18.290225	66	44.231115
22	19.044237	67	44.654330
23	19.788634	68	45.072148
24	20.523538	69	45.484638
25	21.249071	70	45.891868
26	21.965352	71	46.293905
27	22.672499	72	46.690816
28	23.370628	73	47.082665
29	24.059855	74	47.469517
30	24.740293	75	47.851436
31	25.412054	76	48.228484
32	26.075249	77	48.600725
33	26.729986	78	48.968219
34	27.376375	79	49.331027
35	28.014520	80	49.689208
36	28.644529	81	50.042821
37	29.266503	82	50.391925
38	29.880546	83	50.736578
39	30.486759	84	51.076836
40	31.085241	85	51.412754
41	31.676091	86	51.744389
42	32.259407	87	52.071795
43	32.835285	88	52.395026
44	33.403819	89	52.714135
45	33.965103	90	53.029175

yearly interest rate = 15.50%

term (months)	constant	term (months)	constant
91	53.340197	136	63.904107
92	53.647254	137	64.076453
93	53.950394	138	64.246601
94	54.249670	139	64.414579
95	54.545128	140	64.580416
96	54.836819	141	64.744137
97	55.124791	142	64.905771
98	55.409090	143	65.065344
99	55.689764	144	65.222881
100	55.966859	145	65.378410
101	56.240420	146	65.531956
102	56.510493	147	65.683543
103	56.777122	148	65.833198
104	57.040350	149	65.980944
105	57.300223	150	66.126806
106	57.556781	151	66.270808
107	57.810067	152	66.412974
108	58.060124	153	66.553327
109	58.306992	154	66.691890
110	58.550712	155	66.828686
111	58.791324	156	66.963738
112	59.028868	157	67.097067
113	59.263383	158	67.228697
114	59.494907	159	67.358647
115	59.723478	160	67.486941
116	59.949135	161	67.613599
117	60.171915	162	67.738641
118	60.391853	163	67.862089
119	60.608987	164	67.983963
120	60.823352	165	68.104283
121	61.034984	166	68.223068
122	61.243917	167	68.340339
123	61.450185	168	68.456114
124	61.653823	169	68.570413
125	61.854865	170	68.683254
126	62.053342	171	68.794656
127	62.249289	172	68.904638
128	62.442737	173	69.013218
129	62.633718	174	69.120412
130	62.822264	175	69.226240
131	63.008405	176	69.330718
132	63.192173	177	69.433864
133	63.373597	178	69.535695
134	63.552708	179	69.636227
135	63.729535	180	69.735477

yearly interest rate = 15.50%

term (months)	constant	term (months)	constant
181	69.833461	226	73.161514
182	69.930916	227	73.215809
183	70.025698	228	73.269413
184	70.119981	229	73.322333
185	70.213063	230	73.374578
186	70.304957	231	73.426156
187	70.395679	232	73.477078
188	70.485245	233	73.527349
189	70.573668	234	73.576980
190	70.660964	235	73.625978
191	70.747147	236	73.674351
192	70.832231	237	73.722107
193	70.916229	238	73.769254
194	70.999157	239	73.815800
195	71.081027	240	73.861752
196	71.161853	241	73.907119
197	71.241648	242	73.951907
198	71.320426	243	73.996123
199	71.398199	244	74.039776
200	71.474981	245	74.082872
201	71.550783	246	74.125419
202	71.625619	247	74.167423
203	71.699501	248	74.208892
204	71.772440	249	74.249831
205	71.844449	250	74.290249
206	71.915540	251	74.330151
207	71.985724	252	74.369545
208	72.055014	253	74.408436
209	72.123420	254	74.446831
210	72.190953	255	74.484736
211	72.257625	256	74.522158
212	72.323448	257	74.559103
213	72.388430	258	74.595577
214	72.452585	259	74.631586
215	72.515921	260	74.667135
216	72.578449	261	74.702231
217	72.640180	262	74.736880
218	72.701124	263	74.771087
219	72.761290	264	74.804857
220	72.820690	265	74.838197
221	72.879332	266	74.871112
222	72.937226	267	74.903607
223	72.994382	268	74.935688
224	73.050809	269	74.967360
225	73.106516	270	74.998627

yearly interest rate = 15.50%

term (months)	constant	term (months)	constant
271	75.029496	316	76.077965
272	75.059972	317	76.095071
273	75.090058	318	76.111958
274	75.119761	319	76.128630
275	75.149086	320	76.145089
276	75.178036	321	76.161338
277	75.206617	322	76.177380
278	75.234834	323	76.193218
279	75.262691	324	76.208854
280	75.290193	325	76.224290
281	75.317344	326	76.239529
282	75.344148	327	76.254574
283	75.370611	328	76.269428
284	75.396737	329	76.284092
285	75.422529	330	76.298568
286	75.447993	331	76.312861
287	75.473131	332	76.326971
288	75.497949	333	76.340901
289	75.522451	334	76.354653
290	75.546640	335	76.368230
291	75.570521	336	76.381634
292	75.594097	337	76.394867
293	75.617373	338	76.407931
294	75.640352	339	76.420829
295	75.663038	340	76.433562
296	75.685434	341	76.446133
297	75.707545	342	76.458543
298	75.729374	343	76.470795
299	75.750924	344	76.482891
300	75.772200	345	76.494833
301	75.793205	346	76.506623
302	75.813941	347	76.518262
303	75.834413	348	76.529752
304	75.854624	349	76.541097
305	75.874578	350	76.552296
306	75.894277	351	76.563353
307	75.913724	352	76.574268
308	75.932924	353	76.585045
309	75.951879	354	76.595684
310	75.970592	355	76.606187
311	75.989067	356	76.616557
312	76.007306	357	76.626794
313	76.025312	358	76.636901
314	76.043089	359	76.646879
315	76.060639	360	76.656729

yearly interest rate = 15.75%

term (months)	constant	term (months)	constant
1	0.9870450	46	34.368822
2	1.9613029	47	34.910620
3	2.9229394	48	35.445399
4	3.8721178	49	35.973250
5	4.8089997	50	36.494263
6	5.7337443	51	37.008526
7	6.6465089	52	37.516127
8	7.5474486	53	38.017152
9	8.4367167	54	38.511686
10	9.3144644	55	38.999814
11	10.180841	56	39.481617
12	11.035993	57	39.957179
13	11.880068	58	40.426580
14	12.713207	59	40.889900
15	13.535553	60	41.347218
16	14.347245	61	41.798611
17	15.148422	62	42.244157
18	15.939220	63	42.683930
19	16.719773	64	43.118006
20	17.490214	65	43.546459
21	18.250674	66	43.969361
22	19.001282	67	44.386785
23	19.742166	68	44.798801
24	20.473452	69	45.205479
25	21.195264	70	45.606888
26	21.907725	71	46.003098
27	22.610956	72	46.394174
28	23.305077	73	46.780184
29	23.990206	74	47.161193
30	24.666458	75	47.537267
31	25.333950	76	47.908468
32	25.992795	77	48.274861
33	26.643104	78	48.636506
34	27.284989	79	48.993467
35	27.918558	80	49.345804
36	28.543919	81	49.693575
37	29.161178	82	50.036842
38	29.770441	83	50.375661
39	30.371811	84	50.710091
40	30.965390	85	51.040189
41	31.551280	86	51.366010
42	32.129579	87	51.687610
43	32.700386	88	52.005044
44	33.263799	89	52.318365
45	33.819913	90	52.627628

yearly interest rate = 15.75%

term (months)	constant	term (months)	constant
91	52.932884	136	63.256612
92	53.234185	137	63.424169
93	53.531583	138	63.589556
94	53.825128	139	63.752801
95	54.114870	140	63.913931
96	54.400859	141	64.072973
97	54.683143	142	64.229955
98	54.961770	143	64.384903
99	55.236787	144	64.537844
100	55.508241	145	64.688803
101	55.776179	146	64.837807
102	56.040645	147	64.984880
103	56.301686	148	65.130048
104	56.559344	149	65.273336
105	56.813665	150	65.414767
106	57.064691	151	65.554366
107	57.312465	152	65.692156
108	57.557029	153	65.828162
109	57.798425	154	65.962405
110	58.036693	155	66.094910
111	58.271875	156	66.225697
112	58.504009	157	66.354791
113	58.733137	158	66.482212
114	58.959296	159	66.607982
115	59.182526	160	66.732123
116	59.402863	161	66.854655
117	59.620346	162	66.975601
118	59.835011	163	67.094979
119	60.046896	164	67.212811
120	60.256035	165	67.329116
121	60.462466	166	67.443915
122	60.666221	167	67.557226
123	60.867338	168	67.669070
124	61.065848	169	67.779464
125	61.261787	170	67.888429
126	61.455188	171	67.995981
127	61.646083	172	68.102141
128	61.834505	173	68.206925
129	62.020486	174	68.310352
130	62.204058	175	68.412438
131	62.385252	176	68.513203
132	62.564098	177	68.612661
133	62.740627	178	68.710832
134	62.914870	179	68.807730
135	63.086855	180	68.903373

yearly interest rate = 15.75%

term (months)	constant	term (months)	constant
181	68.997778	226	72.190518
182	69.090959	227	72.242338
183	69.182933	228	72.293486
184	69.273715	229	72.343971
185	69.363322	230	72.393802
186	69.451767	231	72.442988
187	69.539067	232	72.491537
188	69.625236	233	72.539456
189	69.710288	234	72.586755
190	69.794239	235	72.633441
191	69.877102	236	72.679523
192	69.958891	237	72.725007
193	70.039621	238	72.769902
194	70.119306	239	72.814215
195	70.197957	240	72.857955
196	70.275590	241	72.901127
197	70.352217	242	72.943741
198	70.427852	243	72.985802
199	70.502506	244	73.027319
200	70.576194	245	73.068297
201	70.648927	246	73.108745
202	70.720717	247	73.148669
203	70.791578	248	73.188075
204	70.861520	249	73.226971
205	70.930557	250	73.265363
206	70.998699	251	73.303258
207	71.065958	252	73.340662
208	71.132346	253	73.377581
209	71.197874	254	73.414022
210	71.262553	255	73.449991
211	71.326394	256	73.485494
212	71.389408	257	73.520537
213	71.451606	258	73.555126
214	71.512998	259	73.589267
215	71.573594	260	73.622965
216	71.633406	261	73.656227
217	71.692443	262	73.689058
218	71.750714	263	73.721464
219	71.808231	264	73.753450
220	71.865003	265	73.785022
221	71.921040	266	73.816184
222	71.976350	267	73.846943
223	72.030944	268	73.877303
224	72.084830	269	73.907271
225	72.138019	270	73.936849

yearly interest rate = 15.75%

term (months)	constant	term (months)	constant
271	73.966045	316	74.953440
272	73.994862	317	74.969465
273	74.023307	318	74.985284
274	74.051382	319	75.000897
275	74.079094	320	75.016308
276	74.106447	321	75.031519
277	74.133446	322	75.046533
278	74.160094	323	75.061353
279	74.186398	324	75.075981
280	74.212361	325	75.090419
281	74.237987	326	75.104670
282	74.263281	327	75.118737
283	74.288248	328	75.132621
284	74.312891	329	75.146326
285	74.337216	330	75.159853
286	74.361224	331	75.173204
287	74.384922	332	75.186383
288	74.408313	333	75.199391
289	74.431401	334	75.212231
290	74.454190	335	75.224904
291	74.476683	336	75.237413
292	74.498886	337	75.249760
293	74.520800	338	75.261946
294	74.542431	339	75.273976
295	74.563781	340	75.285849
296	74.584855	341	75.297568
297	74.605656	342	75.309136
298	74.626187	343	75.320554
299	74.646452	344	75.331823
300	74.666455	345	75.342947
301	74.686199	346	75.353927
302	74.705686	347	75.364764
303	74.724922	348	75.375461
304	74.743908	349	75.386020
305	74.762648	350	75.396442
306	74.781146	351	75.406728
307	74.799404	352	75.416882
308	74.817425	353	75.426904
309	74.835213	354	75.436796
310	74.852770	355	75.446560
311	74.870100	356	75.456197
312	74.887205	357	75.465710
313	74.904089	358	75.475099
314	74.920754	359	75.484367
315	74.937204	360	75.493514

yearly interest rate = 16.00%

term (months)	constant	term (months)	constant
1	0.9868421	46	34.219351
2	1.9606994	47	34.755938
3	2.9217429	48	35.285465
4	3.8701410	49	35.808025
5	4.8060602	50	36.323709
6	5.7296647	51	36.832608
7	6.6411164	52	37.334810
8	7.5405754	53	37.830405
9	8.4281994	54	38.319478
10	9.3041442	55	38.802117
11	10.168563	56	39.278405
12	11.021609	57	39.748426
13	11.863429	58	40.212262
14	12.694174	59	40.669996
15	13.513987	60	41.121706
16	14.323014	61	41.567473
17	15.121395	62	42.007375
18	15.909272	63	42.441488
19	16.686781	64	42.869890
20	17.454060	65	43.292654
21	18.211244	66	43.709856
22	18.958464	67	44.121569
23	19.695853	68	44.527864
24	20.423539	69	44.928813
25	21.141650	70	45.324487
26	21.850313	71	45.714954
27	22.549651	72	46.100283
28	23.239787	73	46.480543
29	23.920842	74	46.855799
30	24.592937	75	47.226117
31	25.256187	76	47.591563
32	25.910711	77	47.952200
33	26.556623	78	48.308093
34	27.194036	79	48.659302
35	27.823062	80	49.005890
36	28.443811	81	49.347918
37	29.056392	82	49.685445
38	29.660913	83	50.018531
39	30.257480	84	50.347235
40	30.846198	85	50.671613
41	31.427169	86	50.991724
42	32.000496	87	51.307622
43	32.566279	88	51.619364
44	33.124617	89	51.927004
45	33.675609	90	52.230596

yearly interest rate = 16.00%

term (months)	constant	term (months)	constant
91	52.530193	136	62.619319
92	52.825849	137	62.782223
93	53.117614	138	62.942983
94	53.405540	139	63.101628
95	53.689678	140	63.258185
96	53.970077	141	63.412683
97	54.246786	142	63.565148
98	54.519855	143	63.715606
99	54.789330	144	63.864085
100	55.055260	145	64.010610
101	55.317691	146	64.155207
102	55.576669	147	64.297902
103	55.832239	148	64.438719
104	56.084446	149	64.577683
105	56.333335	150	64.714819
106	56.578949	151	64.850151
107	56.821331	152	64.983701
108	57.060524	153	65.115495
109	57.296570	154	65.245554
110	57.529510	155	65.373902
111	57.759385	156	65.500561
112	57.986235	157	65.625554
113	58.210100	158	65.748902
114	58.431020	159	65.870627
115	58.649033	160	65.990750
116	58.864177	161	66.109293
117	59.076491	162	66.226276
118	59.286011	163	66.341719
119	59.492774	164	66.455644
120	59.696816	165	66.568070
121	59.898174	166	66.679016
122	60.096882	167	66.788503
123	60.292976	168	66.896549
124	60.486489	169	67.003173
125	60.677456	170	67.108395
126	60.865911	171	67.212232
127	61.051886	172	67.314702
128	61.235414	173	67.415825
129	61.416527	174	67.515616
130	61.595256	175	67.614095
131	61.771635	176	67.711278
132	61.945692	177	67.807182
133	62.117459	178	67.901825
134	62.286966	179	67.995222
135	62.454243	180	68.087390

yearly interest rate = 16.00%

term (months)	constant	term (months)	constant
181	68.178345	226	71.241324
182	68.268104	227	71.290780
183	68.356681	228	71.339585
184	68.444094	229	71.387749
185	68.530355	230	71.435278
186	68.615482	231	71.482183
187	68.699489	232	71.528470
188	68.782391	233	71.574148
189	68.864201	234	71.619225
190	68.944935	235	71.663709
191	69.024607	236	71.707607
192	69.103231	237	71.750928
193	69.180820	238	71.793679
194	69.257388	239	71.835868
195	69.332949	240	71.877501
196	69.407515	241	71.918586
197	69.481101	242	71.959131
198	69.553718	243	71.999143
199	69.625379	244	72.038628
200	69.696098	245	72.077593
201	69.765886	246	72.116046
202	69.834756	247	72.153993
203	69.902720	248	72.191440
204	69.969789	249	72.228395
205	70.035976	250	72.264863
206	70.101292	251	72.300852
207	70.165749	252	72.336367
208	70.229358	253	72.371415
209	70.292129	254	72.406001
210	70.354075	255	72.440133
211	70.415206	256	72.473815
212	70.475532	257	72.507055
213	70.535064	258	72.539857
214	70.593813	259	72.572227
215	70.651790	260	72.604171
216	70.709003	261	72.635695
217	70.765463	262	72.666805
218	70.821181	263	72.697505
219	70.876165	264	72.727801
220	70.930426	265	72.757698
221	70.983973	266	72.787202
222	71.036816	267	72.816318
223	71.088963	268	72.845050
224	71.140424	269	72.873405
225	71.191208	270	72.901386

yearly interest rate = 16.00%

term (months)	constant	term (months)	constant
271	72.929000	316	73.858896
272	72.956250	317	73.873910
273	72.983141	318	73.888727
274	73.009679	319	73.903349
275	73.035867	320	73.917779
276	73.061711	321	73.932019
277	73.087215	322	73.946071
278	73.112383	323	73.959938
279	73.137220	324	73.973623
280	73.161731	325	73.987128
281	73.185918	326	74.000456
282	73.209788	327	74.013608
283	73.233343	328	74.026586
284	73.256589	329	74.039395
285	73.279528	330	74.052034
286	73.302166	331	74.064507
287	73.324506	332	74.076816
288	73.346552	333	74.088964
289	73.368308	334	74.100951
290	73.389778	335	74.112780
291	73.410965	336	74.124454
292	73.431873	337	74.135975
293	73.452506	338	74,147344
294	73.472868	339	74.158563
295	73.492962	340	74.169634
296	73.512791	341	74.180560
297	73.532360	342	74.191342
298	73.551671	343	74.201982
299	73.570728	344	74.212483
300	73.589534	345	74.222845
301	73.608093	346	74.233070
302	73.626407	347	74.243162
303	73.644481	348	74.253120
304	73.662317	349	74.262947
305	73.679918	350	74.272645
306	73.697287	351	74.282216
307	73.714428	352	74.291660
308	73.731344	353	74.300981
309	73.748037	354	74.310178
310	73.764510	355	74.319255
311	73.780766	356	74.328212
312	73.796809	357	74.337051
313	73.812640	358	74.345774
314	73.828263	359	74.354383
315	73.843681	360	74.362878

yearly interest rate = 16.25%

term (months)	constant	term (months)	constant
1	0.9866393	46	34.070810
2	1.9600963	47	34.602238
3	2.9205472	48	35.126565
4	3.8681658	49	35.643888
5	4.8031235	50	36.154298
6	5.7255895	51	36.657889
7	6.6357306	52	37.154752
8	7.5337116	53	37.644976
9	8.4196949	54	38.128651
10	9.2938408	55	38.605863
11	10.156308	56	39.076700
12	11.007251	57	39.541245
13	11.846825	58	39.999584
14	12.675182	59	40.451799
15	13.492472	60	40.897973
16	14.298841	61	41.338185
17	15.094438	62	41.772515
18	15.879404	63	42.201043
19	16.653883	64	42.623845
20	17.418014	65	43.040998
21	18.171935	66	43.452578
22	18.915784	67	43.858658
23	19.649695	68	44.259314
24	20.373799	69	44.654616
25	21.088230	70	45.044636
26	21.793115	71	45.429446
27	22.488582	72	45.809114
28	23.174757	73	46.183710
29	23.851764	74	46.553300
30	24.519726	75	46.917953
31	25.178764	76	47.277734
32	25.828996	77	47.632707
33	26.470541	78	47.982939
34	27.103514	79	48.328490
35	27.728030	80	48.669425
36	28.344203	81	49.005805
37	28.952142	82	49.337690
38	29.551960	83	49.665141
39	30.143763	84	49.988218
40	30.727659	85	50.306977
41	31.303754	86	50.621478
42	31.872152	87	50.931777
43	32.432956	88	51.237930
44	32.986267	89	51.539993
45	33.532185	90	51.838020

yearly interest rate = 16.25%

term (months)	constant
91	52.132064
92	52.422181
93	52.708421
94	52.990837
95	53.269479
96	53.544399
97	53.815645
98	54.083268
99	54.347314
100	54.607833
101	54.864872
102	55.118476
103	55.368691
104	55.615564
105	55.859138
106	56.099458
107	56.336567
108	56.570508
109	56.801323
110	57.029055
111	57.253744
112	57.475431
113	57.694155
114	57.909958
115	58.122878
116	58.332952
117	58.540220
118	58.744719
119	58.946485
120	59.145556
121	59.341966
122	59.535753
123	59.726951
124	59.915594
125	60.101716
126	60.285352
127	60.466534
128	60.645296
129	60.821669
130	60.995686
131	61.167378
132	61.336776
133	61.503910
134	61.668812
135	61.831510

term (months)	constant
136	61.992035
137	62.150414
138	62.306678
139	62.460854
140	62.612970
141	62.763054
142	62.911132
143	63.057232
144	63.201380
145	63.343602
146	63.483924
147	63.622371
148	63.758968
149	63.893741
150	64.026712
151	64.157907
152	64.287349
153	64.415062
154	64.541068
155	64.665391
156	64.788053
157	64.909076
158	65.028482
159	65.146293
160	65.262529
161	65.377213
162	65.490364
163	65.602004
164	65.712152
165	65.820828
166	65.928052
167	66.033844
168	66.138222
169	66.241206
170	66.342813
171	66.443064
172	66.541974
173	66.639564
174	66.735849
175	66.830848
176	66.924578
177	67.017055
178	67.108297
179	67.198320
180	67.287140

yearly interest rate = 16.25%

term (months)	constant	term (months)	constant
181	67.374773	226	70.313308
182	67.461235	227	70.360510
183	67.546543	228	70.407081
184	67.630710	229	70.453029
185	67.713753	230	70.498364
186	67.795686	231	70.543093
187	67.876525	232	70.587224
188	67.956284	233	70.630766
189	68.034977	234	70.673726
190	68.112618	235	70.716112
191	68.189223	236	70.757931
192	68.264803	237	70.799192
193	68.339374	238	70.839902
194	68.412949	239	70.880068
195	68.485541	240	70.919697
196	68.557162	241	70.958797
197	68.627827	242	70.997374
198	68.697548	243	71.035436
199	68.766337	244	71.072989
200	68.834207	245	71.110040
201	68.901171	246	71.146597
202	68.967239	247	71.182665
203	69.032425	248	71.218251
204	69.096740	249	71.253362
205	69.160196	250	71.288003
206	69.222804	251	71.322182
207	69.284575	252	71.355904
208	69.345521	253	71.389176
209	69.405653	254	71.422003
210	69.464981	255	71.454391
211	69.523517	256	71.486347
212	69.581271	257	71.517876
213	69.638253	258	71.548983
214	69.694473	259	71.579675
215	69.749943	260	71.609957
216	69.804671	261	71.639834
217	69.858668	262	71.669312
218	69.911944	263	71.698397
219	69.964508	264	71.727092
220	70.016370	265	71.755405
221	70.067539	266	71.783339
222	70.118024	267	71.810899
223	70.167834	268	71.838092
224	70.216979	269	71.864921
225	70.265468	270	71.891392

yearly interest rate = 16.25%

term (months)	constant	term (months)	constant
271	71.917509	316	72.793271
272	71.943277	317	72.807338
273	71.968701	318	72.821218
274	71.993785	319	72.834912
275	72.018534	320	72.848423
276	72.042952	321	72.861753
277	72.067044	322	72.874905
278	72.090815	323	72.887882
279	72.114267	324	72.900685
280	72.137407	325	72.913317
281	72.160237	326	72.925781
282	72.182762	327	72.938078
283	72.204986	328	72.950210
284	72.226913	329	72.962181
285	72.248547	330	72.973991
286	72.269893	331	72.985644
287	72.290953	332	72.997141
288	72.311731	333	73.008484
289	72.332232	334	73.019676
290	72.352459	335	73.030719
291	72.372416	336	73.041613
292	72.392106	337	73.052363
293	72.411534	338	73.062968
294	72.430701	339	73.073432
295	72.449613	340	73.083756
296	72.468272	341	73.093943
297	72.486681	342	73.103993
298	72.504845	343	73.113909
299	72.522765	344	73.123692
300	72.540447	345	73.133345
301	72.557892	346	73.142868
302	72.575104	347	73.152265
303	72.592086	348	73.161535
304	72.608842	349	73.170682
305	72.625373	350	73.179707
306	72.641684	351	73.188611
307	72.657776	352	73.197397
308	72.673654	353	73.206065
309	72.689319	354	73.214617
310	72.704775	355	73.223054
311	72.720025	356	73.231380
312	72.735071	357	73.239593
313	72.749916	358	73.247697
314	72.764562	359	73.255693
315	72.779013	360	73.263582

yearly interest rate = 16.50%

term (months)	constant	term (months)	constant
1	0.9864365	46	33.923191
2	1.9594935	47	34.449510
3	2.9193524	48	34.968691
4	3.8661922	49	35.480829
5	4.8001896	50	35.986022
6	5.7215187	51	36.484362
7	6.6303514	52	36.975942
8	7.5268571	53	37.460856
9	8.4112031	54	37.939192
10	9.2835542	55	38.411040
11	10.144073	56	38.876488
12	10.992921	57	39.335623
13	11.830255	58	39.788531
14	12.656231	59	40.235296
15	13.471005	60	40.676001
16	14.274728	61	41.110728
17	15.067549	62	41.539559
18	15.849617	63	41.962574
19	16.621077	64	42.379851
20	17.382073	65	42.791468
21	18.132748	66	43.197503
22	18.873241	67	43.598030
23	19.603690	68	43.993124
24	20.324232	69	44.382860
25	21.035001	70	44.767309
26	21.736129	71	45.146545
27	22.427747	72	45.520636
28	23.109985	73	45.889653
29	23.782969	74	46.253665
30	24.446825	75	46.612740
31	25.101677	76	46.966944
32	25.747647	77	47.316345
33	26.384855	78	47.661006
34	27.013421	79	48.000992
35	27.633461	80	48.336367
36	28.245091	81	48.667193
37	28.848425	82	48.993532
38	29.443576	83	49.315445
39	30.030654	84	49.632991
40	30.609770	85	49.946231
41	31.181031	86	50.255221
42	31.744543	87	50.560021
43	32.300413	88	50.860687
44	32.848742	89	51.157274
45	33.389635	90	51.449839

yearly interest rate = 16.50%

term (months)	constant	term (months)	constant
91	51.738435	136	61.374568
92	52.023117	137	61.528550
93	52.303938	138	61.680444
94	52.580950	139	61.830278
95	52.854205	140	61.978079
96	53.123753	141	62.123876
97	53.389646	142	62.267695
98	53.651932	143	62.409563
99	53.910660	144	62.549508
100	54.165879	145	62.687554
101	54.417637	146	62.823728
102	54.665979	147	62.958054
103	54.910954	148	63.090559
104	55.152605	149	63.221267
105	55.390980	150	63.350201
106	55.626120	151	63.477387
107	55.858072	152	63.602848
108	56.086877	153	63.726607
109	56.312579	154	63.848688
110	56.535220	155	63.969113
111	56.754841	156	64.087904
112	56.971483	157	64.205084
113	57.185187	158	64.320675
114	57.395992	159	64.434698
115	57.603938	160	64.547174
116	57.809063	161	64.658125
117	58.011406	162	64.767571
118	58.211005	163	64.875532
119	58.407896	164	64.982029
120	58.602117	165	65.087082
121	58.793704	166	65.190710
122	58.982692	167	65.292932
123	59.169117	168	65.393767
124	59.353013	169	65.493235
125	59.534414	170	65.591354
126	59.713356	171	65.688142
127	59.889870	172	65.783618
128	60.063990	173	65.877798
129	60.235749	174	65.970701
130	60.405177	175	66.062344
131	60.572308	176	66.152743
132	60.737172	177	66.241917
133	60.899800	178	66.329881
134	61.060222	179	66.416652
135	61.218468	180	66.502246

yearly interest rate = 16.50%

term (months)	constant	term (months)	constant
181	66.586679	226	69.405872
182	66.669967	227	69.450922
183	66.752126	228	69.495360
184	66.833170	229	69.539196
185	66.913114	230	69.582438
186	66.991975	231	69.625093
187	67.069765	232	69.667169
188	67.146501	233	69.708675
189	67.222196	234	69.749618
190	67.296864	235	69.790005
191	67.370519	236	69.829845
192	67.443176	237	69.869144
193	67.514846	238	69.907910
194	67.585545	239	69.946151
195	67.655285	240	69.983873
196	67.724079	241	70.021083
197	67.791940	242	70.057788
198	67.858880	243	70.093996
199	67.924913	244	70.129712
200	67.990049	245	70.164944
201	68.054303	246	70.199698
202	68.117685	247	70.233981
203	68.180207	248	70.267799
204	68.241881	249	70.301158
205	68.302719	250	70.334064
206	68.362731	251	70.366525
207	68.421929	252	70.398545
208	68.480325	253	70.430130
209	68.537928	254	70.461288
210	68.594751	255	70.492022
211	68.650802	256	70.522340
212	68.706093	257	70.552247
213	68.760635	258	70.581748
214	68.814436	259	70.610849
215	68.867508	260	70.639555
216	68.919860	261	70.667872
217	68.971502	262	70.695804
218	69.022443	263	70.723358
219	69.072694	264	70.750538
220	69.122262	265	70.777350
221	69.171159	266	70.803797
222	69.219392	267	70.829886
223	69.266971	268	70.855622
224	69.313905	269	70.881008
225	69.360202	270	70.906050

yearly interest rate = 16.50%

term (months)	constant	term (months)	constant
271	70.930752	316	71.755548
272	70.955119	317	71.768728
273	70.979156	318	71.781729
274	71.002866	319	71.794554
275	71.026255	320	71.807205
276	71.049327	321	71.819684
277	71.072086	322	71.831994
278	71.094536	323	71.844138
279	71.116681	324	71.856116
280	71.138527	325	71.867932
281	71.160076	326	71.879588
282	71.181332	327	71.891085
283	71.202301	328	71.902427
284	71.222985	329	71.913615
285	71.243388	330	71.924651
286	71.263515	331	71.935537
287	71.283368	332	71.946276
288	71.302953	333	71.956869
289	71.322272	334	71.967318
290	71.341328	335	71.977626
291	71.360127	336	71.987794
292	71.378670	337	71.997824
293	71.396962	338	72.007717
294	71.415005	339	72.017477
295	71.432804	340	72.027104
296	71.450362	341	72.036601
297	71.467681	342	72.045969
298	71.484766	343	72.055210
299	71.501618	344	72.064325
300	71.518243	345	72.073317
301	71.534641	346	72.082187
302	71.550818	347	72.090937
303	71.566774	348	72.099568
304	71.582515	349	72.108082
305	71.598042	350	72.116480
306	71.613358	351	72.124765
307	71.628467	352	72.132937
308	71.643370	353	72.140998
309	71.658072	354	72.148950
310	71.672574	355	72.156794
311	71.686879	356	72.164532
312	71.700991	357	72.172164
313	71.714911	358	72.179694
314	71.728642	359	72.187121
315	71.742187	360	72.194447

yearly interest rate = 16.75%

term (months)	constant	term (months)	constant
1	0.9862338	46	33.776489
2	1.9588910	47	34.297749
3	2.9181583	48	34.811834
4	3.8642203	49	35.318842
5	4.7972585	50	35.818870
6	5.7174524	51	36.312015
7	6.6249788	52	36.798371
8	7.5200119	53	37.278032
9	8.4027239	54	37.751090
10	9.2732843	55	38.217635
11	10.131860	56	38.677758
12	10.978617	57	39.131547
13	11.813717	58	39.579089
14	12.637321	59	40.020470
15	13.449588	60	40.455775
16	14.250672	61	40.885087
17	15.040728	62	41.308489
18	15.819909	63	41.726063
19	16.588363	64	42.137888
20	17.346238	65	42.544044
21	18.093681	66	42.944609
22	18.830834	67	43.339660
23	19.557839	68	43.729272
24	20.274835	69	44.113521
25	20.981963	70	44.492480
26	21.679355	71	44.866222
27	22.367147	72	45.234820
28	23.045471	73	45.598343
29	23.714456	74	45.956861
30	24.374233	75	46.310445
31	25.024926	76	46.659161
32	25.666663	77	47.003076
33	26.299565	78	47.342257
34	26.923754	79	47.676769
35	27.539350	80	48.006676
36	28.146473	81	48.332041
37	28.745237	82	48.652927
38	29.335759	83	48.969396
39	29.918151	84	49.281508
40	30.492526	85	49.589324
41	31.058994	86	49.892902
42	31.617665	87	50.192301
43	32.168644	88	50.487579
44	32.712038	89	50.778792
45	33.247952	90	51.065995

yearly interest rate = 16.75%

term (months)	constant	term (months)	constant
91	51.349246	136	60.766732
92	51.628596	137	60.916440
93	51.904102	138	61.064087
94	52.175814	139	61.209702
95	52.443786	140	61.353312
96	52.708070	141	61.494945
97	52.968715	142	61.634628
98	53.225772	143	61.772388
99	53.479290	144	61.908252
100	53.729318	145	62.042246
101	53.975904	146	62.174395
102	54.219096	147	62.304725
103	54.458940	148	62.433261
104	54.695482	149	62.560027
105	54.928768	150	62.685048
106	55.158843	151	62.808348
107	55.385750	152	62.929951
108	55.609534	153	63.049880
109	55.830237	154	63.168158
110	56.047901	155	63.284807
111	56.262570	156	63.399851
112	56.474283	157	63.513311
113	56.683081	158	63.625209
114	56.889006	159	63.735567
115	57.092095	160	63.844405
116	57.292389	161	63.951746
117	57.489925	162	64.057608
118	57.684742	163	64.162013
119	57.876878	164	64.264981
120	58.066368	165	64.366532
121	58.253250	166	64.466684
122	58.437559	167	64.565458
123	58.619331	168	64.662872
124	58.798600	169	64.758945
125	58.975402	170	64.853696
126	59.149770	171	64.947142
127	59.321737	172	65.039302
128	59.491337	173	65.130193
129	59.658603	174	65.219833
130	59.823565	175	65.308238
131	59.986257	176	65.395427
132	60.146709	177	65.481416
133	60.304953	178	65.566221
134	60.461018	179	65.649858
135	60.614934	180	65.732344

yearly interest rate = 16.75%

term (months)	constant	term (months)	constant
181	65.813695	226	68.518433
182	65.893925	227	68.561429
183	65.973051	228	68.603834
184	66.051088	229	68.645655
185	66.128051	230	68.686901
186	66.203954	231	68.727578
187	66.278812	232	68.767696
188	66.352640	233	68.807261
189	66.425451	234	68.846282
190	66.497260	235	68.884765
191	66.568081	236	68.922719
192	66.637927	237	68.960150
193	66.706811	238	68.997066
194	66.774747	239	69.033474
195	66.841747	240	69.069380
196	66.907825	241	69.104793
197	66.972994	242	69.139717
198	67.037266	243	69.174161
199	67.100652	244	69.208131
200	67.163166	245	69.241633
201	67.224820	246	69.274674
202	67.285625	247	69.307261
203	67.345593	248	69.339398
204	67.404735	249	69.371093
205	67.463063	250	69.402352
206	67.520588	251	69.433181
207	67.577321	252	69.463585
208	67.633273	253	69.493570
209	67.688455	254	69.523143
210	67.742878	255	69.552309
211	67.796551	256	69.581073
212	67.849485	257	69.609441
213	67.901691	258	69.637419
214	67.953178	259	69.665011
215	68.003956	260	69.692224
216	68.054035	261	69.719062
217	68.103425	262	69.745531
218	68.152134	263	69.771635
219	68.200174	264	69.797380
220	68.247552	265	69.822771
221	68.294277	266	69.847812
222	68.340360	267	69.872508
223	68.385808	268	69.896864
224	68.430630	269	69.920885
225	68.474836	270	69.944575

yearly interest rate = 16.75%

term (months)	constant	term (months)	constant
271	69.967940	316	70.744751
272	69.990982	317	70.757099
273	70.013707	318	70.769278
274	70.036120	319	70.781289
275	70.058224	320	70.793135
276	70.080024	321	70.804818
277	70.101523	322	70.816340
278	70.122727	323	70.827703
279	70.143638	324	70.838910
280	70.164262	325	70.849963
281	70.184602	326	70.860863
282	70.204662	327	70.871614
283	70.224446	328	70.882216
284	70.243957	329	70.892672
285	70.263200	330	70.902985
286	70.282178	331	70.913155
287	70.300895	332	70.923186
288	70.319354	333	70.933078
289	70.337559	334	70.942835
290	70.355513	335	70.952457
291	70.373220	336	70.961946
292	70.390683	337	70.971305
293	70.407906	338	70.980535
294	70.424892	339	70.989638
295	70.441644	340	70.998616
296	70.458166	341	71.007470
297	70.474460	342	71.016202
298	70.490530	343	71.024814
299	70.506378	344	71.033307
300	70.522008	345	71.041684
301	70.537423	346	71.049945
302	70.552626	347	71.058092
303	70.567620	348	71.066128
304	70.582407	349	71.074052
305	70.596991	350	71.081868
306	70.611374	351	71.089576
307	70.625559	352	71.097178
308	70.639548	353	71.104675
309	70.653345	354	71.112069
310	70.666953	355	71.119361
311	70.680372	356	71.126553
312	70.693607	357	71.133646
313	70.706660	358	71.140641
314	70.719533	359	71.147540
315	70.732229	360	71.154344

yearly interest rate = 17.00%

term (months)	constant	term (months)	constant
1	0.9860312	46	33.630696
2	1.9582888	47	34.146948
3	2.9169651	48	34.655988
4	3.8622499	49	35.157918
5	4.7943303	50	35.652836
6	5.7133906	51	36.140841
7	6.6196127	52	36.622028
8	7.5131761	53	37.096495
9	8.3942574	54	37.564333
10	9.2630311	55	38.025637
11	10.119669	56	38.480496
12	10.964341	57	38.929002
13	11.797214	58	39.371243
14	12.618452	59	39.807306
15	13.428219	60	40.237278
16	14.226675	61	40.661244
17	15.013977	62	41.079287
18	15.790281	63	41.491491
19	16.555741	64	41.897937
20	17.310509	65	42.298705
21	18.054734	66	42.693875
22	18.788563	67	43.083525
23	19.512141	68	43.467733
24	20.225611	69	43.846573
25	20.929115	70	44.220121
26	21.622792	71	44.588451
27	22.306780	72	44.951637
28	22.981212	73	45.309748
29	23.646224	74	45.662858
30	24.301947	75	46.011035
31	24.948510	76	46.354348
32	25.586041	77	46.692866
33	26.214666	78	47.026655
34	26.834511	79	47.355782
35	27.445697	80	47.680311
36	28.048345	81	48.000306
37	28.642575	82	48.315832
38	29.228505	83	48.626950
39	29.806250	84	48.933722
40	30.375924	85	49.236209
41	30.937641	86	49.534471
42	31.491511	87	49.828566
43	32.037644	88	50.118554
44	32.576149	89	50.404490
45	33.107131	90	50.686432

yearly interest rate = 17.00%

term (months)	constant	term (months)	constant
91	50.964436	136	60.168345
92	51.238556	137	60.313898
93	51.508848	138	60.457418
94	51.775363	139	60.598933
95	52.038156	140	60.738471
96	52.297278	141	60.876061
97	52.552780	142	61.011728
98	52.804714	143	61.145500
99	53.053128	144	61.277403
100	53.298072	145	61.407464
101	53.539594	146	61.535708
102	53.777743	147	61.662161
103	54.012565	148	61.786847
104	54.244107	149	61.909792
105	54.472414	150	62.031019
106	54.697532	151	62.150553
107	54.919506	152	62.268417
108	55.138379	153	62.384635
109	55.354194	154	62.499229
110	55.566995	155	62.612223
111	55.776824	156	62.723638
112	55.983721	157	62.833497
113	56.187728	158	62.941821
114	56.388886	159	63.048632
115	56.587233	160	63.153951
116	56.782810	161	63.257799
117	56.975655	162	63.360196
118	57.165806	163	63.461163
119	57.353301	164	63.560719
120	57.538177	165	63.658885
121	57.720470	166	63.755680
122	57.900217	167	63.851122
123	58.077453	168	63.945231
124	58.252213	169	64.038026
125	58.424533	170	64.129524
126	58.594445	171	64.219745
127	58.761983	172	64.308705
128	58.927181	173	64.396422
129	59.090072	174	64.482914
130	59.250687	175	64.568198
131	59.409059	176	64.652290
132	59.565218	177	64.735208
133	59.719196	178	64.816968
134	59.871024	179	64.897585
135	60.020730	180	64.977077

yearly interest rate = 17.00%

term (months)	constant	term (months)	constant
181	65.055458	226	67.650428
182	65.132744	227	67.691466
183	65.208951	228	67.731930
184	65.284093	229	67.771829
185	65.358185	230	67.811171
186	65.431242	231	67.849963
187	65.503279	232	67.888214
188	65.574310	233	67.925930
189	65.644348	234	67.963119
190	65.713408	235	67.999788
191	65.781504	236	68.035946
192	65.848648	237	68.071598
193	65.914854	238	68.106753
194	65.980135	239	68.141416
195	66.044505	240	68.175595
196	66.107975	241	68.209297
197	66.170559	242	68.242527
198	66.232269	243	68.275294
199	66.293116	244	68.307603
200	66.353114	245	68.339461
201	66.412273	246	68.370873
202	66.470606	247	68.401847
203	66.528124	248	68.432388
204	66.584839	249	68.462503
205	66.640762	250	68.492197
206	66.695903	251	68.521476
207	66.750274	252	68.550346
208	66.803886	253	68.578813
209	66.856749	254	68.606882
210	66.908873	255	68.634559
211	66.960269	256	68.661849
212	67.010947	257	68.688759
213	67.060918	258	68.715292
214	67.110190	259	68.741455
215	67.158774	260	68.767252
216	67.206679	261	68.792689
217	67.253916	262	68.817771
218	67.300492	263	68.842502
219	67.346418	264	68.866888
220	67.391702	265	68.890933
221	67.436354	266	68.914642
222	67.480382	267	68.938020
223	67.523794	268	68.961071
224	67.566601	269	68.983801
225	67.608809	270	69.006213

yearly interest rate = 17.00%

term (months)	constant	term (months)	constant
271	69.028312	316	69.759944
272	69.050102	317	69.771514
273	69.071588	318	69.782922
274	69.092774	319	69.794172
275	69.113663	320	69.805264
276	69.134261	321	69.816201
277	69.154572	322	69.826985
278	69.174598	323	69.837619
279	69.194345	324	69.848104
280	69.213816	325	69.858443
281	69.233015	326	69.868637
282	69.251946	327	69.878689
283	69.270612	328	69.888601
284	69.289017	329	69.898374
285	69.307166	330	69.908010
286	69.325061	331	69.917512
287	69.342706	332	69.926881
288	69.360104	333	69.936120
289	69.377260	334	69.945229
290	69.394176	335	69.954211
291	69.410855	336	69.963067
292	69.427302	337	69.971800
293	69.443519	338	69.980411
294	69.459509	339	69.988902
295	69.475276	340	69.997274
296	69.490823	341	70.005529
297	69.506152	342	70.013668
298	69.521267	343	70.021694
299	69.536172	344	70.029608
300	69.550868	345	70.037411
301	69.565358	346	70.045106
302	69.579647	347	70.052693
303	69.593736	348	70.060174
304	69.607628	349	70.067550
305	69.621325	350	70.074823
306	69.634832	351	70.081995
307	69.648150	352	70.089067
308	69.661282	353	70.096039
309	69.674230	354	70.102915
310	69.686998	355	70.109694
311	69.699587	356	70.116379
312	69.712000	357	70.122970
313	69.724240	358	70.129469
314	69.736309	359	70.135878
315	69.748209	360	70.142196

yearly interest rate = 17.25%

term (months)	constant	term (months)	constant
1	0.9858287	46	33.485807
2	1.9576870	47	33.997098
3	2.9157727	48	34.501144
4	3.8602812	49	34.998047
5	4.7914047	50	35.487909
6	5.7093331	51	35.970828
7	6.6142532	52	36.446904
8	7.5063494	53	36.916233
9	8.3858035	54	37.378911
10	9.2527946	55	37.835033
11	10.107499	56	38.284690
12	10.950092	57	38.727975
13	11.780744	58	39.164979
14	12.599624	59	39.595789
15	13.406900	60	40.020495
16	14.202735	61	40.439182
17	14.987293	62	40.851935
18	15.760733	63	41.258839
19	16.523211	64	41.659977
20	17.274885	65	42.055430
21	18.015906	66	42.445279
22	18.746426	67	42.829604
23	19.466594	68	43.208482
24	20.176556	69	43.581991
25	20.876457	70	43.950207
26	21.566439	71	44.313204
27	22.246644	72	44.671058
28	22.917209	73	45.023840
29	23.578271	74	45.371623
30	24.229966	75	45.714477
31	24.872425	76	46.052473
32	25.505779	77	46.385679
33	26.130158	78	46.714163
34	26.745689	79	47.037992
35	27.352497	80	47.357232
36	27.950705	81	47.671947
37	28.540436	82	47.982203
38	29.121810	83	48.288062
39	29.694946	84	48.589587
40	30.259959	85	48.886839
41	30.816965	86	49.179878
42	31.366077	87	49.468764
43	31.907408	88	49.753557
44	32.441068	89	50.034314
45	32.967165	90	50.311092

yearly interest rate = 17.25%

term (months)	constant	term (months)	constant
91	50.583948	136	59.579228
92	50.852937	137	59.720743
93	51.118114	138	59.860251
94	51.379533	139	59.997783
95	51.637247	140	60.133366
96	51.891310	141	60.267028
97	52.141772	142	60.398795
98	52.388685	143	60.528695
99	52.632098	144	60.656754
100	52.872062	145	60.782999
101	53.108626	146	60.907454
102	53.341837	147	61.030146
103	53.571743	148	61.151098
104	53.798391	149	61.270337
105	54.021827	150	61.387887
106	54.242097	151	61.503770
107	54.459246	152	61.618011
108	54.673317	153	61.730633
109	54.884354	154	61.841659
110	55.092401	155	61.951112
111	55.297499	156	62.059014
112	55.499691	157	62.165386
113	55.699018	158	62.270251
114	55.895520	159	62.373630
115	56.089237	160	62.475544
116	56.280209	161	62.576014
117	56.468475	162	62.675060
118	56.654072	163	62.772703
119	56.837040	164	62.868961
120	57.017415	165	62.963856
121	57.195233	166	63.057406
122	57.370532	167	63.149630
123	57.543346	168	63.240547
124	57.713711	169	63.330176
125	57.881663	170	63.418534
126	58.047234	171	63.505641
127	58.210458	172	63.591513
128	58.371370	173	63.676168
129	58.530001	174	63.759623
130	58.686384	175	63.841896
131	58.840551	176	63.923003
132	58.992534	177	64.002960
133	59.142362	178	64.081785
134	59.290068	179	64.159492
135	59.435680	180	64.236098

yearly interest rate = 17.25%

term (months)	constant	term (months)	constant
181	64.311618	226	66.801315
182	64.386069	227	66.840483
183	64.459464	228	66.879096
184	64.531819	229	66.917162
185	64.603149	230	66.954688
186	64.673468	231	66.991683
187	64.742790	232	67.028153
188	64.811130	233	67.064106
189	64.878502	234	67.099550
190	64.944918	235	67.134492
191	65.010394	236	67.168938
192	65.074942	237	67.202897
193	65.138575	238	67.236374
194	65.201306	239	67.269377
195	65.263148	240	67.301912
196	65.324114	241	67.333986
197	65.384216	242	67.365605
198	65.443466	243	67.396776
199	65.501877	244	67.427506
200	65.559459	245	67.457800
201	65.616226	246	67.487665
202	65.672188	247	67.517107
203	65.727358	248	67.546131
204	65.781745	249	67.574744
205	65.835362	250	67.602952
206	65.888219	251	67.630759
207	65.940326	252	67.658173
208	65.991696	253	67.685198
209	66.042337	254	67.711841
210	66.092261	255	67.738105
211	66.141477	256	67.763998
212	66.189996	257	67.789524
213	66.237827	258	67.814687
214	66.284981	259	67.839495
215	66.331466	260	67.863950
216	66.377292	261	67.888060
217	66.422469	262	67.911827
218	66.467006	263	67.935258
219	66.510912	264	67.958356
220	66.554195	265	67.981128
221	66.596865	266	68.003576
222	66.638931	267	68.025707
223	66.680400	268	68.047524
224	66.721281	269	68.069031
225	66.761584	270	68.090234

yearly interest rate = 17.25%

term (months)	constant	term (months)	constant
271	68.111136	316	68.800230
272	68.131743	317	68.811071
273	68.152057	318	68.821758
274	68.172083	319	68.832294
275	68.191826	320	68.842680
276	68.211288	321	68.852919
277	68.230475	322	68.863014
278	68.249390	323	68.872965
279	68.268037	324	68.882775
280	68.286420	325	68.892446
281	68.304542	326	68.901980
282	68.322408	327	68.911379
283	68.340020	328	68.920645
284	68.357382	329	68.929779
285	68.374499	330	68.938784
286	68.391373	331	68.947661
287	68.408008	332	68.956413
288	68.424407	333	68.965041
289	68.440574	334	68.973546
290	68.456511	335	68.981931
291	68.472223	336	68.990196
292	68.487712	337	68.998345
293	68.502982	338	69.006379
294	68.518035	339	69.014298
295	68.532875	340	69.022105
296	68.547505	341	69.029802
297	68.561927	342	69.037389
298	68.576145	343	69.044869
299	68.590161	344	69.052243
300	68.603979	345	69.059513
301	68.617601	346	69.066679
302	68.631030	347	69.073744
303	68.644269	348	69.080709
304	68.657320	349	69.087575
305	68.670186	350	69.094344
306	68.682870	351	69.101017
307	68.695374	352	69.107595
308	68.707700	353	69.114080
309	68.719853	354	69.120474
310	68.731833	355	69.126776
311	68.743643	356	69.132989
312	68.755285	357	69.139115
313	68.766763	358	69.145153
314	68.778078	359	69.151106
315	68.789233	360	69.156974

yearly interest rate = 17.50%

term (months)	constant	term (months)	constant
1	0.9856263	46	33.341813
2	1.9570854	47	33.848194
3	2.9145811	48	34.347296
4	3.8583141	49	34.839224
5	4.7884820	50	35.324081
6	5.7052800	51	35.801969
7	6.6089002	52	36.272988
8	7.4995321	53	36.737236
9	8.3773622	54	37.194812
10	9.2425746	55	37.645811
11	10.095351	56	38.090327
12	10.935869	57	38.528453
13	11.764307	58	38.960283
14	12.580836	59	39.385905
15	13.385629	60	39.805409
16	14.178854	61	40.218884
17	14.960677	62	40.626415
18	15.731263	63	41.028089
19	16.490773	64	41.423989
20	17.239365	65	41.814199
21	17.977198	66	42.198800
22	18.704425	67	42.577872
23	19.421199	68	42.951496
24	20.127671	69	43.319750
25	20.823987	70	43.682710
26	21.510296	71	44.040454
27	22.186739	72	44.393055
28	22.853459	73	44.740588
29	23.510597	74	45.083126
30	24.158288	75	45.420740
31	24.796670	76	45.753502
32	25.425876	77	46.081480
33	26.046038	78	46.404744
34	26.657286	79	46.723362
35	27.259748	80	47.037400
36	27.853550	81	47.346924
37	28.438818	82	47.651999
38	29.015672	83	47.952689
39	29.584236	84	48.249057
40	30.144626	85	48.541165
41	30.696962	86	48.829074
42	31.241359	87	49.112845
43	31.777931	88	49.392537
44	32.306790	89	49.668209
45	32.828048	90	49.939919

yearly interest rate = 17.50%

term (months)	constant	term (months)	constant
91	50.207723	136	58.999207
92	50.471677	137	59.136795
93	50.731838	138	59.272406
94	50.988259	139	59.406067
95	51.240995	140	59.537808
96	51.490098	141	59.667654
97	51.735620	142	59.795635
98	51.977613	143	59.921775
99	52.216128	144	60.046103
100	52.451214	145	60.168644
101	52.682922	146	60.289423
102	52.911298	147	60.408466
103	53.136393	148	60.525798
104	53.358252	149	60.641444
105	53.576921	150	60.755427
106	53.792448	151	60.867772
107	54.004877	152	60.978502
108	54.214253	153	61.087641
109	54.420619	154	61.195211
110	54.624018	155	61.301235
111	54.824494	156	61.405734
112	55.022089	157	61.508732
113	55.216843	158	61.610249
114	55.408798	159	61.710307
115	55.597994	160	61.808927
116	55.784471	161	61.906129
117	55.968267	162	62.001934
118	56.149421	163	62.096362
119	56.327972	164	62.189433
120	56.503956	165	62.281166
121	56.677410	166	62.371581
122	56.848371	167	62.460695
123	57.016875	168	62.548529
124	57.182957	169	62.635101
125	57.346652	170	62.720428
126	57.507993	171	62.804529
127	57.667016	172	62.887420
128	57.823753	173	62.969121
129	57.978237	174	63.049647
130	58.130501	175	63.129015
131	58.280576	176	63.207243
132	58.428493	177	63.284346
133	58.574285	178	63.360341
134	58.717981	179	63.435244
135	58.859612	180	63.509070

yearly interest rate = 17.50%

term (months)	constant	term (months)	constant
181	63.581835	226	65.970565
182	63.653554	227	66.007949
183	63.724242	228	66.044796
184	63.793914	229	66.081113
185	63.862585	230	66.116908
186	63.930268	231	66.152188
187	63.996979	232	66.186962
188	64.062731	233	66.221235
189	64.127538	234	66.255016
190	64.191413	235	66.288312
191	64.254370	236	66.321129
192	64.316422	237	66.353474
193	64.377582	238	66.385354
194	64.437864	239	66.416776
195	64.497278	240	66.447747
196	64.555839	241	66.478272
197	64.613558	242	66.508358
198	64.670447	243	66.538012
199	64.726519	244	66.567240
200	64.781784	245	66.596048
201	64.836256	246	66.624441
202	64.889944	247	66.652427
203	64.942861	248	66.680010
204	64.995017	249	66.707197
205	65.046423	250	66.733992
206	65.097090	251	66.760403
207	65.147030	252	66.786434
208	65.196251	253	66.812091
209	65.244765	254	66.837380
210	65.292581	255	66.862304
211	65.339710	256	66.886871
212	65.386162	257	66.911084
213	65.431946	258	66.934950
214	65.477072	259	66.958472
215	65.521550	260	66.981656
216	65.565388	261	67.004507
217	65.608596	262	67.027029
218	65.651183	263	67.049228
219	65.693158	264	67.071108
220	65.734529	265	67.092673
221	65.775306	266	67.113928
222	65.815497	267	67.134878
223	65.855109	268	67.155527
224	65.894153	269	67.175878
225	65.932635	270	67.195938

yearly interest rate = 17.50%

term (months)	constant	term (months)	constant
271	67.215708	316	67.864749
272	67.235195	317	67.874907
273	67.254402	318	67.884918
274	67.273332	319	67.894786
275	67.291991	320	67.904512
276	67.310381	321	67.914098
277	67.328507	322	67.923546
278	67.346372	323	67.932859
279	67.363981	324	67.942037
280	67.381337	325	67.951084
281	67.398443	326	67.960001
282	67.415303	327	67.968789
283	67.431921	328	67.977451
284	67.448300	329	67.985989
285	67.464443	330	67.994404
286	67.480355	331	68.002698
287	67.496037	332	68.010873
288	67.511495	333	68.018930
289	67.526730	334	68.026871
290	67.541746	335	68.034699
291	67.556547	336	68.042414
292	67.571134	337	68.050017
293	67.585512	338	68.057512
294	67.599683	339	68.064899
295	67.613651	340	68.072180
296	67.627418	341	68.079356
297	67.640987	342	68.086429
298	67.654361	343	68.093400
299	67.667542	344	68.100271
300	67.680535	345	68.107043
301	67.693340	346	68.113718
302	67.705961	347	68.120297
303	67.718401	348	68.126782
304	67.730663	349	68.133173
305	67.742747	350	68.139472
306	67.754659	351	68.145681
307	67.766399	352	68.151801
308	67.777970	353	68.157832
309	67.789375	354	68.163777
310	67.800616	355	68.169637
311	67.811695	356	68.175412
312	67.822616	357	68.181104
313	67.833379	358	68.186715
314	67.843987	359	68.192244
315	67.854443	360	68.197695

yearly interest rate = 17.75%

term (months)	constant	term (months)	constant
1	0.9854239	46	33.198710
2	1.9564843	47	33.700227
3	2.9133904	48	34.194435
4	3.8563486	49	34.681438
5	4.7855621	50	35.161344
6	5.7012314	51	35.634254
7	6.6035539	52	36.100270
8	7.4927240	53	36.559495
9	8.3689335	54	37.012025
10	9.2323713	55	37.457959
11	10.083224	56	37.897394
12	10.921674	57	38.330423
13	11.747903	58	38.757140
14	12.562089	59	39.177638
15	13.364407	60	39.592006
16	14.155030	61	40.000334
17	14.934130	62	40.402711
18	15.701873	63	40.799222
19	16.458425	64	41.189954
20	17.203950	65	41.574991
21	17.938608	66	41.954415
22	18.662558	67	42.328309
23	19.375955	68	42.696753
24	20.078954	69	43.059826
25	20.771706	70	43.417607
26	21.454360	71	43.770174
27	22.127064	72	44.117601
28	22.789962	73	44.459964
29	23.443198	74	44.797337
30	24.086913	75	45.129792
31	24.721244	76	45.457401
32	25.346330	77	45.780235
33	25.962304	78	46.098363
34	26.569300	79	46.411855
35	27.167448	80	46.720777
36	27.756878	81	47.025196
37	28.337716	82	47.325177
38	28.910087	83	47.620786
39	29.474116	84	47.912087
40	30.029923	85	48.199141
41	30.577629	86	48.482011
42	31.117352	87	48.760759
43	31.649207	88	49.035443
44	32.173310	89	49.306123
45	32.689774	90	49.572858

yearly interest rate = 17.75%

term (months)	constant	term (months)	constant
91	49.835705	136	58.428109
92	50.094720	137	58.561882
93	50.349960	138	58.693704
94	50.601480	139	58.823605
95	50.849334	140	58.951612
96	51.093575	141	59.077754
97	51.334255	142	59.202057
98	51.571428	143	59.324548
99	51.805144	144	59.445253
100	52.035453	145	59.564200
101	52.262405	146	59.681412
102	52.486048	147	59.796916
103	52.706432	148	59.910736
104	52.923604	149	60.022898
105	53.137610	150	60.133424
106	53.348497	151	60.242339
107	53.556310	152	60.349667
108	53.761094	153	60.455431
109	53.962893	154	60.559652
110	54.161750	155	60.662355
111	54.357709	156	60.763561
112	54.550812	157	60.863291
113	54.741100	158	60.961568
114	54.928614	159	61.058412
115	55.113395	160	61.153845
116	55.295482	161	61.247887
117	55.474916	162	61.340558
118	55.651734	163	61.431878
119	55.825975	164	61.521867
120	55.997676	165	61.610544
121	56.166874	166	61.697929
122	56.333606	167	61.784040
123	56.497908	168	61.868896
124	56.659815	169	61.952515
125	56.819362	170	62.034915
126	56.976583	171	62.116114
127	57.131513	172	62.196130
128	57.284184	173	62.274979
129	57.434631	174	62.352679
130	57.582884	175	62.429247
131	57.728976	176	62.504698
132	57.872939	177	62.579050
133	58.014803	178	62.652317
134	58.154600	179	62.724517
135	58.292359	180	62.795665

yearly interest rate = 17.75%

term (months)	constant	term (months)	constant
181	62.865775	226	65.157669
182	62.934864	227	65.193350
183	63.002945	228	65.228512
184	63.070034	229	65.263161
185	63.136145	230	65.297305
186	63.201293	231	65.330951
187	63.265491	232	65.364107
188	63.328753	233	65.396780
189	63.391093	234	65.428976
190	63.452524	235	65.460703
191	63.513060	236	65.491968
192	63.572714	237	65.522777
193	63.631498	238	65.553137
194	63.689425	239	65.583054
195	63.746508	240	65.612535
196	63.802759	241	65.641587
197	63.858190	242	65.670215
198	63.912813	243	65.698426
199	63.966640	244	65.726225
200	64.019682	245	65.753620
201	64.071951	246	65.780615
202	64.123458	247	65.807216
203	64.174215	248	65.833430
204	64.224231	249	65.859262
205	64.273519	250	65.884717
206	64.322088	251	65.909801
207	64.369949	252	65.934520
208	64.417113	253	65.958878
209	64.463589	254	65.982881
210	64.509387	255	66.006535
211	64.554518	256	66.029843
212	64.598992	257	66.052812
213	64.642817	258	66.075446
214	64.686003	259	66.097750
215	64.728560	260	66.119729
216	64.770496	261	66.141388
217	64.811821	262	66.162731
218	64.852544	263	66.183763
219	64.892673	264	66.204488
220	64.932217	265	66.224911
221	64.971185	266	66.245037
222	65.009585	267	66.264869
223	65.047425	268	66.284412
224	65.084714	269	66.303670
225	65.121459	270	66.322648

yearly interest rate = 17.75%

term (months)	constant	term (months)	constant
271	66.341348	316	66.952676
272	66.359777	317	66.962194
273	66.377936	318	66.971573
274	66.395831	319	66.980815
275	66.413466	320	66.989922
276	66.430843	321	66.998897
277	66.447967	322	67.007741
278	66.464841	323	67.016456
279	66.481469	324	67.025043
280	66.497855	325	67.033506
281	66.514002	326	67.041846
282	66.529914	327	67.050063
283	66.545593	328	67.058161
284	66.561045	329	67.066141
285	66.576271	330	67.074005
286	66.591275	331	67.081754
287	66.606060	332	67.089390
288	66.620630	333	67.096915
289	66.634987	334	67.104330
290	66.649136	335	67.111637
291	66.663078	336	67.118838
292	66.676816	337	67.125933
293	66.690355	338	67.132925
294	66.703696	339	67.139816
295	66.716843	340	67.146605
296	66.729798	341	67.153296
297	66.742564	342	67.159890
298	66.755144	343	67.166387
299	66.767541	344	67.172789
300	66.779757	345	67.179098
301	66.791795	346	67.185316
302	66.803658	347	67.191442
303	66.815347	348	67.197479
304	66.826867	349	67.203429
305	66.838218	350	67.209291
306	66.849404	351	67.215068
307	66.860427	352	67.220761
308	66.871289	353	67.226371
309	66.881993	354	67.231899
310	66.892541	355	67.237347
311	66.902935	356	67.242715
312	66.913177	357	67.248005
313	66.923271	358	67.253218
314	66.933217	359	67.258355
315	66.943018	360	67.263417

yearly interest rate = 18.00%

term (months)	constant	term (months)	constant
1	0.9852217	46	33.056490
2	1.9558834	47	33.553192
3	2.9122004	48	34.042554
4	3.8543847	49	34.524683
5	4.7826450	50	34.999688
6	5.6971872	51	35.467673
7	6.5982140	52	35.928742
8	7.4859251	53	36.382997
9	8.3605173	54	36.830539
10	9.2221846	55	37.271467
11	10.071118	56	37.705879
12	10.907505	57	38.133871
13	11.731532	58	38.555538
14	12.543382	59	38.970973
15	13.343233	60	39.380269
16	14.131264	61	39.783516
17	14.907649	62	40.180804
18	15.672561	63	40.572221
19	16.426168	64	40.957853
20	17.168639	65	41.337786
21	17.900137	66	41.712105
22	18.620824	67	42.080891
23	19.330861	68	42.444228
24	20.030405	69	42.802195
25	20.719611	70	43.154872
26	21.398632	71	43.502337
27	22.067617	72	43.844667
28	22.726717	73	44.181938
29	23.376076	74	44.514224
30	24.015838	75	44.841600
31	24.646146	76	45.164138
32	25.267139	77	45.481910
33	25.878954	78	45.794985
34	26.481729	79	46.103433
35	27.075595	80	46.407324
36	27.660684	81	46.706723
37	28.237127	82	47.001697
38	28.805052	83	47.292313
39	29.364583	84	47.578633
40	29.915845	85	47.860722
41	30.458961	86	48.138643
42	30.994050	87	48.412456
43	31.521232	88	48.682222
44	32.040622	89	48.948002
45	32.552337	90	49.209855

yearly interest rate = 18.00%

term (months)	constant	term (months)	constant
91	49.467837	136	57.865769
92	49.722007	137	57.995831
93	49.972421	138	58.123971
94	50.219134	139	58.250218
95	50.462201	140	58.374599
96	50.701675	141	58.497142
97	50.937611	142	58.617874
98	51.170060	143	58.736822
99	51.399074	144	58.854011
100	51.624704	145	58.969469
101	51.846999	146	59.083221
102	52.066009	147	59.195292
103	52.281782	148	59.305706
104	52.494366	149	59.414489
105	52.703809	150	59.521664
106	52.910157	151	59.627255
107	53.113455	152	59.731286
108	53.313749	153	59.833779
109	53.511083	154	59.934758
110	53.705500	155	60.034244
111	53.897044	156	60.132260
112	54.085758	157	60.228828
113	54.271683	158	60.323968
114	54.454860	159	60.417703
115	54.635330	160	60.510052
116	54.813133	161	60.601036
117	54.988308	162	60.690676
118	55.160895	163	60.778991
119	55.330931	164	60.866001
120	55.498454	165	60.951725
121	55.663502	166	61.036183
122	55.826110	167	61.119392
123	55.986315	168	61.201371
124	56.144153	169	61.282139
125	56.299658	170	61.361713
126	56.452865	171	61.440112
127	56.603808	172	61.517352
128	56.752520	173	61.593450
129	56.899035	174	61.668423
130	57.043384	175	61.742289
131	57.185600	176	61.815063
132	57.325714	177	61.886762
133	57.463758	178	61.957401
134	57.599761	179	62.026996
135	57.733755	180	62.095562

yearly interest rate = 18.00%

term (months)	constant	term (months)	constant
181	62.163116	226	64.362132
182	62.229671	227	64.396189
183	62.295242	228	64.429743
184	62.359844	229	64.462801
185	62.423492	230	64.495371
186	62.486199	231	64.527459
187	62.547979	232	64.559073
188	62.608846	233	64.590219
189	62.668814	234	64.620906
190	62.727896	235	64.651139
191	62.786104	236	64.680925
192	62.843452	237	64.710271
193	62.899953	238	64.739183
194	62.955619	239	64.767668
195	63.010462	240	64.795732
196	63.064495	241	64.823381
197	63.117729	242	64.850622
198	63.170176	243	64.877460
199	63.221848	244	64.903902
200	63.272757	245	64.929952
201	63.322913	246	64.955618
202	63.372328	247	64.980904
203	63.421013	248	65.005817
204	63.468978	249	65.030362
205	63.516235	250	65.054544
206	63.562793	251	65.078368
207	63.608663	252	65.101841
208	63.653855	253	65.124966
209	63.698380	254	65.147750
210	63.742246	255	65.170197
211	63.785464	256	65.192312
212	63.828043	257	65.214101
213	63.869993	258	65.235567
214	63.911323	259	65.256716
215	63.952043	260	65.277553
216	63.992160	261	65.298082
217	64.031685	262	65.318307
218	64.070626	263	65.338234
219	64.108991	264	65.357866
220	64.146789	265	65.377208
221	64.184029	266	65.396264
222	64.220718	267	65.415038
223	64.256865	268	65.433535
224	64.292478	269	65.451759
225	64.327564	270	65.469713

yearly interest rate = 18.00%

term (months)	constant	term (months)	constant
271	65.487402	316	66.063219
272	65.504830	317	66.072137
273	65.522000	318	66.080923
274	65.538916	319	66.089580
275	65.555582	320	66.098108
276	65.572002	321	66.106510
277	65.588179	322	66.114789
278	65.604118	323	66.122944
279	65.619820	324	66.130980
280	65.635291	325	66.138896
281	65.650533	326	66.146696
282	65.665550	327	66.154380
283	65.680345	328	66.161951
284	65.694921	329	66.169410
285	65.709281	330	66.176758
286	65.723430	331	66.183998
287	65.737370	332	66.191131
288	65.751103	333	66.198159
289	65.764633	334	66.205083
290	65.777964	335	66.211904
291	65.791098	336	66.218625
292	65.804037	337	66.225246
293	65.816785	338	66.231770
294	65.829345	339	66.238197
295	65.841719	340	66.244529
296	65.853911	341	66.250767
297	65.865922	342	66.256914
298	65.877755	343	66.262969
299	65.889414	344	66.268935
300	65.900901	345	66.274813
301	65.912217	346	66.280604
302	65.923367	347	66.286309
303	65.934352	348	66.291930
304	65.945174	349	66.297468
305	65.955836	350	66.302924
306	65.966341	351	66.308300
307	65.976691	352	66.313596
308	65.986888	353	66.318814
309	65.996934	354	66.323954
310	66.006831	355	66.329019
311	66.016582	356	66.334009
312	66.026190	357	66.338925
313	66.035655	358	66.343768
314	66.044980	359	66.348540
315	66.054168	360	66.353242

yearly interest rate = 18.25%

term (months)	constant	term (months)	constant
1	0.9850195	46	32.915147
2	1.9552829	47	33.407081
3	2.9110113	48	33.891645
4	3.8524223	49	34.368951
5	4.7797306	50	34.839106
6	5.6931473	51	35.302218
7	6.5928806	52	35.758393
8	7.4791354	53	36.207733
9	8.3521137	54	36.650343
10	9.2120143	55	37.086322
11	10.059033	56	37.515769
12	10.893363	57	37.938784
13	11.715195	58	38.355461
14	12.524715	59	38.765896
15	13.322108	60	39.170183
16	14.107555	61	39.568413
17	14.881236	62	39.960678
18	15.643327	63	40.347067
19	16.394002	64	40.727667
20	17.133431	65	41.102565
21	17.861783	66	41.471847
22	18.579224	67	41.835598
23	19.285917	68	42.193899
24	19.982024	69	42.546832
25	20.667703	70	42.894479
26	21.343110	71	43.236917
27	22.008399	72	43.574226
28	22.663721	73	43.906482
29	23.309227	74	44.233760
30	23.945062	75	44.556135
31	24.571373	76	44.873681
32	25.188301	77	45.186471
33	25.795987	78	45.494574
34	26.394569	79	45.798062
35	26.984185	80	46.097003
36	27.564967	81	46.391466
37	28.137050	82	46.681518
38	28.700562	83	46.967225
39	29.255633	84	47.248652
40	29.802388	85	47.525863
41	30.340953	86	47.798921
42	30.871449	87	48.067888
43	31.393999	88	48.332826
44	31.908721	89	48.593796
45	32.415731	90	48.850856

yearly interest rate = 18.25%

term (months)	constant	term (months)	constant
91	49.104065	136	57.312020
92	49.353480	137	57.438477
93	49.599160	138	57.563039
94	49.841159	139	57.685735
95	50.079533	140	57.806593
96	50.314336	141	57.925640
97	50.545621	142	58.042905
98	50.773441	143	58.158412
99	50.997849	144	58.272189
100	51.218895	145	58.384262
101	51.436630	146	58.494656
102	51.651103	147	58.603396
103	51.862362	148	58.710507
104	52.070458	149	58.816013
105	52.275435	150	58.919939
106	52.477342	151	59.022308
107	52.676225	152	59.123144
108	52.872128	153	59.222469
109	53.065096	154	59.320306
110	53.255174	155	59.416677
111	53.442404	156	59.511605
112	53.626829	157	59.605110
113	53.808492	158	59.697215
114	53.987433	159	59.787940
115	54.163693	160	59.877306
116	54.337313	161	59.965333
117	54.508332	162	60.052042
118	54.676790	163	60.137452
119	54.842723	164	60.221582
120	55.006171	165	60.304452
121	55.167170	166	60.386080
122	55.325758	167	60.466485
123	55.481969	168	60.545686
124	55.635841	169	60.623701
125	55.787408	170	60.700547
126	55.936704	171	60.776241
127	56.083763	172	60.850802
128	56.228619	173	60.924246
129	56.371306	174	60.996590
130	56.511855	175	61.067849
131	56.650298	176	61.138042
132	56.786667	177	61.207182
133	56.920994	178	61.275287
134	57.053308	179	61.342372
135	57.183640	180	61.408452

yearly interest rate = 18.25%

term (months)	constant	term (months)	constant
181	61.473542	226	63.583478
182	61.537657	227	63.615985
183	61.600811	228	63.648005
184	61.663019	229	63.679545
185	61.724296	230	63.710613
186	61.784654	231	63.741215
187	61.844108	232	63.771359
188	61.902672	233	63.801051
189	61.960358	234	63.830299
190	62.017180	235	63.859108
191	62.073151	236	63.887486
192	62.128283	237	63.915439
193	62.182590	238	63.942973
194	62.236082	239	63.970094
195	62.288774	240	63.996810
196	62.340676	241	64.023125
197	62.391801	242	64.049045
198	62.442160	243	64.074578
199	62.491764	244	64.099728
200	62.540625	245	64.124501
201	62.588755	246	64.148903
202	62.636163	247	64.172940
203	62.682861	248	64.196616
204	62.728860	249	64.219938
205	62.774169	250	64.242910
206	62.818800	251	64.265538
207	62.862762	252	64.287828
208	62.906066	253	64.309783
209	62.948721	254	64.331410
210	62.990737	255	64.352712
211	63.032123	256	64.373696
212	63.072890	257	64.394365
213	63.113045	258	64.414724
214	63.152600	259	64.434778
215	63.191561	260	64.454532
216	63.229939	261	64.473990
217	63.267742	262	64.493157
218	63.304979	263	64.512036
219	63.341658	264	64.530633
220	63.377788	265	64.548951
221	63.413376	266	64.566995
222	63.448431	267	64.584768
223	63.482961	268	64.602275
224	63.516974	269	64.619520
225	63.550477	270	64.636506

yearly interest rate = 18.25%

term (months)	constant	term (months)	constant
271	64.653238	316	65.195618
272	64.669720	317	65.203975
273	64.685954	318	65.212206
274	64.701945	319	65.220313
275	64.717697	320	65.228300
276	64.733213	321	65.236166
277	64.748496	322	65.243915
278	64.763550	323	65.251548
279	64.778379	324	65.259066
280	64.792986	325	65.266472
281	64.807374	326	65.273767
282	64.821546	327	65.280952
283	64.835506	328	65.288030
284	64.849257	329	65.295002
285	64.862802	330	65.301869
286	64.876144	331	65.308634
287	64.889286	332	65.315297
288	64.902231	333	65.321860
289	64.914983	334	65.328325
290	64.927543	335	65.334694
291	64.939915	336	65.340966
292	64.952102	337	65.347145
293	64.964106	338	65.353232
294	64.975930	339	65.359227
295	64.987578	340	65.365132
296	64.999050	341	65.370949
297	65.010351	342	65.376678
298	65.021483	343	65.382322
299	65.032448	344	65.387882
300	65.043248	345	65.393358
301	65.053887	346	65.398752
302	65.064367	347	65.404065
303	65.074689	348	65.409298
304	65.084857	349	65.414454
305	65.094872	350	65.419532
306	65.104738	351	65.424533
307	65.114455	352	65.429460
308	65.124027	353	65.434314
309	65.133456	354	65.439094
310	65.142744	355	65.443803
311	65.151892	356	65.448441
312	65.160903	357	65.453010
313	65.169779	358	65.457510
314	65.178523	359	65.461943
315	65.187135	360	65.466310

yearly interest rate = 18.50%

term (months)	constant	term (months)	constant
1	0.9848174	46	32.774675
2	1.9546827	47	33.261887
3	2.9098229	48	33.741703
4	3.8504617	49	34.214233
5	4.7768190	50	34.679589
6	5.6891119	51	35.137880
7	6.5875538	52	35.589213
8	7.4723550	53	36.033694
9	8.3437226	54	36.471426
10	9.2018606	55	36.902512
11	10.046970	56	37.327054
12	10.879248	57	37.745149
13	11.698890	58	38.156897
14	12.506088	59	38.562394
15	13.301030	60	38.961734
16	14.083904	61	39.355010
17	14.854891	62	39.742316
18	15.614172	63	40.123742
19	16.361926	64	40.499377
20	17.098327	65	40.869308
21	17.823547	66	41.233623
22	18.537757	67	41.592407
23	19.241123	68	41.945743
24	19.933810	69	42.293715
25	20.615980	70	42.636404
26	21.287793	71	42.973890
27	21.949407	72	43.306252
28	22.600975	73	43.633568
29	23.242651	74	43.955914
30	23.874584	75	44.273366
31	24.496923	76	44.585999
32	25.109814	77	44.893885
33	25.713399	78	45.197096
34	26.307820	79	45.495704
35	26.893216	80	45.789778
36	27.469724	81	46.079388
37	28.037480	82	46.364600
38	28.596616	83	46.645482
39	29.147262	84	46.922100
40	29.689548	85	47.194518
41	30.223601	86	47.462800
42	30.749545	87	47.727008
43	31.267505	88	47.987205
44	31.777600	89	48.243452
45	32.279951	90	48.495809

yearly interest rate = 18.50%

term (months)	constant	term (months)	constant
91	48.744333	136	56.766704
92	48.989085	137	56.889655
93	49.230121	138	57.010739
94	49.467497	139	57.129985
95	49.701269	140	57.247421
96	49.931492	141	57.363074
97	50.158219	142	57.476970
98	50.381504	143	57.589138
99	50.601399	144	57.699602
100	50.817956	145	57.808389
101	51.031225	146	57.915525
102	51.241255	147	58.021034
103	51.448097	148	58.124941
104	51.651798	149	58.227271
105	51.852407	150	58.328047
106	52.049970	151	58.427293
107	52.244534	152	58.525032
108	52.436143	153	58.621287
109	52.624843	154	58.716081
110	52.810679	155	58.809435
111	52.993693	156	58.901372
112	53.173928	157	58.991914
113	53.351427	158	59.081080
114	53.526231	159	59.168893
115	53.698381	160	59.255373
116	53.867917	161	59.340540
117	54.034879	162	59.424413
118	54.199307	163	59.507014
119	54.361238	164	59.588360
120	54.520710	165	59.668471
121	54.677761	166	59.747366
122	54.832428	167	59.825063
123	54.984746	168	59.901580
124	55.134752	169	59.976935
125	55.282481	170	60.051147
126	55.427966	171	60.124232
127	55.571243	172	60.196207
128	55.712344	173	60.267089
129	55.851303	174	60.336895
130	55.988153	175	60.405642
131	56.122924	176	60.473344
132	56.255650	177	60.540019
133	56.386360	178	60.605681
134	56.515086	179	60.670347
135	56.641857	180	60.734031

yearly interest rate = 18.50%

term (months)	constant	term (months)	constant
181	60.796747	226	62.821243
182	60.858512	227	62.852270
183	60.919339	228	62.882827
184	60.979242	229	62.912919
185	61.038236	230	62.942555
186	61.096334	231	62.971741
187	61.153550	232	63.000483
188	61.209898	233	63.028789
189	61.265390	234	63.056666
190	61.320039	235	63.084119
191	61.373859	236	63.111155
192	61.426861	237	63.137781
193	61.479059	238	63.164003
194	61.530465	239	63.189826
195	61.581089	240	63.215258
196	61.630946	241	63.240303
197	61.680045	242	63.264968
198	61.728399	243	63.289259
199	61.776019	244	63.313181
200	61.822915	245	63.336739
201	61.869100	246	63.359940
202	61.914583	247	63.382789
203	61.959376	248	63.405291
204	62.003489	249	63.427451
205	62.046932	250	63.449274
206	62.089716	251	63.470767
207	62.131850	252	63.491933
208	62.173344	253	63.512777
209	62.214208	254	63.533306
210	62.254452	255	63.553522
211	62.294085	256	63.573432
212	62.333116	257	63.593039
213	62.371555	258	63.612349
214	62.409410	259	63.631365
215	62.446690	260	63.650093
216	62.483404	261	63.668536
217	62.519561	262	63.686700
218	62.555169	263	63.704587
219	62.590236	264	63.722203
220	62.624771	265	63.739552
221	62.658781	266	63.756637
222	62.692275	267	63.773463
223	62.725261	268	63.790033
224	62.757746	269	63.806352
225	62.789737	270	63.822423

yearly interest rate = 18.50%

term (months)	constant	term (months)	constant
271	63.838250	316	64.349144
272	63.853837	317	64.356974
273	63.869187	318	64.364685
274	63.884304	319	64.372279
275	63.899191	320	64.379758
276	63.913852	321	64.387123
277	63.928291	322	64.394376
278	63.942511	323	64.401520
279	63.956515	324	64.408554
280	63.970306	325	64.415482
281	63.983888	326	64.422305
282	63.997263	327	64.429024
283	64.010436	328	64.435642
284	64.023408	329	64.442158
285	64.036183	330	64.448576
286	64.048765	331	64.454896
287	64.061156	332	64.461121
288	64.073358	333	64.467251
289	64.085375	334	64.473288
290	64.097210	335	64.479233
291	64.108865	336	64.485088
292	64.120343	337	64.490854
293	64.131647	338	64.496532
294	64.142779	339	64.502124
295	64.153742	340	64.507632
296	64.164539	341	64.513055
297	64.175171	342	64.518397
298	64.185643	343	64.523657
299	64.195955	344	64.528838
300	64.206111	345	64.533939
301	64.216112	346	64.538964
302	64.225962	347	64.543912
303	64.235662	348	64.548785
304	64.245215	349	64.553583
305	64.254623	350	64.558310
306	64.263888	351	64.562964
307	64.273013	352	64.567547
308	64.281999	353	64.572062
309	64.290848	354	64.576507
310	64.299563	355	64.580885
311	64.308146	356	64.585197
312	64.316598	357	64.589443
313	64.324922	358	64.593624
314	64.333120	359	64.597742
315	64.341193	360	64.601798

yearly interest rate = 18.75%

term (months)	constant	term (months)	constant
1	0.9846154	46	32.635066
2	1.9540828	47	33.117604
3	2.9086354	48	33.592718
4	3.8485026	49	34.060522
5	4.7739102	50	34.521129
6	5.6850808	51	34.974650
7	6.5822334	52	35.421194
8	7.4655837	53	35.860868
9	8.3353439	54	36.293778
10	9.1917233	55	36.720028
11	10.034928	56	37.139719
12	10.865159	57	37.552955
13	11.682618	58	37.959832
14	12.487501	59	38.360450
15	13.280001	60	38.754905
16	14.060309	61	39.143291
17	14.828612	62	39.525702
18	15.585095	63	39.902229
19	16.329939	64	40.272964
20	17.063325	65	40.637996
21	17.785428	66	40.997411
22	18.496421	67	41.351297
23	19.196476	68	41.699739
24	19.885761	69	42.042820
25	20.564442	70	42.380622
26	21.232681	71	42.713228
27	21.890640	72	43.040717
28	22.538476	73	43.363167
29	23.176346	74	43.680657
30	23.804402	75	43.993262
31	24.422796	76	44.301058
32	25.031676	77	44.604119
33	25.631189	78	44.902517
34	26.221478	79	45.196325
35	26.802686	80	45.485612
36	27.374952	81	45.770449
37	27.938415	82	46.050903
38	28.493208	83	46.327043
39	29.039467	84	46.598935
40	29.577321	85	46.866644
41	30.106901	86	47.130234
42	30.628333	87	47.389769
43	31.141743	88	47.645311
44	31.647255	89	47.896921
45	32.144989	90	48.144661

yearly interest rate = 18.75%

term (months)	constant	term (months)	constant
91	48.388589	136	56.229662
92	48.628765	137	56.349205
93	48.865245	138	56.466910
94	49.098088	139	56.582804
95	49.327348	140	56.696914
96	49.553081	141	56.809269
97	49.775341	142	56.919896
98	49.994182	143	57.028821
99	50.209656	144	57.136070
100	50.421815	145	57.241669
101	50.630711	146	57.345643
102	50.836392	147	57.448018
103	51.038909	148	57.548817
104	51.238310	149	57.648066
105	51.434644	150	57.745788
106	51.627957	151	57.842007
107	51.818296	152	57.936745
108	52.005707	153	58.030026
109	52.190235	154	58.121872
110	52.371923	155	58.212305
111	52.550817	156	58.301346
112	52.726958	157	58.389018
113	52.900390	158	58.475341
114	53.071153	159	58.560335
115	53.239289	160	58.644022
116	53.404838	161	58.726422
117	53.567841	162	58.807554
118	53.728336	163	58.887438
119	53.886361	164	58.966093
120	54.041956	165	59.043537
121	54.195156	166	59.119791
122	54.346000	167	59.194871
123	54.494523	168	59.268796
124	54.640761	169	59.341584
125	54.784750	170	59.413252
126	54.926523	171	59.483817
127	55.066115	172	59.553297
128	55.203559	173	59.621707
129	55.338889	174	59.689066
130	55.472137	175	59.755388
131	55.603335	176	59.820690
132	55.732514	177	59.884987
133	55.859706	178	59.948295
134	55.984941	179	60.010629
135	56.108250	180	60.072003

yearly interest rate = 18.75%

term (months)	constant	term (months)	constant
181	60.132434	226	62.074979
182	60.191935	227	62.104595
183	60.250521	228	62.133755
184	60.308205	229	62.162466
185	60.365002	230	62.190736
186	60.420925	231	62.218571
187	60.475988	232	62.245977
188	60.530203	233	62.272962
189	60.583585	234	62.299532
190	60.636145	235	62.325693
191	60.687897	236	62.351452
192	60.738852	237	62.376814
193	60.789024	238	62.401786
194	60.838423	239	62.426374
195	60.887063	240	62.450584
196	60.934954	241	62.474421
197	60.982109	242	62.497891
198	61.028538	243	62.521001
199	61.074253	244	62.543754
200	61.119264	245	62.566158
201	61.163583	246	62.588217
202	61.207220	247	62.609937
203	61.250186	248	62.631323
204	61.292491	249	62.652379
205	61.334145	250	62.673112
206	61.375158	251	62.693526
207	61.415540	252	62.713625
208	61.455301	253	62.733416
209	61.494450	254	62.752901
210	61.532997	255	62.772088
211	61.570951	256	62.790979
212	61.608321	257	62.809579
213	61.645116	258	62.827893
214	61.681345	259	62.845925
215	61.717017	260	62.863680
216	61.752140	261	62.881162
217	61.786722	262	62.898375
218	61.820773	263	62.915323
219	61.854299	264	62.932011
220	61.887310	265	62.948441
221	61.919813	266	62.964619
222	61.951816	267	62.980548
223	61.983326	268	62.996232
224	62.014352	269	63.011674
225	62.044900	270	63.026879

yearly interest rate = 18.75%

term (months)	constant	term (months)	constant
271	63.041851	316	63.523096
272	63.056591	317	63.530433
273	63.071105	318	63.537657
274	63.085396	319	63.544770
275	63.099467	320	63.551774
276	63.113321	321	63.558669
277	63.126962	322	63.565459
278	63.140394	323	63.572144
279	63.153618	324	63.578727
280	63.166640	325	63.585208
281	63.179461	326	63.591589
282	63.192084	327	63.597872
283	63.204514	328	63.604059
284	63.216752	329	63.610150
285	63.228802	330	63.616148
286	63.240667	331	63.622054
287	63.252349	332	63.627868
288	63.263851	333	63.633593
289	63.275176	334	63.639230
290	63.286327	335	63.644781
291	63.297307	336	63.650245
292	63.308118	337	63.655626
293	63.318762	338	63.660924
294	63.329243	339	63.666141
295	63.339562	340	63.671277
296	63.349723	341	63.676334
297	63.359727	342	63.681314
298	63.369577	343	63.686217
299	63.379276	344	63.691044
300	63.388826	345	63.695797
301	63.398228	346	63.700477
302	63.407486	347	63.705085
303	63.416602	348	63.709623
304	63.425577	349	63.714090
305	63.434415	350	63.718489
306	63.443116	351	63.722820
307	63.451683	352	63.727084
308	63.460119	353	63.731283
309	63.468425	354	63.735417
310	63.476603	355	63.739487
311	63.484655	356	63.743495
312	63.492584	357	63.747441
313	63.500390	358	63.751327
314	63.508076	359	63.755153
315	63.515644	360	63.758919

yearly interest rate = 19.00%

term (months)	constant	term (months)	constant
1	0.9844135	46	32.496317
2	1.9534833	47	32.974225
3	2.9074487	48	33.444684
4	3.8465451	49	33.907810
5	4.7710042	50	34.363718
6	5.6810541	51	34.812520
7	6.5769196	52	35.254326
8	7.4588216	53	35.689246
9	8.3269778	54	36.117388
10	9.1816024	55	36.538856
11	10.022906	56	36.953755
12	10.851097	57	37.362187
13	11.666380	58	37.764253
14	12.468955	59	38.160052
15	13.259020	60	38.549682
16	14.036771	61	38.933239
17	14.802400	62	39.310818
18	15.556095	63	39.682511
19	16.298043	64	40.048412
20	17.028426	65	40.408609
21	17.747425	66	40.763191
22	18.455217	67	41.112247
23	19.151978	68	41.455863
24	19.837878	69	41.794123
25	20.513087	70	42.127110
26	21.177773	71	42.454907
27	21.832098	72	42.777595
28	22.476224	73	43.095254
29	23.110311	74	43.407961
30	23.734515	75	43.715795
31	24.348989	76	44.018830
32	24.953886	77	44.317142
33	25.549354	78	44.610804
34	26.135542	79	44.899889
35	26.712592	80	45.184468
36	27.280649	81	45.464612
37	27.839851	82	45.740389
38	28.390337	83	46.011868
39	28.932243	84	46.279115
40	29.465703	85	46.542197
41	29.990848	86	46.801178
42	30.507808	87	47.056123
43	31.016710	88	47.307094
44	31.517680	89	47.554153
45	32.010842	90	47.797362

yearly interest rate = 19.00%

term (months)	constant	term (months)	constant
91	48.036779	136	55.700740
92	48.272465	137	55.816971
93	48.504478	138	55.931391
94	48.732874	139	56.044027
95	48.957710	140	56.154908
96	49.179042	141	56.264060
97	49.396924	142	56.371511
98	49.611410	143	56.477288
99	49.822553	144	56.581415
100	50.030405	145	56.683920
101	50.235017	146	56.784827
102	50.436440	147	56.884161
103	50.634724	148	56.981947
104	50.829917	149	57.078208
105	51.022067	150	57.172970
106	51.211223	151	57.266254
107	51.397430	152	57.358084
108	51.580735	153	57.448483
109	51.761183	154	57.537473
110	51.938819	155	57.625076
111	52.113685	156	57.711314
112	52.285826	157	57.796207
113	52.455284	158	57.879777
114	52.622101	159	57.962045
115	52.786318	160	58.043030
116	52.947975	161	58.122754
117	53.107112	162	58.201234
118	53.263769	163	58.278491
119	53.417984	164	58.354544
120	53.569796	165	58.429412
121	53.719241	166	58.503113
122	53.866357	167	58.575665
123	54.011180	168	58.647086
124	54.153746	169	58.717394
125	54.294090	170	58.786606
126	54.432246	171	58.854739
127	54.568248	172	58.921810
128	54.702131	173	58.987836
129	54.833928	174	59.052833
130	54.963669	175	59.116817
131	55.091389	176	59.179803
132	55.217118	177	59.241808
133	55.340887	178	59.302846
134	55.462727	179	59.362933
135	55.582669	180	59.422084

yearly interest rate = 19.00%

term (months)	constant	term (months)	constant
181	59.480312	226	61.344252
182	59.537633	227	61.372520
183	59.594060	228	61.400348
184	59.649608	229	61.427742
185	59.704290	230	61.454709
186	59.758120	231	61.481256
187	59.811111	232	61.507389
188	59.863275	233	61.533115
189	59.914627	234	61.558439
190	59.965178	235	61.583369
191	60.014942	236	61.607911
192	60.063930	237	61.632070
193	60.112154	238	61.655852
194	60.159626	239	61.679264
195	60.206359	240	61.702310
196	60.252363	241	61.724998
197	60.297651	242	61.747332
198	60.342232	243	61.769318
199	60.386118	244	61.790961
200	60.429321	245	61.812267
201	60.471850	246	61.833240
202	60.513716	247	61.853887
203	60.554930	248	61.874212
204	60.595501	249	61.894220
205	60.635440	250	61.913917
206	60.674756	251	61.933306
207	60.713460	252	61.952393
208	60.751560	253	61.971183
209	60.789066	254	61.989679
210	60.825988	255	62.007888
211	60.862335	256	62.025812
212	60.898114	257	62.043458
213	60.933337	258	62.060828
214	60.968010	259	62.077927
215	61.002143	260	62.094760
216	61.035743	261	62.111331
217	61.068820	262	62.127643
218	61.101382	263	62.143701
219	61.133436	264	62.159509
220	61.164990	265	62.175070
221	61.196052	266	62.190389
222	61.226631	267	62.205469
223	61.256733	268	62.220314
224	61.286365	269	62.234928
225	61.315536	270	62.249314

yearly interest rate = 19.00%

term (months)	constant	term (months)	constant
271	62.263476	316	62.716801
272	62.277416	317	62.723677
273	62.291140	318	62.730445
274	62.304650	319	62.737107
275	62.317949	320	62.743666
276	62.331041	321	62.750122
277	62.343929	322	62.756478
278	62.356616	323	62.762735
279	62.369105	324	62.768894
280	62.381399	325	62.774957
281	62.393502	326	62.780926
282	62.405416	327	62.786801
283	62.417145	328	62.792585
284	62.428691	329	62.798279
285	62.440056	330	62.803884
286	62.451245	331	62.809402
287	62.462259	332	62.814834
288	62.473102	333	62.820181
289	62.483775	334	62.825445
290	62.494283	335	62.830627
291	62.504626	336	62.835728
292	62.514808	337	62.840749
293	62.524832	338	62.845692
294	62.534699	339	62.850558
295	62.544412	340	62.855349
296	62.553974	341	62.860064
297	62.563387	342	62.864707
298	62.572654	343	62.869276
299	62.581776	344	62.873775
300	62.590755	345	62.878203
301	62.599595	346	62.882563
302	62.608297	347	62.886854
303	62.616863	348	62.891079
304	62.625296	349	62.895238
305	62.633598	350	62.899331
306	62.641770	351	62.903362
307	62.649814	352	62.907329
308	62.657733	353	62.911234
309	62.665529	354	62.915079
310	62.673203	355	62.918864
311	62.680758	356	62.922589
312	62.688195	357	62.926257
313	62.695516	358	62.929867
314	62.702723	359	62.933421
315	62.709817	360	62.936920

yearly interest rate = 19.25%

term (months)	constant	term (months)	constant
1	0.9842116	46	32.358419
2	1.9528841	47	32.831743
3	2.9062628	48	33.297594
4	3.8445892	49	33.756090
5	4.7681009	50	34.207347
6	5.6770319	51	34.651480
7	6.5716122	52	35.088600
8	7.4520686	53	35.518819
9	8.3186241	54	35.942245
10	9.1714979	55	36.358987
11	10.010906	56	36.769148
12	10.837062	57	37.172834
13	11.650174	58	37.570146
14	12.450448	59	37.961186
15	13.238087	60	38.346051
16	14.013290	61	38.724840
17	14.776254	62	39.097649
18	15.527173	63	39.464571
19	16.266235	64	39.825700
20	16.993629	65	40.181128
21	17.709539	66	40.530944
22	18.414145	67	40.875237
23	19.107627	68	41.214095
24	19.790160	69	41.547602
25	20.461916	70	41.875843
26	21.123067	71	42.198903
27	21.773779	72	42.516861
28	22.414218	73	42.829800
29	23.044545	74	43.137798
30	23.664920	75	43.440933
31	24.275501	76	43.739282
32	24.876441	77	44.032921
33	25.467894	78	44.321923
34	26.050008	79	44.606363
35	26.622932	80	44.886311
36	27.186810	81	45.161840
37	27.741786	82	45.433019
38	28.287999	83	45.699916
39	28.825589	84	45.962599
40	29.354691	85	46.221135
41	29.875439	86	46.475589
42	30.387965	87	46.726026
43	30.892400	88	46.972509
44	31.388870	89	47.215100
45	31.877502	90	47.453861

yearly interest rate = 19.25%

term (months)	constant	term (months)	constant
91	47.688852	136	55.179789
92	47.920133	137	55.292800
93	48.147763	138	55.404027
94	48.371799	139	55.513498
95	48.592297	140	55.621241
96	48.809314	141	55.727282
97	49.022905	142	55.831649
98	49.233124	143	55.934369
99	49.440024	144	56.035467
100	49.643657	145	56.134968
101	49.844075	146	56.232899
102	50.041328	147	56.329283
103	50.235468	148	56.424146
104	50.426542	149	56.517511
105	50.614599	150	56.609402
106	50.799688	151	56.699842
107	50.981854	152	56.788854
108	51.161144	153	56.876461
109	51.337603	154	56.962684
110	51.511276	155	57.047546
111	51.682208	156	57.131069
112	51.850440	157	57.213273
113	52.016017	158	57.294179
114	52.178979	159	57.373807
115	52.339368	160	57.452178
116	52.497225	161	57.529312
117	52.652590	162	57.605228
118	52.805502	163	57.679946
119	52.955999	164	57.753484
120	53.104120	165	57.825861
121	53.249903	166	57.897095
122	53.393384	167	57.967204
123	53.534600	168	58.036207
124	53.673586	169	58.104120
125	53.810378	170	58.170961
126	53.945010	171	58.236746
127	54.077517	172	58.301493
128	54.207931	173	58.365218
129	54.336287	174	58.427936
130	54.462616	175	58.489664
131	54.586950	176	58.550418
132	54.709321	177	58.610213
133	54.829760	178	58.669063
134	54.948298	179	58.726984
135	55.064964	180	58.783991

yearly interest rate = 19.25%

term (months)	constant	term (months)	constant
181	58.840098	226	60.628641
182	58.895319	227	60.655624
183	58.949668	228	60.682181
184	59.003159	229	60.708318
185	59.055805	230	60.734043
186	59.107621	231	60.759361
187	59.158618	232	60.784280
188	59.208810	233	60.808806
189	59.258209	234	60.832944
190	59.306829	235	60.856701
191	59.354681	236	60.880083
192	59.401778	237	60.903096
193	59.448130	238	60.925745
194	59.493752	239	60.948037
195	59.538652	240	60.969977
196	59.582844	241	60.991571
197	59.626338	242	61.012823
198	59.669146	243	61.033740
199	59.711277	244	61.054327
200	59.752744	245	61.074589
201	59.793555	246	61.094531
202	59.833723	247	61.114158
203	59.873256	248	61.133475
204	59.912165	249	61.152487
205	59.950460	250	61.171199
206	59.988150	251	61.189616
207	60.025245	252	61.207742
208	60.061754	253	61.225581
209	60.097687	254	61.243139
210	60.133053	255	61.260420
211	60.167860	256	61.277428
212	60.202118	257	61.294167
213	60.235835	258	61.310643
214	60.269019	259	61.326858
215	60.301680	260	61.342817
216	60.333825	261	61.358524
217	60.365462	262	61.373983
218	60.396600	263	61.389198
219	60.427246	264	61.404172
220	60.457408	265	61.418911
221	60.487095	266	61.433416
222	60.516312	267	61.447693
223	60.545068	268	61.461744
224	60.573370	269	61.475573
225	60.601226	270	61.489184

yearly interest rate = 19.25%

term (months)	constant	term (months)	constant
271	61.502580	316	61.929615
272	61.515765	317	61.936057
273	61.528741	318	61.942398
274	61.541513	319	61.948639
275	61.554083	320	61.954781
276	61.566454	321	61.960826
277	61.578631	322	61.966775
278	61.590614	323	61.972631
279	61.602409	324	61.978394
280	61.614018	325	61.984067
281	61.625443	326	61.989649
282	61.636688	327	61.995144
283	61.647755	328	62.000552
284	61.658647	329	62.005874
285	61.669368	330	62.011112
286	61.679919	331	62.016268
287	61.690304	332	62.021342
288	61.700525	333	62.026337
289	61.710584	334	62.031252
290	61.720485	335	62.036090
291	61.730229	336	62.040851
292	61.739819	337	62.045537
293	61.749258	338	62.050149
294	61.758548	339	62.054689
295	61.767692	340	62.059156
296	61.776690	341	62.063554
297	61.785547	342	62.067881
298	61.794264	343	62.072141
299	61.802844	344	62.076333
300	61.811288	345	62.080459
301	61.819598	346	62.084520
302	61.827778	347	62.088516
303	61.835828	348	62.092450
304	61.843751	349	62.096322
305	61.851549	350	62.100132
306	61.859224	351	62.103882
307	61.866778	352	62.107573
308	61.874212	353	62.111206
309	61.881529	354	62.114781
310	61.888731	355	62.118300
311	61.895819	356	62.121764
312	61.902795	357	62.125172
313	61.909661	358	62.128527
314	61.916418	359	62.131829
315	61.923069	360	62.135079

yearly interest rate = 19.50%

term (months)	constant	term (months)	constant
1	0.9840098	46	32.221366
2	1.9522852	47	32.690151
3	2.9050777	48	33.151440
4	3.8426349	49	33.605353
5	4.7652004	50	34.052008
6	5.6730139	51	34.491521
7	6.5663113	52	34.924006
8	7.4453248	53	35.349575
9	8.3102827	54	35.768340
10	9.1614098	55	36.180408
11	9.9989272	56	36.585888
12	10.823053	57	36.984883
13	11.634000	58	37.377499
14	12.431980	59	37.763836
15	13.217201	60	38.143997
16	13.989866	61	38.518078
17	14.750175	62	38.886177
18	15.498327	63	39.248391
19	16.234517	64	39.604813
20	16.958934	65	39.955535
21	17.671768	66	40.300650
22	18.373203	67	40.640246
23	19.063423	68	40.974412
24	19.742605	69	41.303234
25	20.410928	70	41.626799
26	21.068563	71	41.945189
27	21.715684	72	42.258489
28	22.352456	73	42.566779
29	22.979047	74	42.870139
30	23.595618	75	43.168648
31	24.202330	76	43.462385
32	24.799341	77	43.751424
33	25.386805	78	44.035842
34	25.964876	79	44.315711
35	26.533703	80	44.591106
36	27.093435	81	44.862097
37	27.644216	82	45.128754
38	28.186191	83	45.391148
39	28.719499	84	45.649346
40	29.244279	85	45.903416
41	29.760669	86	46.153423
42	30.268801	87	46.399432
43	30.768807	88	46.641508
44	31.260819	89	46.879712
45	31.744963	90	47.114108

yearly interest rate = 19.50%

term (months)	constant	term (months)	constant
91	47.344756	136	54.666659
92	47.571715	137	54.776540
93	47.795046	138	54.884665
94	48.014805	139	54.991060
95	48.231051	140	55.095754
96	48.443838	141	55.198774
97	48.653223	142	55.300146
98	48.859260	143	55.399898
99	49.062003	144	55.498055
100	49.261503	145	55.594642
101	49.457814	146	55.689684
102	49.650985	147	55.783207
103	49.841068	148	55.875235
104	50.028111	149	55.965791
105	50.212164	150	56.054898
106	50.393273	151	56.142582
107	50.571486	152	56.228862
108	50.746850	153	56.313764
109	50.919410	154	56.397308
110	51.089210	155	56.479515
111	51.256295	156	56.560409
112	51.420709	157	56.640009
113	51.582493	158	56.718336
114	51.741691	159	56.795410
115	51.898343	160	56.871252
116	52.052490	161	56.945882
117	52.204172	162	57.019318
118	52.353429	163	57.091580
119	52.500299	164	57.162686
120	52.644820	165	57.232655
121	52.787031	166	57.301506
122	52.926968	167	57.369256
123	53.064667	168	57.435922
124	53.200164	169	57.501522
125	53.333495	170	57.566073
126	53.464694	171	57.629593
127	53.593795	172	57.692096
128	53.720831	173	57.753600
129	53.845836	174	57.814121
130	53.968843	175	57.873673
131	54.089882	176	57.932274
132	54.208986	177	57.989937
133	54.326186	178	58.046679
134	54.441511	179	58.102513
135	54.554992	180	58.157454

yearly interest rate = 19.50%

term (months)	constant	term (months)	constant
181	58.211517	226	59.927740
182	58.264716	227	59.953496
183	58.317063	228	59.978840
184	58.368574	229	60.003778
185	58.419261	230	60.028318
186	58.469138	231	60.052466
187	58.518217	232	60.076227
188	58.566511	233	60.099608
189	58.614033	234	60.122616
190	58.660795	235	60.145255
191	58.706809	236	60.167533
192	58.752088	237	60.189454
193	58.796642	238	60.211025
194	58.840484	239	60.232251
195	58.883625	240	60.253138
196	58.926077	241	60.273690
197	58.967849	242	60.293914
198	59.008954	243	60.313815
199	59.049401	244	60.333397
200	59.089201	245	60.352666
201	59.128365	246	60.371627
202	59.166903	247	60.390285
203	59.204825	248	60.408645
204	59.242140	249	60.426711
205	59.278859	250	60.444488
206	59.314990	251	60.461980
207	59.350544	252	60.479194
208	59.385529	253	60.496131
209	59.419955	254	60.512798
210	59.453830	255	60.529199
211	59.487163	256	60.545337
212	59.519964	257	60.561217
213	59.552240	258	60.576844
214	59.584000	259	60.592220
215	59.615252	260	60.607351
216	59.646005	261	60.622239
217	59.676265	262	60.636890
218	59.706042	263	60.651306
219	59.735343	264	60.665492
220	59.764175	265	60.679451
221	59.792546	266	60.693186
222	59.820464	267	60.706703
223	59.847935	268	60.720003
224	59.874967	269	60.733090
225	59.901566	270	60.745968

yearly interest rate = 19.50%

term (months)	constant	term (months)	constant
271	60.758640	316	61.160915
272	60.771109	317	61.166952
273	60.783380	318	61.172893
274	60.795453	319	61.178738
275	60.807334	320	61.184490
276	60.819025	321	61.190150
277	60.830529	322	61.195720
278	60.841849	323	61.201200
279	60.852988	324	61.206593
280	60.863949	325	61.211900
281	60.874734	326	61.217122
282	60.885347	327	61.222260
283	60.895791	328	61.227316
284	60.906067	329	61.232291
285	60.916179	330	61.237187
286	60.926130	331	61.242005
287	60.935921	332	61.246745
288	60.945556	333	61.251410
289	60.955036	334	61.256000
290	60.964365	335	61.260516
291	60.973545	336	61.264961
292	60.982578	337	61.269334
293	60.991467	338	61.273637
294	61.000214	339	61.277872
295	61.008820	340	61.282039
296	61.017289	341	61.286139
297	61.025623	342	61.290174
298	61.033823	343	61.294144
299	61.041893	344	61.298050
300	61.049833	345	61.301895
301	61.057646	346	61.305677
302	61.065334	347	61.309400
303	61.072900	348	61.313062
304	61.080344	349	61.316667
305	61.087669	350	61.320213
306	61.094878	351	61.323703
307	61.101971	352	61.327137
308	61.108950	353	61.330516
309	61.115818	354	61.333841
310	61.122576	355	61.337113
311	61.129226	356	61.340333
312	61.135770	357	61.343501
313	61.142209	358	61.346618
314	61.148545	359	61.349686
315	61.154780	360	61.352704

yearly interest rate = 19.75%

term (months)	constant	term (months)	constant
1	0.9838082	46	32.085154
2	1.9516866	47	32.549444
3	2.9038934	48	33.006217
4	3.8406822	49	33.455593
5	4.7623026	50	33.897694
6	5.6690003	51	34.332636
7	6.5610169	52	34.760535
8	7.4385901	53	35.181506
9	8.3019538	54	35.595661
10	9.1513380	55	36.003110
11	9.9869691	56	36.403961
12	10.809070	57	36.798322
13	11.617859	58	37.186298
14	12.413553	59	37.567991
15	13.196363	60	37.943504
16	13.966497	61	38.312937
17	14.724162	62	38.676388
18	15.469559	63	39.033955
19	16.202887	64	39.385731
20	16.924340	65	39.731812
21	17.634112	66	40.072289
22	18.332391	67	40.407253
23	19.019364	68	40.736793
24	19.695214	69	41.060997
25	20.360120	70	41.379952
26	21.014261	71	41.693743
27	21.657809	72	42.002452
28	22.290938	73	42.306163
29	22.913814	74	42.604957
30	23.526606	75	42.898912
31	24.129475	76	43.188108
32	24.722582	77	43.472621
33	25.306086	78	43.752527
34	25.880142	79	44.027902
35	26.444903	80	44.298817
36	27.000520	81	44.565346
37	27.547140	82	44.827559
38	28.084909	83	45.085526
39	28.613971	84	45.339316
40	29.134466	85	45.588998
41	29.646533	86	45.834636
42	30.150309	87	46.076297
43	30.645929	88	46.314045
44	31.133523	89	46.547943
45	31.613222	90	46.778054

yearly interest rate = 19.75%

term (months)	constant	term (months)	constant
91	47.004440	136	54.161207
92	47.227159	137	54.268046
93	47.446273	138	54.373154
94	47.661838	139	54.476561
95	47.873914	140	54.578293
96	48.082555	141	54.678378
97	48.287818	142	54.776842
98	48.489757	143	54.873713
99	48.688427	144	54.969014
100	48.883880	145	55.062773
101	49.076168	146	55.155013
102	49.265342	147	55.245760
103	49.451454	148	55.335038
104	49.634552	149	55.422870
105	49.814685	150	55.509279
106	49.991902	151	55.594290
107	50.166249	152	55.677924
108	50.337773	153	55.760204
109	50.506520	154	55.841152
110	50.672534	155	55.920789
111	50.835861	156	55.999136
112	50.996543	157	56.076215
113	51.154623	158	56.152046
114	51.310144	159	56.226649
115	51.463146	160	56.300044
116	51.613671	161	56.372251
117	51.761759	162	56.443289
118	51.907449	163	56.513176
119	52.050779	164	56.581932
120	52.191790	165	56.649574
121	52.330516	166	56.716121
122	52.466997	167	56.781591
123	52.601268	168	56.846000
124	52.733365	169	56.909367
125	52.863322	170	56.971708
126	52.991176	171	57.033039
127	53.116959	172	57.093377
128	53.240706	173	57.152738
129	53.362449	174	57.211138
130	53.482221	175	57.268593
131	53.600053	176	57.325117
132	53.715978	177	57.380726
133	53.830025	178	57.435434
134	53.942226	179	57.489257
135	54.052610	180	57.542208

yearly interest rate = 19.75%

term (months)	constant	term (months)	constant
181	57.594302	226	59.241154
182	57.645552	227	59.265739
183	57.695973	228	59.289925
184	57.745577	229	59.313721
185	57.794378	230	59.337130
186	57.842388	231	59.360161
187	57.889622	232	59.382819
188	57.936090	233	59.405110
189	57.981806	234	59.427040
190	58.026782	235	59.448614
191	58.071030	236	59.469840
192	58.114561	237	59.490722
193	58.157387	238	59.511266
194	58.199520	239	59.531477
195	58.240971	240	59.551361
196	58.281750	241	59.570923
197	58.321870	242	59.590168
198	58.361339	243	59.609101
199	58.400170	244	59.627728
200	58.438372	245	59.646054
201	58.475955	246	59.664082
202	58.512929	247	59.681819
203	58.549305	248	59.699268
204	58.585092	249	59.716435
205	58.620300	250	59.733325
206	58.654938	251	59.749940
207	58.689014	252	59.766287
208	58.722539	253	59.782368
209	58.755521	254	59.798190
210	58.787969	255	59.813755
211	58.819892	256	59.829068
212	58.851297	257	59.844134
213	58.882195	258	59.858955
214	58.912592	259	59.873536
215	58.942496	260	59.887882
216	58.971917	261	59.901995
217	59.000861	262	59.915879
218	59.029337	263	59.929539
219	59.057351	264	59.942977
220	59.084912	265	59.956198
221	59.112026	266	59.969205
222	59.138702	267	59.982001
223	59.164946	268	59.994590
224	59.190764	269	60.006976
225	59.216165	270	60.019160

yearly interest rate = 19.75%

term (months)	constant	term (months)	constant
271	60.031148	316	60.410107
272	60.042941	317	60.415764
273	60.054543	318	60.421330
274	60.065958	319	60.426805
275	60.077187	320	60.432192
276	60.088235	321	60.437492
277	60.099104	322	60.442705
278	60.109797	323	60.447835
279	60.120317	324	60.452881
280	60.130666	325	60.457846
281	60.140848	326	60.462730
282	60.150865	327	60.467535
283	60.160720	328	60.472262
284	60.170415	329	60.476913
285	60.179953	330	60.481489
286	60.189337	331	60.485990
287	60.198569	332	60.490419
288	60.207651	333	60.494775
289	60.216587	334	60.499062
290	60.225377	335	60.503279
291	60.234026	336	60.507427
292	60.242534	337	60.511509
293	60.250905	338	60.515524
294	60.259140	339	60.519474
295	60.267241	340	60.523361
296	60.275212	341	60.527184
297	60.283053	342	60.530946
298	60.290768	343	60.534646
299	60.298357	344	60.538287
300	60.305824	345	60.541869
301	60.313170	346	60.545392
302	60.320396	347	60.548859
303	60.327506	348	60.552270
304	60.334501	349	60.555625
305	60.341382	350	60.558926
306	60.348152	351	60.562174
307	60.354813	352	60.565369
308	60.361365	353	60.568512
309	60.367812	354	60.571604
310	60.374154	355	60.574646
311	60.380393	356	60.577639
312	60.386531	357	60.580584
313	60.392570	358	60.583481
314	60.398511	359	60.586331
315	60.404356	360	60.589135

yearly interest rate = 20.00%

term (months)	constant	term (months)	constant
1	0.9836066	46	31.949775
2	1.9510884	47	32.409614
3	2.9027099	48	32.861916
4	3.8387311	49	33.306802
5	4.7594076	50	33.744396
6	5.6649911	51	34.174815
7	6.5557290	52	34.598179
8	7.4318646	53	35.014602
9	8.2936373	54	35.424199
10	9.1412826	55	35.827081
11	9.9750320	56	36.223358
12	10.795113	57	36.613139
13	11.601751	58	36.996531
14	12.395165	59	37.373637
15	13.175572	60	37.744561
16	13.943186	61	38.109404
17	14.698215	62	38.468266
18	15.440868	63	38.821245
19	16.171345	64	39.168438
20	16.889848	65	39.509939
21	17.596571	66	39.845842
22	18.291710	67	40.176238
23	18.975452	68	40.501218
24	19.647986	69	40.820870
25	20.309494	70	41.135282
26	20.960158	71	41.444539
27	21.600156	72	41.748727
28	22.229661	73	42.047928
29	22.848847	74	42.342225
30	23.457882	75	42.631696
31	24.056934	76	42.916423
32	24.646164	77	43.196481
33	25.225735	78	43.471949
34	25.795805	79	43.742901
35	26.356530	80	44.009410
36	26.908062	81	44.271551
37	27.450553	82	44.529395
38	27.984150	83	44.783011
39	28.509000	84	45.032470
40	29.025246	85	45.277839
41	29.533029	86	45.519186
42	30.032487	87	45.756577
43	30.523758	88	45.990075
44	31.006975	89	46.219746
45	31.482271	90	46.445652

yearly interest rate = 20.00%

term (months)	constant	term (months)	constant
91	46.667854	136	53.663291
92	46.886414	137	53.767172
93	47.101391	138	53.869349
94	47.312844	139	53.969852
95	47.520830	140	54.068707
96	47.725406	141	54.165941
97	47.926629	142	54.261581
98	48.124553	143	54.355654
99	48.319233	144	54.448184
100	48.510721	145	54.539197
101	48.699070	146	54.628719
102	48.884331	147	54.716773
103	49.066555	148	54.803383
104	49.245792	149	54.888573
105	49.422090	150	54.972367
106	49.595498	151	55.054787
107	49.766064	152	55.135856
108	49.933834	153	55.215597
109	50.098853	154	55.294029
110	50.261167	155	55.371176
111	50.420820	156	55.447059
112	50.577855	157	55.521697
113	50.732317	158	55.595112
114	50.884246	159	55.667323
115	51.033685	160	55.738351
116	51.180673	161	55.808214
117	51.325252	162	55.876932
118	51.467461	163	55.944523
119	51.607339	164	56.011006
120	51.744924	165	56.076399
121	51.880253	166	56.140721
122	52.013363	167	56.203988
123	52.144292	168	56.266217
124	52.273074	169	56.327427
125	52.399745	170	56.387633
126	52.524339	171	56.446852
127	52.646891	172	56.505101
128	52.767434	173	56.562394
129	52.886000	174	56.618748
130	53.002623	175	56.674178
131	53.117335	176	56.728700
132	53.230165	177	56.782328
133	53.341146	178	56.835077
134	53.450308	179	56.886961
135	53.557680	180	56.937994

yearly interest rate = 20.00%

term (months)	constant	term (months)	constant
181	56.988191	226	58.568501
182	57.037565	227	58.591968
183	57.086129	228	58.615050
184	57.133898	229	58.637755
185	57.180883	230	58.660086
186	57.227098	231	58.682052
187	57.272556	232	58.703658
188	57.317268	233	58.724909
189	57.361247	234	58.745813
190	57.404505	235	58.766373
191	57.447054	236	58.786596
192	57.488906	237	58.806488
193	57.530071	238	58.826054
194	57.570562	239	58.845299
195	57.610389	240	58.864229
196	57.649563	241	58.882848
197	57.688095	242	58.901162
198	57.725995	243	58.919175
199	57.763273	244	58.936894
200	57.799941	245	58.954322
201	57.836008	246	58.971464
202	57.871483	247	58.988325
203	57.906377	248	59.004910
204	57.940698	249	59.021223
205	57.974457	250	59.037269
206	58.007663	251	59.053051
207	58.040324	252	59.068575
208	58.072450	253	59.083844
209	58.104049	254	59.098863
210	58.135130	255	59.113636
211	58.165702	256	59.128166
212	58.195772	257	59.142459
213	58.225350	258	59.156517
214	58.254443	259	59.170344
215	58.283058	260	59.183945
216	58.311205	261	59.197323
217	58.338890	262	59.210482
218	58.366121	263	59.223425
219	58.392906	264	59.236156
220	58.419252	265	59.248678
221	58.445166	266	59.260994
222	58.470655	267	59.273109
223	58.495726	268	59.285025
224	58.520386	269	59.296746
225	58.544642	270	59.308275

yearly interest rate = 20.00%

term (months)	constant	term (months)	constant
271	59.319615	316	59.676616
272	59.330769	317	59.681917
273	59.341740	318	59.687132
274	59.352531	319	59.692261
275	59.363145	320	59.697306
276	59.373585	321	59.702268
277	59.383854	322	59.707149
278	59.393955	323	59.711950
279	59.403890	324	59.716672
280	59.413663	325	59.721317
281	59.423275	326	59.725885
282	59.432729	327	59.730379
283	59.442029	328	59.734799
284	59.451176	329	59.739146
285	59.460173	330	59.743423
286	59.469023	331	59.747629
287	59.477727	332	59.751766
288	59.486289	333	59.755835
289	59.494710	334	59.759838
290	59.502994	335	59.763775
291	59.511142	336	59.767648
292	59.519156	337	59.771457
293	59.527038	338	59.775203
294	59.534792	339	59.778889
295	59.542418	340	59.782513
296	59.549920	341	59.786079
297	59.557298	342	59.789586
298	59.564555	343	59.793035
299	59.571694	344	59.796428
300	59.578715	345	59.799765
301	59.585621	346	59.803048
302	59.592415	347	59.806276
303	59.599096	348	59.809452
304	59.605668	349	59.812576
305	59.612133	350	59.815649
306	59.618491	351	59.818671
307	59.624746	352	59.821643
308	59.630897	353	59.824567
309	59.636948	354	59.827443
310	59.642900	355	59.830272
311	59.648754	356	59.833054
312	59.654512	357	59.835791
313	59.660176	358	59.838483
314	59.665747	359	59.841131
315	59.671226	360	59.843735

INDEX

INDEX

INDEX

INDEX

INDEX

INDEX

INDEX

INDEX

INDEX

INDEX